MARRIAGES AND DEATHS

FROM THE

NEWSPAPERS

OF

ALLEGANY AND WASHINGTON COUNTIES MARYLAND

1820–1830

COMPILED BY

F. Edward Wright

HERITAGE BOOKS
2011

HERITAGE BOOKS
AN IMPRINT OF HERITAGE BOOKS, INC.

Books, CDs, and more—Worldwide

For our listing of thousands of titles see our website
at
www.HeritageBooks.com

Published 2011 by
HERITAGE BOOKS, INC.
Publishing Division
100 Railroad Ave. #104
Westminster, Maryland 21157

Originally published 1987

All rights reserved. No part of this book may be reproduced or transmitted in any form or by any means, electronic or mechanical, including photocopying, recording or by any information storage and retrieval system without written permission from the author, except for the inclusion of brief quotations in a review.

International Standard Book Numbers
Paperbound: 978-1-58549-276-3
Clothbound: 978-0-7884-8948-8

INTRODUCTION

These newspaper items were compiled from issues held by the Maryland Historical Society and the Library of Congress, in addition to microfilm rolls of the Maryland Historical Society and the George Peabody Library.

Noting the dearth of marriage and death notices in earlier issues, I find that this collection is abundant with announcements of marriages and obituaries, not only for prominent persons but for those of lesser prominence as well. In addition I have included those advertisements of Equity (or Chancery) cases in which heirs are listed. It seems that only those Equity cases were listed in the local papers in which at lease one of the heirs was residing outside the state. These cases provide excellent leads in tracing persons back to Maryland.

The first newspaper in Allegany County for which I have found any issues was the Maryland Advocate. It began in 1823. In 1828 another newspaper was founded in Cumberland - The Weekly Civilian.

Hagerstown began publishing newspapers in 1797 with the Maryland Herald. During the period of this book, 1820-1830, there were two newspapers, the Maryland Herald, with changes in its name occurring during the period, and the Torchlight, called at this point The Torchlight and Public Advertiser. The Torchlight may have been established in Hagerstown as early as 1814. Eventually the two papers merged. The Hagerstown Mail was founded in 1828.

Williams-Port introduced its first newspaper, Republican Banner, on January 2nd 1830.

At the beginning of each issue is a trigraph indicating the name and location of the newspaper.

MAL - Maryland Advocate, issues held by the Library of Congress
EAM - Maryland Herald, issues held by the Maryland Historical Society
TLM - The Torchlight, issues held by the Maryland Historical Society
RBL - Republican Banner, issues held by the Library of Congress
HMM - The Hagerstown Mail, issues held by the Maryland Historical Society
FRL - The Farmers' Register and Maryland Herald, issues held by the Library of Congress

Comments and suggestions are welcome.

F. Edward Wright
Silver Spring, Maryland

Abbreviations

In order to save space certain abbreviations have been used.

AA - Anne Arundel
agnst - against
Balt - Baltimore
co - county
dau(s) - daughter(s)
decd - deceased
est - estate
esq. - esquire
exec - executor, executrix
Fred - Frederick (county)
ft - feet
inch - inches

inst - instant, meaning this month
m - married
Md - Maryland
Mont - Montgomery (county)
Pa - Pennsylvania
Phila - Philadelphia
PG - Prince George's (county)
res - resides, resident, residence
ult - ultimo, meaning last month
Va - Virginia
Wash - Washington
yrs - years

MARYLAND ADVOCATE, Cumberland

1. MAL Oct 20 1823/Died Wed last, Mrs. Rabecca Pollard, consort of Thomas Pollard, Esq. in the 46th year of her age/Died Sun 12th inst. Mrs. Harriet Clise, consort of John Clise in 18th year of her age/Lewis R. Fechtig is dead (long memorial submitted by J.J.J.)

2. MAL Nov 3 1823/Equity Court - Wm. Hoblitzell vs Rebecca Hoblitzell, John B. French and Juliana his wife, Joseph Knesely & Christiana his wife, Hannah Hoblitzell, Adrian Hoblitzell, William Hoblitzell & Caroline Hoblitzell, which said defendants are the widow and heirs at law of John Hoblitzell, decd - to obtain decree for the sale of real est in Allegany Co, whereof John Hoblitzell died intestate in 1818. Rebecca Hoblitzell and William Hoblitzell were appointed administrators. J. Hoblitzell left Rebecca his widow and 6 children: Juliana, Christiana, Hannah, Adrian, William and Caroline, his heirs at law. Juliana hath since m John B. French and Christiana hath m Joseph Knesely. All said children are minors under age of 21 and each res out of Md.

3. MAL Nov 10 1823/Married Thurs evening last by Rev Hyer, Gustavus Beall to Rachael Tomlinson, dau of Benjamin Tomlinson, all of this co.

4. MAL Dec 1 1823/Died Tues 25th ult. Capt. Thomas Beall (of Samuel) at an advanced age; he participated in the struggles of the Rev, and was proprietor of the town of Cumberland/Died Sun last, James M. Cresap, citizen of this co, aged upwards of 50 years (testimonial in issue dated Dec 8 1823).

5. MAL Dec 8 1823/Married Thurs evening last by Rev R. Kennedy, Benjamin C. Payne, to Miss Maria Bryan, both of this town.

6. MAL Jan 26 1824/Died at his res near Frost-town Tues evening last, Christian Musselman, in the 69th year of his age.

7. MAL Feb 23 1824/Died Wed last, George Moor, in the 84th year of his age, long a citizen of Cumberland.

8. MAL Apr 12 1824/Died Tues night 30th ult., Upton Lawrence, Esq. Attorney at Law, of Hagers town, in the 45th year of his age; remains deposited in family vault with Masonic honors.

9. MAL May 10 1824/Equity court - Michael C. Sprigg vs Jacob Lantz, George Lantz, Sophia Lantz, Clarissa Lantz, Jacob Taylor and Mary his wife, Margaret Lantz, Eliza Lantz, Susan Lantz and Julian Lantz, heirs of Daniel Lantz. Bill to obtain decree for sale of parcel of land, part of two tracts, Good Hope and The Resurvey on Good Hope. The bill states that Osborn Sprigg, of Hampshire Co, Va, some years since, sold parcel lying at the mouth of Town creek, in Allegany Co, to Daniel Lantz and Jacob Lantz. Both Osborn Sprigg and Daniel Lantz have died intestate and Michael C. Sprigg appointed administrator of estate of Osborn Sprigg and Margaret Lantz and Jacob Lantz administrator of estate of Daniel Lantz. A portion of the purchase money unpaid. At the time of his death Daniel Lantz left 10 children: Jacob, John, George, Sophia, Clarissa, Margaret, Eliza, Susan, Juliana, and Mary who had earlier m Jacob Taylor; John Lantz shortly after the death of his father, died leaving his aforesaid brothers and sister his heirs. Margaret, Eliza, Susan and Juliana Lantz are minors under age of 21. Jacob Taylor and Mary his wife do not res in Md. Clarissa Lantz hath m George Catlett since the filing of the

MARYLAND ADVOCATE, Cumberland

bill in this cause who both res out of the state of Md. George Lantz hath removed from the said state to parts unknown./John Hardin, Knox Co, Ohio, cautions that his wife Elizabeth has left his bed and board /Mary A. O'Neale vs Ann Jackson, Henry Shelhorn, John Shelhorn, Jacob Shelhorn, Baltzer Shelhorn, James Black and Polly his wife, Gabriel Kimmel and Nancy his wife. Object of bill to obtain decree for sale of real est of John Shelhorn, Allegany Co, decd. The bill states that Francis Jameson and Mary A. O'Neale were adminstrators d.b.n. of Lawrence O'Neale, late of Montgomery Co, decd, obtained a judgment agnst Ann Jackson, surviving acting exec of John Shelhorn, decd in Allegany Co Court. Francis Jameson hath died since leaving said Mary A. O'Neale surviving adminstratrix d.b.n. John Shelhorn died some years ago with last will and testament and appt Daniel Lantz, Daniel Fetter and Ann Jackson (then Ann Shelhorn) as executors. John Shelhorn, at the time of his death, was seized in fee, of real est in Allegany co. John Shelhorn left Ann Jackson his widow and relict and their 6 children: John, Henry, Jacob, Baltzer, Polly and Nancy, his heirs at law and devisees. Polly Shelhorn hath m with James Black, Nancy Shelhorn hath m Gabriel Kimmel. John, Henry and Baltzer Shelhorn and Gabriel Kimmel and Nancy his wife res out of the state of Md. Jacob Shelhorn is deaf and dumb and incapable of answering the complainant's bill.

10. MAL May 24 1824/Married at Bedford, Pa, on Tues last by Rev H. Gerhart, William Townsend, to Louisa second dau of Elijah Adams, esq. all of that place/Married Thurs by same, Henry Williams, to Miss --- Henry, dau of Geo. Henry, esq. all of the same place/George Witner, farmer of this co, res about 8 miles west of Cumberland, suddenly hurried into Eternity on Mon last, while repairing one of the cog wheels in his mill, leaving his numerous family.

11. MAL Jul 5 1824/James King, Allegany Co, cautions that his wife Rabecca has left his bed and board

12. MAL Jul 19 1824/Reward for apprentice boy, Isaac Gross, about 20 year of age, about 5 ft 10-11 inch, fair complexion - Casper Yenter, Old-Town /Married Tues evening last by Rev Heyer, Sylvenus Bennett, to Miss Rabecca Rizer, both of this place.

13. MAL Aug 30 1824/Died Tues 7th inst, in Virginia, about 6 miles below Cumberland, Catharine B. Sanford, wife of Thornton Sanford, in the 29th year of her age, leaving a husband, 3 children, aged parents and other relatives.

14. MAL Sep 6 1824/Died in this town on Fri last, Henry M'Kinley, long an inhabitant of this place.

15. MAL Sep 20 1824/Died at Paddytown, Hampshire Co, 24th ult., Col. Edward M'Carty, old and respectable inhabitant of that co, aged 68, one of the few remaining heroes of the Rev, served from 1776 until shortly before the siege of Yorktown, received an honourable discharge, returned to co of Hampshire and raised a company of volunteers, at the head of which he witnessed the surrender of Cornwallis/Died near Old-Town Sat the 11th inst, Mrs. Prather, aged upwards of 70 years, one of the first settlers of Allegany Co/Died Wed night last, Mrs. Mary M'Clary, old and respectable inhabitant of this town.

MARYLAND ADVOCATE (Cumberland)

16. MAL Sep 27 1824/Died Sun morning last, in this town, Edward Frethy, in the 60th year of his age/Died Mon morning, Owen Edwards, of a protracted pulmonary complaint, leaving widow and several small children/Died Wed morning, Mrs. Charlotte Dunn, consort of Richard Dunn/Died same day at Old-town, Md., Jacob Rahouser/Died 13th inst. at Green-Castle, Pa, Rev John X. Clarke /Died 20th inst at Hagers-town, Rev John Lind; remains interred on fol day in the Presby burying ground in Green-Castle, Pa.

17. MAL Oct 4 1824/Died at Frederick-town, Wed 22d inst. Robert Ritchie, Esq. editor of the Political Intelligencer or Republican Gazette.

18. MAL Oct 11 1824/Married at Fountain Rock, near Hagers-town, Tues 28th ult, by Rev George Lemon, William Schley, Esq. Attorney at law, of Frederick, to Miss Ann Cadwalader, third dau of Gen. Samuel Ringgold/Married Tues last, in this town, by Rev Hyer, Robert A. Robison to Miss Hannah Neff, dau of Jacob Neff, all of this place/Died at his res about 8 miles from this place on morning of Wed, 6th inst, William Hilleary, Esq. aged about 56 years, res of this co for many years.

19. Oct 18 1824/Married Thurs 14th inst by Rev Sigler, David W. Walton, of this town, to Miss Mary, dau of William Vickroy, of Cumberland Valley, Bedford Co, Pa./Married at Chambersburg, Pa, on 30th ult, by Rev David Denny, Kenton Harper, editor of the Staunton Spectator, to Miss Eleanor, dau of Capt. Samuel Calhoun, of that place/Died in this town, Fri night last, after a short illness, Randolph Campbell, aged about 30 years, son of Capt. William Campbell, of Frederick Co, Md.

20. MAL Oct 25 1824/Married Thurs last by Rev J. J. Jacob, Alexander Carlisle to Miss Ellen Cresap, dau of Thomas Cresap, Esq., all of this co /Died Wed last at the res of her father, about 5 miles from this town, Miss Harriet Carter, in the 20th year of her age/Died same day in this town, Mrs. Louderbaugh, aged about 88 years.

21. MAL Nov 1 1824/Married Tues evening last by Rev Heyer, Daniel Allbright to Miss Catharine Myers, all of this place.

22. MAL Nov 22 1824/Married Tues night last, in this town, by Rev Kennedy, John Johnson, of Flintstone, to Mrs. Mary Reid, of this place/Married Thurs evening last by Rev Heyer, John Clise to Miss Jane M'Clary, both of this place.

23. MAL Dec 6 1824/Married in Hagers-town Tues evening last by Rev J. R. Reily, Capt. George Shafer to Miss Martha B. Swearingen, dau of John V. Swearingen, Esq. late Sheriff of Wash Co.

24. MAL Dec 20 1824/Died at Western-Port Monday, 6th inst, after a lingering illness, James Morrison, in the 65th year of his age.

25. MAL Jan 10 1825/Married this morning by Rev Sigler, Euriah Fisher to Miss Amanda Rager, both of Virginia.

26. MAL Jan 17 1825/Died at Union-town, Pa, on morning of 8th inst, after a short illness, Mrs. Elizabeth Shriver, consort of James Shriver, esq. of that place.

MARYLAND ADVOCATE (Cumberland)

26A. MAL Jan 24 1825/Miss Lydia Olds of Allegany Co, Pa, aged about 18 years killed herself, swallowing three ounces of arsenic, in the 6th attempt of suicide in the past 2 years. She said she was tired of life./Died Wed last the 19th inst, at the res of her son Peter M'Cleery, in this co, Mrs. Margaret M'Cleery, after a lingering illness of 2 years, in the 53d year of her age.

27. MAL Feb 7 1825/Married Tues evening last by Rev J. J. Jacobs, Samuel Jacobs of Wellsburg, Va, to Miss Mary Ann Shryer, first dau of John Shryer of this place/Married same evening by Rev Heyer, Solomon Stover to Miss Harriet L. Shryer, 2nd dau of John Shryer, all of this town.

28. MAL Feb 14 1825/Married Thurs evening last by Rev Martin, Samuel Hendrixon to Miss Elleanora Kealhofer, all of this place.

29. MAL Feb 21 1825/Married Thurs evening last by Rev Robert Kennedy, David Kearnes of Springfield, Va, to Miss Sophia Yantz, of this place/Died in this town Fri last, Thomas Pollard, son of Thomas Pollard, Esq. formerly of this place, aged 17 years, 34 days.

30. MAL Mar 7 1825/Married Tues 1st inst by Rev John Miller, Jacob Fechtig, youngest son of Christian Fechtig, of Hagers-town, to Miss Matilda Ann Hilleary, only dau of late William Hilleary, Esq. of this co/Married Thurs last by same, Archibald M'Neil to Miss Elizabeth Zigler, both of Cumberland.

31. MAL Mar 14 1825/Died Tues evening last, Miss Abigail Cresap, aged about 15 years, dau of James D. Cresap, Esq. of this co/John S. Dugan, proprietor of the line of stages from Wheeling to Zanesville, returning from Washington city of Wheeling, with one of his own stages, upset, about 4 miles east of this place, on Thursday evening last, severely injured and died in a few hours.

32. MAL Mar 21 1825/Married at Phila on 10th inst by Rev Skinner, James Espy, merchant of Harrisburg, Pa, to Miss Mary H. Pollard, dau of Thos. Pollard, Esq. of Cumberland/Married Sun morning 13th inst, in this town, by Rev Adam Sigler, John T. Sigler, to Miss Mary Carlton, dau of James P. Carlton, all of this place.

33. MAL Apr 4 1825/Married Mon evening last by Rev Robt. Kennedy, Jonathan Butler to Miss Catharine Hoffman, dau of George Hoffman, Esq. all of this place.

34. MAL Apr 11 1825/Accident - A gentleman and his wife and five children were removing from Virginia to a farm in this co, on Mon morning whilst in the act of crossing the Potomac at M'Laughlin's fording on the south Branch, about 3 miles from Old Town, Mrs. Conroy and her five children were drowned. They were in a wagon, the body of which, floated free of the moving part and carried off down river/Married Tues last by Rev A. Sigler, Samuel Wright to Miss Margaret Hoffman, dau of Valentine Hoffman, Esq. all of this co/Married yesterday evening by Rev T. Ryan, Baptist Mattingly to Miss Ann Timmonds, both of this town.

35. MAL Apr 18 1825/Died yesterday afternoon, after an illness of a few days, Matthias Bartgis, Esq., aged about 74 years, original proprietor of

MARYLAND ADVOCATE (Cumberland)

the Republican Gazette, the helm of which he held for 30 years, the first paper established in Frederick. In 1821 he relinquished his vocation and sought retirement on his farm a few miles from Frederick.

36. MAL Apr 25 1825/Married Thurs last by Rev Geo. Lemon, of Hagerstown, Thomas Turner, Esq. of George-town, D. C. to Miss Ellenor T. Pratt, dau of Thomas Pratt, Esq. of this co.

37. MAL May 9 1825/Accident - During the storm on Fri evening 29th ult, the gable end of the brick stable belonging to the tavern occupied by Mr. Delong, in this place, was forced out, the bricks of which fell on two men - one of whom, Patrick O'Ferrall, was so severely injured, that he expired the following morning. He was one of the hands employed at repairing the turnpike.

38. MAL May 16 1825/Sun 8th inst, George H. Drake of this co shot a Dennis M. Athey, about 8 miles north of this place. Although there was an argument Drake contends that the shooting was an accident. Drake has been committed to prison to await his trial.

39. MAL May 23 1825/Married Thurs evening last, by Rev Sigler, William Shryer to Miss Gertrude Snyder, dau of Jacob Snyder, Esq. all of that place.

40. MAL Jun 6 1825/Died at his res in London, 11 Apr last, in the 77th year of his age, William Murdoch, merchant of that city, native of Prince George's co, Md/Married Thurs 26th ult. by Rev Leakin, John Withney of Hagers-town, to Miss Margaret Osborn, dau of Capt. Wm. Osborn, of this co.

41. MAL Jun 13 1825/Equity court - The Cumberland Bank of Allegany, Roger Perry, David Lynn, Thomas Blair, and Henry Winour, complainants agnst Isaac Beall, William T. Beall, Benjamin M. Beall, Jesse T. Beall, Joseph T. Beall, Isaac W. Beall, Samuel B. Beall, Daniel Beall and Elizabeth B. Beall, Richard Beall and Gustavus Beall, Defendants. Object of the bill to obtain decree for sale of real est of Thomas Beall (of Samuel), Allegany Co, decd. The bill states that Thomas Beall of Samuel seized in fee of sundry tracts and ground rents in Cumberland, devised a small piece of land to his negro man Basil and the remainder of his estate to his right grand children, to wit: William T. Beall, Benjamin M. Beall, Jesse T. Beall, Joseph T. Beall, Isaac M. Beall, Samuel B. Beall, Daniel Beall, and Elizabeth B. Beall and appointed Isaac Beall, the exec of his Will who neglected to take out letters testamentary, and that letters of administration, with the will annexed, was granted to Richard Beall and Gustavus Beall, of Allegany Co. Complainants were creditors of said Thomas Beall (of Samuel) at the time of his death and had obtained judgments agnst him. Isaac Beall, William T. Beal, Benjamin M. Beall, Jesse T. Beall, Joseph T. Beall, Isaac W. Beall, Samuel B. Beall, Daniel Beall, and Elizabeth B. Beall, res out of the state of Md.

42. MAL Jun 20 1825/Married Tues evening last by Rev A. Sigler, William Taylor to Miss Mary Ann W. Clifton, all of this town/Married Thurs last by same, Jacob Shafer to Miss Rosa Isahart, both of this co/Married in Balt Co, Thrus 28 Apr last by Rev Austin, Rev Lewis R. Porter, D.D. to Miss Sophia Hooper, all of that co/Died Sat 11th inst in this place, Mrs. Sophia Duck-

MARYLAND ADVOCATE (Cumberland)

ett, in the 54th year of her age, after a severe and distressing illness of 4 months.

43. MAL Jul 4 1825/Died suddenly on 23d ult at his dwelling in Charles St., Gen. John Stricker, Pres of the Bank of Balt/John Reynolds, Jr. eldest son of Col. John Reynolds of Hagers-town, died Sat morning 25th ult., about 7 o'clock after a rapid consumption of five months, proceeding from a violent cold he contracted by over exertion at a fire in the first part of Feb last /Died suddenly Mon last, in the 69th year of her age, Mrs. Anna Catharine Butler, widow of the late Rev John George Butler/Died Tues last after a long and painful illness, Mrs. Rice, widow of late John Rice, Esqr. of this co, decd.

44. MAL Jul 11 1825/ Reward offered for Edward Mopps, apprentice to the saddle and harness making business, 21st year of his age, 5 ft 8-9 inch, dark complexion - Jacob Saylar, Cumberland.

45. MAL Jul 25 1825/Married Thurs evening 13th inst, by Rev Eli Sigler, Emanuel Easter, to Miss Mary Neff, dau of Jacob Neff, all of this town.

46. MAL Aug 1 1825/Married Mon 25th ult. Wm. H. Littrell, to Miss Angelina Renalds, both of this place.

47. MAL Sep 5 1825/Hagers-Town, Aug. 30 - Sat evening last, Thomas Stoner of this town was killed in a well. - Herald/Died at the res of his father, at 3 o'clock on Mon morning, 28th ult., after a severe illness, James Michael, son of Michael C. Sprigg, esq. of this co, aged 6 years and 2 months.

48. MAL Sep 12 1825/Died in Hagers-town, Sat 3d inst. at the res of Elie Beatty, Esq. Miss Nancy Hoye, dau of late Paul Hoye, Esq. of Washington Co /Died this morning in this town, Mrs. Catharine Boose, wife of John Boose, and her infant child.

49. MAL Oct 3 1825/Married Tues last by Rev Ryan, of Hagerstown, Wm. Logsdon to Miss Elizabeth Majors, both of this co/Married same day by Rev Sigler, Samuel Scott Porter to Miss Anna Winters, all of this co/Married Thurs last in this town, by Rev Sigler, James Ward to Miss Cordelia Cleary.

50. MAL Oct 24 1825/Married in Chambersburg, Pa, Thurs 13th inst by Rev Rahouser, Joseph Pritts, Printer, formerly of this place, to Mrs. Nancy Sloan, proprietress of the Franklin Republican/Equity case - Francis Twigg, Jr. vs John Jonas and others, heirs at law of John Jonas, Allegany co, decd. The bill states that the complainant purchased of John Jonas, decd, in 1813, a lot. John Jonas died in 1815; letters of admin granted to Lucia Jonas, his widow and Adolph Jonas, his son. John Jonas, at the time of his death left the fol children his heirs at law: Catharine, Ann, Lucia, Elizabeth, Hannah and Susanna, John, William, Samuel and Adolph. Said Catharine hath m Jonathan Clark, Ann with William Barker, Hannah m Joseph Everly, Elizabeth m George Inks and Lucia m John Cummings. Samuel Jonas is an infant under age of 21. Adolph Jonas has died, leaving Rachel Jonas his widow and their five children: John, Jeremiah, George, Elizabeth and Mary, all under age of 21. All defendants res out of the state of Md.

MARYLAND ADVOCATE (Cumberland)

51. MAL Oct 31 1825/Reward offered for William Neill, about 18, about 5 ft, stout made, apprentice to blacksmithing bus. - William Riley, living near Old-town, Md.

52. MAL Nov 7 1825/Died 7th of Oct last on Blue River, about 35 miles above the Falls of the Ohio, Miss Rosanah Shryer, in the 18th year of her age, dau of John Shryer of this place, of a severe Bilous Fever, after an illness of 6 days/Died in this co Thurs night last, captain William Helm, aged 90. He emigrated in the valley of Virginia when 7 years old, when the Indians navigated our rivers with their canoes and roamed in our woods. He shared the periods of the Rev - Winchester Rep./Died on 17th ult. in Washington Co, Md. Rev Daniel Hitt, elder in the ministry of the Meth Episc Church.

53. MAL Nov 14 1825/Died Tues morning last, at Prattsville, in this co, of bilous fever, after a protracted illness, Mrs. Pratt, consort of Thomas Pratt, Esq.

54. MAL Nov 28 1825/Rev Hero gone! Died at his res in Liberty-town, Mon evening the 14th inst., Maj. General Robert Cumming, commander of the 2nd division of Md. Militia in the 72d year.

55. MAL Dec 12 1825/Died at Circleville, Ohio, on 30th ult, very suddenly, Isreal Welfley, formerly of this place.

56. MAL Dec 26 1825/Died in this town, Fri evening last, after a short illness, John Whitehead, senr. in the 74th year of his age.

57. MAL Jan 9 1826/Married in this town Tues evening last by Rev N.B. Little, Joseph Kelly to Miss Ruth Murrow, all of this co

58. MAL Jan 23 1826/Married at Wash Pa, Tues 10 inst, By Rev Jennings, Henry B. Tomlinson, esq. Attorney at Law, formerly of this place, to Miss Elizabeth McCammant, all of that place

59. MAL Jan 30 1826/Married in this town Tues evening last by Rev N. B. Little, Christopher Stotler to Miss Elizabeth Bomwart, dau of Peter Bomwart, of this place/Died near Frankfort, Va, Fri morning last, Mrs. Seymour, consort of Garret Seymour, Esq.

60. MAL Feb 6 1826/Died in this town Wed morning last after a protracted illness, Peter Gephartt, Cryer of Allegany Co Court, in the 80th year of his age/Benjamin Harwood, Treasurer of the Western Shore of Md., died Sat morning last, 28th inst

61. MAL Feb 27 1826/Married Thurs 14th inst at Springfield, Va, by Rev Foote, John Parker, to Miss Mary Ann Whiteman, both of that place/Married Tues last by Rev Heyer, John Hamond, to Miss Catharine Stoyer, both of Allegany Co/Married Thurs last by Rev Sigler, Samuel Magill to Miss Precilla Beall, dau of Thomas Beall, all of this co/Died at Springfield, Va, Mon night last, Mrs. Elizabeth Abernathy, consort of Wm Abernathy, and dau of John Stump, Esq.

62. MAL Mar 6 1826/Married Tues last by Rev Kurtz, Rev N. B. Little of this place, to Miss Mary Ann Fouke, dau of Henry Fouke, of Wash Co/Died at Phila

MARYLAND ADVOCATE (Cumberland)

Fri 24th ult, Commodore Richard Dale, in the 70th year of his age/Died 16th inst, at his late res in Essex Co, after a severe illness of 13 days' continuance, James Hunter, Esq. a member of the Board of Public Works of the State of Va

63. MAL Mar 13 1826/Died near Springfield, Va, on 1st inst, in the 67th year of her age, Mrs. Elizabeth Isler, wife of Jacob Isler, and mother of George Isler, mail contractor/Died Sun morning last, in this place, William Hoblitzell, in the 34th year of his age, leaving wife and 3 small children

64. MAL Mar 20 1826/Married in George-town, D.C. Tues evening 7th inst, by Rev Balch, Dr. R.H. Beatty of Hancock, Md., to Miss Mary C. Ott, dau of late Dr. John Ott, of the former place/Married in this town, Tues evening last by Rev Little, Joseph Everstine to Miss Mary Clary, all of this place

65. MAL Mar 27 1826/Married Thurs evening last by Rev Sigler, Ephriam Shipley to Miss Nancy Statler, all of this place

66. MAL Apr 3 1826/Married Thurs 16th ult by Rev Heyer, Absalom Stoyer to Miss Juliana Brant, dau of John Brant, of this co/Married Tues last by Rev Nash, Dr. Temple of Romney, Va, to Miss Nancy Cresap, dau of Thomas Cresap, Esq. of this co

67. MAL Apr 10 1826/Married Sun 2d inst by Rev J.J. Jacobs, John Collins to Miss Elizabeth Reily, all of this co/Died in this town, yesterday morning, after a short illness, Jacob Neff, aged 57 years, 5 months and 17 days/Died at his res in Chester Co 15th ult, Walter Kerr, Esq. aged 60 years, Past G.M. of the Grand Lodge of Pa.

68. MAL Apr 17 1826/Married Tues last by Rev Ryan, Peter McCleery, Esq. of this city to Mrs. Hunter, of the Big Crossings, Pa/Died near Frostburg, Sun morning 9th inst, after a short illness, Mrs. Sarah Bevans, wife of Samuel Bevans/Died in this town Thurs morning last, after an illness of about one hour, Michael Kershner, a soldier of the Rev

69. MAL Apr 29 1826/Married Tues last by Rev N.B. Little, John Boose, of this town, to Mrs. Elizabeth Wengert, of this co/Married Tues evening last by same, George Tilghman of Wash Co, to Miss Anna Lynn, dau of Capt. D. Lynn, of this place/Died Tues last after two weeks' sickness, Mrs. Mary Arnold, aged 40 years, consort of Anthony Arnold, of this co, leaving husband and 6 small children/Died lately at his res in Montgomery Co, Md., Washington Bowie, aged about 50, for many years an eminent merchant of Georgetown, D.C./Died in the same co on 30th ult. John B. Magruder, aged 83 yrs/Died in Rockville, same co, 14th inst John A.T. Kilgour, Esq. Attorney at Law, aged 31 yrs

70. MAL May 6 1826/Died Thurs last at the res of her father, Joseph Cresap, Esq. near Cresap-town, in this co, Mrs. Phoebe Cresap, aged about 35 yrs, wife of John Cresap/Died Sat night 29th ult, after an illness of only 4 days, James Scott, in the 55th yr of his age, res of this place for many yrs. He left wife and 3 children; remains deposited in the burial ground on farm on which he lived adj town/Died Mon morning last about 7 o'clock, in the 21st year of her age, Mrs. Mary Ann W. Taylor, consort of William Taylor of this place. She had been unwell for several weeks, occasionally taken

MARYLAND ADVOCATE (Cumberland)

with sudden spasms. On the morning of her death, thinking that a short walk in the cool air would be a relief to her, she left the house, unaccompanied and proceeded down the banks of the river... (apparently taken with a spasm and drowned in about 6 inches of water, observed by man on opposite side of the river, who got to her too late)/Two boys, Richard Kade and Isaac White, aged about 14 and 15 years, who lived with, Samuel Madden on the opp side of the Potomac from this place in Virginia, while ploughing in a field, 8-10 days since, ate of a poisonous root they ploughed up, which caused their deaths within a few days of each other

71. MAL May 13 1826/Equity case - Michael Ream vs Richard Dunn and others, Allegany Court. Object of bill is to obtain decree for sale of mortgaged premises. In 1823 Richard Dunn, being indebted to complainant, it was agreed that complainant should convey house and lot to Charlotte Dunn, wife of said Richard, and that the said Richard and Charlotte, his wife, should execute to the complainant a mortgage. Charlotte Dunn hath died, leaving infant child who survived her a few days only; Mary Soyster, wife of Jonathan Soyster, of Allegany Co, is heir at law to Charlotte Dunn, decd. Jonathan Soyster and Mary have conveyed their interest in premises to James Reside and Reside hath conveyed same to William Hoblitzell. Richard Dunn hath removed to Pa

72. MAL May 20 1826/Died Sat last, Mrs. Selby, wife of Arthur Selby of this co, leaving husband and 2 small twin daus/Equity case - Christian Musselman & others vs Jacob Musselman & others - to obtain decree for sale of real est of which Christian Musselman, late of Allegany Co, died seized, or possessed, in 1824, intestate, leaving children, heirs at law: Christian, Elizabeth wife of Joseph Horb, Anna wife of John Plocher, Jacob, Susanah wife of Henry Arthur, Fanny wife of George Hansel and John, who, after the decease of his father, died in testate, leaving Christiana his widow and the following children: John, Susanah, Elizabeth, Daniel and Andrew. Susannah Musselman is the widow of Christian Musselman. Susannah, John, Elizabeth, Daniel and Andrew, children of said John Musselman, are under age of 21. Said minors and Christiana Musselman, widow fo John Musselman, and Henry, Arthur and Susannah, his wife, do not res within state of Md

73. MAL May 27 1826/Died Wed night 1st inst, about 10 o'clock, Mrs. Elizabeth Isler, companion of Jacob Isler, on Morgan's Run, near Springield, after an indisposition of about 4 weeks (long testimonial)

74. MAL Jun 10 1826/Married Thurs last, by Rev Sigler, Henry Sheetz, to Miss Ann Blair, dau of Col.T. Blair, all of this co

75. MAL Jul 1 1826/Dreadful Accident - Sat last at the raising of a barn of Christ'n Barkley, in Somerset township, as the hands were putting up the rafter, the last work to be done that day, Theophilus Sutton and a son of Jacob Huffman, aged about 19 yrs, who were on the building, were by reason of the plank or board giving way, precipitated to the ground. The former instantly killed and the latter so much injured by the fall that little hopes are entertained. Mr Sutton left a wife and 4 small children/Died Thurs morning 29th ult, Mrs. Elizabeth Beall, consort of Aza Beall, Esq. in the 51st year of her age, after a long and painful illness, leaving husband and children

MARYLAND ADVOCATE (Cumberland)

76. MAL Jul 8 1826/Died in this town, Sun last after a long indisposition, Solomon Davis, in the 51st year of his age

77. MAL Aug 5 1826/Chancery case - Cumberland bank of Allegany vs John Timmonds, Bridjit Hone, Charles Hone, Maria Easter, Henry Easter; Wm., James, Andrew, Nancy, George, Ophilia, Johanna, Jerome, Margaret and Ann Timmonds. Object of the bill is to obtain decree for sale of real est of James Timmonds, decd, to pay his debts. He died lately intestate. John Timmonds, Bridget Hone, Chas. Hone, Wm. Timmonds, Andrew Timmonds, Maria Ester and Henry Ester, res out of the state of Md

78. MAL Aug 12 1826/Died near this town Wed night last Mrs. Beall, wife of William Beall, aged 80 yrs

79. MAL Aug 19 1826/Died in this town Fri night last, after a short illness, Henry Wineour, young man/Died at her res in Prince George's Co, yesterday, 14th inst, in the 45th year of her age, Mrs. Eleanor Lee Kent, consort of the Hon. Joseph Kent, Governor of Md, leaving husband and group of little children/Joseph Shumate cautions whereas his wife Deborah has left his bed and board, leaving him with their 4 small children, 2 of whom are now confined to bed with sickness

80. MAL Aug 26 1826/Died 14th inst at the res of her father in Allegany Co, in the 5th year of her age, Margaret, eldest dau of Michael C. Sprigg, Esq /Died at Fort Wayne, In, 8th inst, of billious fever, James Shriver, Esq. of Union town, Pa; he was attending to his duties as U.S. Engineer in the neighborhood of Brookville - From Balt. American/Died Fri night last after a painful illness, Paul Allen, in the 55th year of his age; during a res of 12 yrs in Balt/Died in Haverhill, N.H. jail where he was confined for a debt of $12.00, Noah Buzzell, aged 70, of Alexandria, soldier of the Rev

81. MAL Sep 2 1826/Died in this town, Thurs last, William, son of Reubin Worthington, in the 2d year of his age

82. MAL Sep 9 1826/Died Tues morning last, after a few days illness, at Walter Slicer's tavern, about 12 miles east of this place, Samuel Thomas, in the 50th (59th?) year of his age, husband and father, twice a member of the general assembly, once from Montgomery co and once from Alegany co, interred Wed morning in the burial ground, near Mr. Slicer's tavern

83. MAL Sep 16 1826/Married Wed 7th inst, by Rev N.B. Little, George Wolford, to Miss Rebecca Street, all of this co/Married Thurs 7th inst, by Rev John Jones, J. Snively, of Hancock, Md. to Miss Harriet Blackwell, dau of David Blackwell, of Prince William Co, Va

84. MAL Sep 23 1826/Married in this town, Thurs night last, by Rev James Riely, Rev Tobias Riely, to Miss Ann Maria M'Neill, dau of John McNeill, Esq. of this place/Died suddenly in this town, Sat morning last, Henry Culver, Esq., of Prince Georges Co, Md

85. MAL Sep 30 1826/Died in this town, Tues morning last, after a short illness, Mrs. Anne Everstine, wife of Lewis Everstine, in the 23d year of her age, leaving husband and 2 small children

MARYLAND ADVOCATE (Cumberland)

86. MAL Oct 7 1826/Died in this town Thurs morning last after a protracted indisposition, Mrs. Catharine Searight, consort of James Searight

87. MAL Oct 14 1826/Died in this town, Tues morning last, after an indisposition of 5 days, Louisiana P.W. Buchanan, aged 7 months, dau of the Editor of this paper (J.M. Buchanan)

88. MAL Oct 21 1826/Died near Old-town Wed morning last, Mrs. Elizabeth Martin, consort of Lenox Martin, Esq./Died at his res in Cecil Co, Md., Col. Wm. C. Miller, late a member of the Senate of this state

89. MAL Oct 28 1826/Allegany Co Equity Court - Margaret Sheetze vs Wm. M. Sheetze. Object of bill is to obtain decree for sale of real est of which Adam Sheetz, late of Allegany Co, decd, died, seized or possessed, in testate, in 1821, leaving children: Wm. M. Sheetze, Joseph Sheetze, Henry Sheetze, Jacob Sheetze, Harriet Sheetze, Elizabeth Willey, wife of Alexander Willey, and Sarah Groves, wife of David Groves. Alexander Willey and Elizabeth his wife and David Groves and Sarah his wife and Jacob Sheetze, do not res within state of Md

90. MAL Nov 4 1826/Allegany Equity court - Robert French, agnst Samuel French and others. Object of bill is to obtain decree for sale of lot westward of Fort Cumberland of which Joseph French, of Allegany Co, died, seized or possessed, intestate, leaving children: Robert French, Samuel French, Phebius French, Daniel French, David French, Mary French, Joseph French, and Anna French, and a widow Annah French. Phebius m David Ruttan of Allegany Co, who died leaving two children, her heirs, Peter and Daniel Ruttan, under age of 21 and who now res in Allegany Co. Mary French m Matthew Molor who lives in Fayette Co, Pa. Anna French m Benjamin Johnson, lives in Ohio. Annah French m Ephram Vansicke, lives in Pa. Samuel French, Daniel French, David French, Joseph French, do not res within state of Md

91. MAL Nov 11 1826/Allegany Equity court - James C. Connelly vs Jonathan France and others - object of the bill is to obtain a decree for sale of tract in Allegany Co, called Rich Hill, sold by Edward Kemp, decd, to Jonathan France. The bill states that Edward Kemp died intestate. James C. Connelly, complainant is administrator of said Edward Kemp. Nancy Hoover, wife of Henry Hoover, Ruth Dean wife of William Dean, Hulda Pierson wife of David Pierson, Oliva Guard widow of Jeremiah Guard, Elizabeth Tissul wife of Isaac Tissul, Sophia Friend wife of John Friend, Edward Kemp, Henry Kemp, Richard Kemp, John Kemp, Lavinia Friend wife of Josiah Friend, Sarah Kemp and Mary Kemp (children of Massey Kemp), Rachael Moore wife of Francis Moore, Daniel McCulloch and Alexander McCulloch (children of Jeremiah McCulloch), Rachael Elliott, dau of Sophia Elliott, Edward Forshey, Oliva Friend, wife of John Friend, John Forshey, Rachel Connelly, wife of James C. Connelly, Abel Forshey and Margaret Forshey (children of Margaret Forshey), Margaret Spencer, Rachel Spencer, Darcus Spencer, Benjamin Spencer, Edward Spencer, and Drusilla Spencer children of Oliva Spencer, are the heirs at law and legal representatives of said Edward Kemp, decd and all said heirs res out of the state of Md

92. MAL Dec 9 1826/John S. Williams, vs. Joseph Williams, Otho H. Williams, Maria Sophia Buchanan, John Buchanan, Catharine K. Gaither, Henry H. Gaither, John I. Stull, Anne B. Stull, Elie W. Stull, John Louis Stull, Matilda

MARYLAND ADVOCATE (Cumberland)

Stull, Naomi Williams, Anne Barbara Williams, Susan Williams, Josias Thompson, Eliza Thompson, Hilleary Thompson, the president, directors and company of the bank of Columbia, Thomas Kennedy, Barclay and McKean, and James Campbell - object of bill to obtain sale of real est of late Elie Williams, Allegany, called Willimas' Sheep Walk. That Elie Williams died, seized of and possesed said tract; that it descended to part of the defendants, as his children and heirs at law. That Josias Thompson and Hilleary Thompson, at the time of the death of Elie Williams, were entitled to an equitable interest in 2/3 of said land; that Otho H. Williams, Maria Sophia Buchanan, John Buchanan, Catharine K. Gaither, Henry H. Gaither, John I. Stull & Prudence H. Stull, Josiah Thompson, Eliza Thompson and Hilleary Thompson have transferred all their interest in said land to complainant; that Naomi Williams, widow of John Conrod Williams has consented as far as she is concerned to have the land sold. The bill states that Joseph Williams, John I. Stull, Anne B. Stull, Elie H. Stull, John Louis Stull, Matilda Stull, Naomi Williams, Anne Barbara Williams, Susan Williams, Josias Thompson, Eliza Thompson, Hilleary Thompson, the president, directors and company of the Bank of Columbia, res out of the state of Md

93. MAL Jan 20 1827/Died in this town last night at the res of Mrs. James Scott, her father Joseph Cresap; for several years he held a seat in the Councils of the State; for a number of yrs he belonged to the Meth Church

94. MAL Jan 27 1827/Died very suddenly at his res in this co, Sun morning last, Charles Uhl, in the 66th year of his age

95. MAL Feb 3 1827/John J. Hoffman offers reward for apprentice to the wagon making bus., named Dicksey Simpkins, about 19 yrs of age, 5 ft 6-7 inch

96. MAL Feb 10 1827/Married Thus last by Rev N.B. Little, Philip Wingert, esq. of Hagerstown, to Miss Martha Tomlinson, dau of Benjamin Tomlinson, Esq. of this co/Allegany Co Equity Court - William Roby vs Martin Engle - to obtain Writ of Injunction to stay proceedings at law on a judgment obtained in Allegany Co court, by Martin Engle agnst William Roby, and for final relief. The bill states that Owen Roby father of this complainant, died in 1799; complainant as exec of said Owen Roby, was empowered to sell real est of decd, which he did, sell est to Daniel Rench. That there was 9 heirs of said Owen Roby and they all received their shares arising from sale of said real estate. Complainant has not received any compensation for expenses as Executor. The bill states further that Statia Roby, heir of Owen Roby, m some yrs since, Martin Engle, defendant in this bill who is not res of this state

97. MAL Mar 3 1827/Died Sat last near Fred Town, Thomas Grahame

98. MAL Mar 10 1827/Married Tues last by Rev T. Ryan, of Hagerstown, Edward Mullan to Miss Ann Blocher, dau of George Blocher, Esq. of this town/Married same day by Rev N.B. Little, George Riely, to Miss Margaret Brant, dau of John Brant, near Westernport, all of this co/Married Thurs last by Rev T. Ryan, Francis Dean, to Miss Mary Arnold, both of this co/Married 15th ult, by Rev Robert Kennedy, of Frankin Co, Pa, Rev John H. Kennedy, Pastor of the 6th Presby Church, Phila, to Miss Harriet McCallmot of Crescentville/Died in Balt Co Thurs, 22d ult, Edward Reside, father of James Reside, Esq. of this

MARYLAND ADVOCATE (Cumberland)

town, a native of Scotland, in the 82d year of his age. He had res in that co 50 yrs

99. MAL Mar 17 1827/Married Tiues 6th inst. by Rev Haus, Jacob Schaeffer, to Miss Sarah Ann Payton, all of this co/Married Sun last by Rev T. Ryan, of Hagers-town, James Mattingly, to Miss Albright, both of this co

100. MAL Mar 24 1827/Married Thurs 15th inst by Rev J.J. Jacob, Reuben Collins to Miss Lucinda Carter, both of this co/Bedford, March 16. - Died on the 27th ult at the seat of Hon. John Taliaferro, near Fredricksburg, Va, Maj. John A. Burd, of the U.S. army, in the 43d year of his age. He was a native of this co and active officer during the late war - True Amer.

102. MAL Apr 7 1827/Married Thurs 29th ult by Rev Sigler, Frederick Rice to Miss Barbara Diffenbaugh, both of Bedford Co, Pa

103. MAL Apr 14 1827/Married in Hagerstown, Tues morning last by Rev Brunner, Samuel J. Downey, merchant, to Miss Ann Maria Conrad, all of that town

104. MAL Apr 21 1827/Died at his res in this co, 26th ult, Henry White, senr., in the 68th year of his age/Married in Wash Co, Wed last by Rev F. Ruthrauff, Benjamin Oswald, editor of the Lancaster (Ohio) Gazette, to Miss Sarah Ann Brennum, of that co

105. MAL Apr 28 1827/Died in this co, Mon last, Mrs. Sarah McCarty, consort of Edward McCarty, aged about 39 yrs, leaving husband and children/Chancery court - David Logsdon, Thomas White and Wenny White, Ralph Payne, Wenny Payne, his wife, Joshua Logsdon, Joseph Logsdon, vs Ralph Logsdon, John Logsdon, Margaret M'Kinsey & John M'Kinsey, Joseph Logsdon of William, Thomas Porter, John Porter of Thomas, Henry Porter, John Porter of Henry, David Porter, Nancy Porter, Henry Porter, jr., Margaret Logsdon. The object of the bill is to obtain decree for sale of real est of William Logsdon, senr, decd, for the benefit of his heirs at law. That some of the complainants and defendants are the heirs at law of said William Logsdon who died intestate, leaving considerable real est in Allegany Co. John Logsdon purchased undivided share of said real est from John Porter of Thomas; John Logsdon, Joseph Logsdon of William, John Porter, of Thomas, Thomas Porter, res out of the state of Md

106. MAL May 5 1827/George Lantz was arrested near Old town for the murder of John Gusler, about 30 miles south east of Cumberland, March 1824

107. MAL May 12 1827/William McMahon, and others vs Mary Cochran and others. Object of bill is to obtain decree for sale of real est of Ninian Cochran, Allegany co, decd. The bill states that Ninian Cochran some yrs since died intestate, leaving his widow, Mary, and following children and heirs at law: Mary who m Isaac Hildebrand both res out of state of Md, and Arabell under age of 21/Died in this co on the 7th inst, Mrs. Honour Shircliff, consort of Leonard Shircliff, Esq.

108. MAL May 26 1827/Hagerstown - Died Sun last in the 72d year of his age, Capt. William Lewis of this town; remains deposited yesterday in the Luth burial ground. He was the late crier of Wash Co court; served at the battles of Trenton, Princeton, Brandywine, Germantown, Monmouth and numerous

MARYLAND ADVOCATE (Cumberland)

skirmishes. When Gen. Wayne organized the U.S. Army and proceeded agnst the Indians in 1793, Lewis was promoted a captain and fought at the Miami. He was deprived of sight for 2 yrs before his death

109. MAL Jun 2 1827/Married in this town, Thurs evening last by Rev N.B. Little, Joseph Rizer, to Miss Elizabeth Fisher, all of this town/Died in Columbus Ohio, on 15th ult, George Nashee, esq., Editor of the Ohio State Journal, aged about 40 yrs, member of the Legislature of Ohio - Lancasster (Ohio) Gazette

110. MAL Jun 9 1827/Married near Old-town, Md. on Thurs 31st ult by Rev J.J. Jacob, Lionel M. Jameson, of Frankfort, Va, to Miss Elizabeth Stump, dau of Jacob Stump, of this co/Allegany co Equity Court - Anne Timmons, Bridget and Charles Hone, Henry and Maria Easter, Nancy and Baptist Mattingly, Wm. Timmonds, Ja's Timmonds, And'w Timmonds, Jno. Timmonds, Geo. Timmonds, Ophelia Timmonds, Joanna Timmonds, Jerome Timmonds, and Margaret Timmonds, complainants vs Sarah Logsdon, Joseph Logsdon, John Porter (of Samuel), William Porter (of Samuel), Henry Porter, Hannah Porter, Benjamin F. Porter, Mary Devore, Cornelius Devore, Nancy Ireland, William Ireland, John Porter (of Michael), Michael Porter (of Michael), Henry Porter, Thomas Porter, Samuel Scott Porter, Polly Porter, Betsy Barkus, John Barkus and William R. Dawson, respondents. Object of bill is to obtain a decree for conveyance of tract called Pine Mountain of which Michael Porter, senr, Allegany Co, died seized. Samuel Porter, decd, of said co, caused to be surveyed for himself, a tract called Pine Mountain. That Michael Porter died leaving children: John, Michael, Henry, Thomas, Samuel, Scott, Polly and Betsy who m John Barkus. That James Timmonds has died leaving Ann Timmonds his widow and following children: John, Andrew, George, Ophelia, Joanna, Jereome, William, James, Margaret, Nancy who m Baptist Mattingly, Maria who m Henry Easter and Bridget who m Charles Hone. Samuel Porter has died leaving Sarah his widow who has since m Joseph Logsdon and following children: John, Michael, William, Hannah, Benjamin F., Mary who m Cornelius Devore, and Nancy who m William Ireland. The following res out of the state of Md.: Michael Porter of Samuel, Mary Devore, Cornelius Devore, Hannah Porter, Benjamin F. Porter, Nancy Ireland, William Ireland, Sarah and Joseph Logsdon, and John Porter of Michael.

111. MAL Jun 16 1827/Died at his res in this co, Sat night last after a protracted and painful illness, William Coddington, in the 77th year of his age/Michael Lane, Cumberland, warns person not to trust his wife Frances, as he is determined not to pay any of her debts

112. MAL Jun 30 1827/Died in this town, Mon, 18th inst, Margaret McKinley, dau of James McKinley, in the 12th year of her age/Died in this town, Sat morning last, Mrs. Catharine Rogers, consort of Arthur Rogers, married just 5 weeks ago; remains interred in Roman Cath burial ground/Died in this town, Thurs morning last Christiana Dorcas, infant dau of Solomon and Harriet Stover

113. MAL Jul 7 1827/Married in this place Tues last by Rev N.B. Little, Malohn Lewis, to Miss Isabella Bogs, both of Va/Died at his res in this co, Fri 29th ult, John Simpkins, Esq. in the 84th year of his age, several yrs a rep from this co in state legislature

MARYLAND ADVOCATE (Cumberland)

114. MAL Jul 14 1827/Died in this co, Sun last, Mrs. Nancy Arnold, consort of Johnzee Arnold/Died a few days since, at his res, near Hancock, in this co, Thomas Beveins, Inn Keeper - Hagerstown, Torch Light

115. MAL Jul 21 1824/Murder committed Wed 11th inst, near Berlin, Somerset Co, Pa, by an Irishman named Burns on the person of John P.H. Walker. Altercation arose from dissatisfaction of Walker with Burns who had been employed to mow for Walker. Burns cut walker in two, his bowels instantly falling on the ground and he expired without a groan. Burns made his escape without delay/Married in this town Tues evening last by Rev N.B. Little, James W. Miller, of Wellsburg, Va, to Miss Elenora Shryer, dau of John Shryer, of this place

116. MAL Jul 28 1827/Married Sun 15th inst, by Rev S. Haslett, Jacob Clemmer, Esq. to Miss Maria Hoffman, dau of David Hoffman, all of this co/Philip Walker, Brothers valley township, Somerset co, Pa, offers $200 reward for Andrew Burns who slew his son, Geo. P.H. Walker. Burns is a native of Ireland, about 5 ft 6-7 inch, dark sandy hair, rather of a dark complexion, supposed to be about 30 yrs of age

117. MAL Aug 18 1827/Died in Hagers-town Fri morning 10th inst, in the 74th year of his age, Col. Adam Ott, Rev officer and former Sheriff of Wash Co

118. MAL Aug 25 1827/Died in this town, Mon last after a protracted illness, Mrs. Mary Moore, wife of Enoch Moore, in the 37th year of her age, for many yrs a member of the Meth Epis church/Died at his res in Yough Glades in this co, Fri night 19th inst, Joseph White, aged about 35 yrs, leaving wife and 2 children/Died at Pittsburg, Pa, Sun morning 12th inst, Col. John McFarland, editor of Allegany Democrat, in the 30th year of his age

119. MAL Sep 1 1827/Married Wed evening last by Rev Butler, Edward McCarty to Miss Ruth Cresap, dau of Robert Cresap, of this co

120. MAL Sep 8 1827/Died at his res Tues evening last after a very short illness, Robert Cresap, old citizen/Died Tues evening last, Mrs. Jemima Bucey, wife of Paul Bucey, aged about 86, for upwards of 36 yrs, an inhabitant of this co/Died Wed morning last near Old Town, in this co, after an illness of about 24 hrs, John Foly, leaving wife and several children/Died Mon 20th ult, near Frostburg, Mrs. Rebecca Vaughn, in the 58th year of her age, consort of Benjamin Vaughn, Esq./Died in this town Sun 26th ult., Mrs. Hook, relict of the late John S. Hook, aged upwards of 70 yrs, for more than 40 yrs a res of this town

121. MAL Sep 15 1827/Married in this town Thurs night last by Rev Sigler, John C. Newman, late of Hampshire Co, Va, to Miss Margaret Bucy, of this town/Died at his res in Smythfield, Somerset Co, Pa, on Tues 4th inst, David Hoffman, sen., in the 75th year of his age/Died in the neighbourhood of Frostburg Fri 14th inst, William Taylor

122. MAL Sep 22 1827/Robert Cresap died at his res on North Branch Tues evening Sep 4, in the 60th year of his age of a protracted nature (long testimonial) /Died Thurs last, Miss Nancy Carter, dau of Joseph Carter, Esq. of this co/Died yesterday evening in this town, Miss Melvina Hays, dau of late Rev John Hays

MARYLAND ADVOCATE (Cumberland)

123. MAL Sep 29 1827/Married Tues evening last at Old town, by Rev J.J. Jacob, George Devicman, to Miss Sophia Lantz, dau of late Daniel Lantz, of this co

124. MAL Oct 6 1827/John McShane gives notice that his wife Mary has left his bed and board

125. MAL Oct 13 1827/Died 28th ult, Mrs. Amelia Kile, consort of Robert Kile of Cresapsburgh, after a long and tedious illness/Died at his res near Western Port in this co, Monday night last after a short illness, John Morrison, in the 30th year of his age, leaving wife and 2 small children

126. MAL Oct 20 1827/Died in this town Sun morning the 7th inst, Mrs. Margaret Neff, relict of late Jacob Neff, aged about 50 yrs, wife and parents /Died morning of 9th inst at the res of his son, 1 miles from Cumberland, George Brown, Senr., in the 87th year of his age. He was born in Phila Co, Pa, his parents who were poor German emigrants, died when he was an infant. At the age of 16 he entered into the British army where he remained 7 yrs; during which period he assisted as a provincical soldier in the taking of Canada from the French. After the cession of that province he returned to his native state, and in a few yrs after settled at Pipe creek, Fred Co, Md. He resided near this town since autumn of 1795. He was bereft of his sight during the last three yrs/Died in this town Tues morning last, George Hughes, Jr/Death of Col. John Eager Howard last eveing at about half past 8 o'clock, hero of Cowpens and Eutaw/Died at Wheatland, at his late res, Talb Co, Md, Maj. Gen. Perry Benson, in the 72d year of his age, after a lingering illness

127. MAL Oct 27 1827/Died Fri morning last, in the 31st year of his age, after a short illness at the res of his brother, Thomas Farmer Van Lear, son of the late Col. William Van Lear, of Williams-Port

128. MAL Nov 3 1827/From Balt. Amer. of Monday last - Death of Bishop Kemp yesterday from injuries in an accident of a stage from New Castle (Del) to Frenchtown, Md./Chancery case - Thomas Dowden vs Mary Grubb, Sarah Lough, Samuel Basnett, Geo. and William Hoblitzell, Winna Basnett, Thomsa Cooper, and Nancy his wife, defendants. Object of the bill is to obtain decree for sale of a lot in Cumberland of which Nehemiah Basnett, of Allegany Co, died, intestate, leaving the defendants, Winna Basnett his widow and four children, viz. Sarah Basnett, Samuel Basnett, Nancy Basnett and Mary Basnett, his heirs at law. Sarah Basnett m George Laugh who is now dead and since the death of said Laugh, Sarah Laugh has conveyed her interest to complainant. Samuel Basnett conveyed his interest to George and William Hoblitzell and they conveyed same to complainant. Nancy Basnett m Thomas Cooper. Winna Basnett, Thomas Cooper and Nancy his wife, Sarah Laugh, Mary Basnett who m Amos Grubb and Samuel Basnet do not res in state of Md

129. MAL Nov 10 1827/Died Mon 26th Oct last at his res near Hancock, Wash Co, Md, Dr. Lancelot Jacques, aged about 72 yrs/Equity court case - Moses T. Spencer and others vs William I. Spencer and others, heirs at law of David Spencer, decd. Object of this bill to obtain decree for sale of real est of David Spencer, of Allegany Co, decd, to effect division of est among the heirs. David Spencer died intestate some yrs ago, leaving Sarah Spencer, his widow and following children: Moses T. Spencer, Amos L. Spencer, William

MARYLAND ADVOCATE (Cumberland)

1. Spencer, John W. Spencer, Joseph W. Spencer, David G. Spencer, Samuel C. Spencer, Daniel S. Spencer, Ann Inskeep, wife of Samuel Inskeep, Abegael Lewellen, wife of John Lewellen, Rachel Rush, wife of John Rush, Rebecca Chamberlin, wife of John Chamberlin, Mary Jacobs, wife of Jacob Jacobs, and Sarah Hobbs, wife of John Hobbs, his heirs at law. David G. Spencer, Samuel C. Spencer, and Daniel S. Spencer are under age of 21. William I. Spencer, John W. Spencer, Joseph W. Spencer, John Hobbs, and Sarah his wife, John Chamberlin and Rebecca his wife and John Lewellen and Abegael his wife, res out of the state of Md/Equity case - Henry Bedinger vs Edward W. Duval and others, heirs at law of Benjamin Duval decd - for the conveyance of 4 lots West of Cumberland. The bill states that Benjamin Duval sold lots to complainant in 1814; he died in 1820 without having conveyed the prop, and leaving Benjamin Duval, Jr. William Duval, Isaac Duval, Gabriel Duval, Edward W. Duval, Griffen Duval, Susannah Nesbit, Juliet Duval, Jefferson Duval, Martha A. Duval and Era Duval, his children. Jefferson Duval, Martha A. Duval and Era Duval are under age of 21. All said heirs of Benjamin Duval res out of state of Md

130. MAL Dec 1 1827/Died in this town, yesterday morning, Henry Neff, son of late Jacob Neff, in the 16th year of his age/Died in Paddy-town, Hampshire Co, Va, on 17th inst, Jacob son of Henry Rafter, in the 6th year of his age

131. MAL Dec 8 1827/Died in this town on Thurs night last, Hannah Elizabeth dau of Burgess Magruder, in the 5th year of her age

132. MAL Dec 15 1827/Equity Court case - Cumberland Bank of Allegany, Roger Perry, David Lynn, Thomas Blair and Henry Winour vs Isaac Beall, William T. Beall, Benjamin M. Beall and others. Object is to obtain decree for sale of est of Thomas Beall, of Samuel, Allegany Co, decd. The bill states Thomas Beall, of Samuel, made his will and died in 1823, seized of certain tracts in Allegany Co. By said will he devised to his negro man Basil a small piece of land and then devised all the residue of his estate to 8 of his grandchildren, to wit: William T. Beall, Benjamin M. Beall, Jesse T. Beall, Joseph T. Beall, Isaac M. Beall, Samuel B. Beall, Daniel Beall, and Elizabeth B. Beall, children of the devisor's son Isaac Beall. Negro man Basil was a slave over age of 45. Devisor (Thomas Beall of Samuel) died, leaving his son Isaac Beall, his, the devisor's grand children, William T. Beall, John J. Beall, Lewis H. Beall, Anna P. Beall, Juliet Beall, Alexander Beall, Elizbeth Beall, Charles F. Beall, Hamilton Beall, Elie R. Beall, Thomas Beall & Geo. Beall, children of the devisor's son John B. Beall, decd; Eleanor Beall, widow of the said John Beall, decd; his, the devisor's grandchild Thomas Beall, son of the devisor's son Josiah Beall, decd; his the devisor's dau Elizabeth who m Aza Beall, who since died, leaving the following children, Thomas Beall, Anna Eckles, wife of Samuel Eckles, Richard Beall, Alpheus Beall, John Beall, Verlinda Beall, Priscilla Beall, children of the devisor's dau Elizabeth Beall, decd; his the devisor's grand children Beal Beatty, Otho Beatty, Lewis Beatty, Thomas Beatty, Brooke Beatty, Louisa Shroyer wife of Lewis Shroyer, children of the devisor's dau Eleanor Beatty, decd; the devisor's daus Lucy English, wife of James English, Priscilla Slicer, wife of Walter Slicer and Nancy Beatty widow of John C. Beatty, decd; all his the devisor's heirs at law. The son Isaac Beall, the son, neglected to take out letters testamentary on the personal estate of said Thomas Beall of Samuel, and that letters of administration, with the will

MARYLAND ADVOCATE (Cumberland)

annexed were in due form of law, granted to Richard Beall and Gustavus Beall. The complainants were creditors of Thomas Beall of Samuel. The following defendants res out of the state of Md: Isaac Beall, William T. Beall, John J. Beall, Lewis H. Beall, Ann P. Beall, Juliet Beall, Alexander Beall, Elizabeth Beall, Charles F. Beall, Hamilton Beall, Elie R. Beall, Thomas Beall, George Bell, children of John B. Beall, decd; Thomas Beall son of Elizabeth Beall, decd, Beal Beatty, Otho Beatty, Lewis Beatty, Thomas Beatty, Brooke Beatty, Louisa Shroyer, Lewis Shroyer, Lucy English, James English, Nancy Beatty, widow of John C. Beatty, decd, and Eleanor Beall, widow of John B. Beall, decd. Alpheus Beall, John Beall and Priscilla Beall, children of Elizabeth Beall, decd, are under age of 21

133. MAL Dec 15 1827/Died in this town Wed morning last after a long illness, Samuel Lingo, long an inhabitant of this place/Died Thurs last week, John McKinney, of Harpers-Ferry in the 26th year of his age. - He had been married but 8 months, and was the 5th husband of Mrs. Mary Jackson, who is yet under the age of 29

134. MAL Dec 19 1827/Died at his res near Frostburg, in this co, Sat last, Jacob Neff, in the 29th year of his age, industrious citzen and member of the Meth Soc

135. MAL Jan 5 1828/Married Thurs evening last by Rev Little, George Deneen, to Mrs. Elizabeth Davis, all of this co/Died Sun 16th ult, at his res near Westminster, Joshua Cockey, late member of the Senate of Md

136. MAL Jan 12 1828/William Greene was killed in his well in this town, Wed evening last. He was near the bottom of the well, engaged in walling it up. Persons who were employed to lower stone to him in a large wooden vessel, let the bucket in which was placed a large stone, fall into the well, which struck Mr. Greene on the left side of the head, and killed him instantly. He left a wife and 3 small children/Married Thurs last by Rev N. B. Little, John Broadmarkle, to Miss Ellen Beall, all of this co

137. MAL Jan 26 1828/Died in this town, yesterday morning, James Ward, Innkeeper, in the 24th year of his age, husband and parent

138. MAL Feb 9 1828/Married near Old-town Tues 29th ult, by Rev James Taylor, John Slicer, of Urbanna, Ohio, to Miss Jemima Harness, dau of late Wm. Harness, of this co/Ambrose Mareshal, Archbishop of Baltimore, died yesterday/Died in Frostburg, Fri night 1st inst., Dennis Beall, Esq. in the 49th year of his age, leaving a wife and 7 children/Washington, Pa. Feb 4 - Robert Carlisle of Woodford Co, Ky, murdered Fri morning last, 1st inst, before day light, on the U.S. Turnpike road, 2 miles from Washington, near the bridge over Chartiers creek. Mr. Carlisle arrived in Washington, Thursday night, from Cumberland, on his way home with a runaway slave. His slave, Kit, has been charged

139. MAL Feb 16 1828/Hagerstown Times - A man by name of Edward Kelly, was killed at Samuel Prather's in this co last week. In the turning of a boat which was launched, his head was caught beneath it and crushed to pieces

140. MAL Feb 23 1828/Died at his res near Paddy-town, Hampshire Co, Va, Sat 2d inst., John Ravenscraft, in 75th year of his age, leaving widow and sev-

MARYLAND ADVOCATE (Cumberland)

eral children/Died in this town Thurs morning, Michael Hays, in the 76th year of his age, upwards of 30 yrs an inhabitant of this co, parent and good citizen/Married Tues evening last, by Rev N. B. Little, Francis Bruce to Miss Ellenor Clary, both of this co

141. MAL May 3 1828/Married Thurs last by Rev Sigler, William Taylor to Miss Levenia Hill, dau of John Hill, all of this co

142. MAL May 10 1828/Married Thurs last by Rev N.B. Little, Ezra Wilson to Miss Elizabeth Burgess, all of this co/Married Mon evening last by Rev Ryan of Hagerstown, Arthur Rogers, to Miss Lucinda Fisher, dau of Michael Fisher of this place/Died one day last week at Cresapsburg, Eleanor Walls, late living relict of Samuel Walls, formerly of this place, but now of "yon and elsewhere!"/Equity case of Allegany co court - Thomas Dowdon agnst Mary Grubb, Sarah Lough, Samuel Basnett, George & William Hoblitzell, Winey Basnett, Thomas Cooper and Nancy his wife, and John J. Hoffman, defendants. Object of the bill is to obtain decree for sale of lot No. 199 in Cumberland, of which Nehemiah Basnett of Allegany Co, died intestate leaving the defendant Winey Basnett, his widow and four children, viz: Sarah Basnett, Samuel Basnett, Nancy Basnett and Mary Basnett, his heirs at law. That Sarah Basnett intermarried with George Lough who is now dead and that since the death of said Lough, Sarah Lough has conveyed all her interest in said lot to the complainant. Samuel Basnett conveyed his interest to George and Wm. Hoblitzell who in turn conveyed their interest to John J. Hoffman who conveyed same to complainant. Nancy Basnett intermarried with Thomas Cooper who have conveyed their right to complainant. Winey Basnett, Thomas Cooper and Nancy his wife, Sarah Lough, Mary Basnett who has intermarried with one Amos Grubb and Samuel Basnett do not res with state of Md/Henry Beddinger vs Edward W. Duvall and others - Object of Bill is to obtain decree for conveyance of 4 lots west of Cumberland. Bill states that Benjamin Duvall sold lots in 1814 to complainant. Benj. Duvall died some time in 1820 without having conveyed the prop and leaving Benjamin Duvall jr., William Duvall, Isaac Duvall, Gabriel Duvall, Edward W. Duvall, Griffin Duvall, Susan Nesbit wife of Nesbit whose Christian name cannot be ascertained, Juliet Duvall, Jefferson Duvall, Matthew A. Duvall and Ezra Duvall his children and heirs at law; it further appears that Jefferson Duvall, Matthew A. Duvall and Ezra Duvall are under age of 21 and all said heirs of Benjamin Duvall res out of the state

143. MAL May 24 1828/Married Thurs last by Rev Voigt, Archibald Uhl, of this co to Miss Leah Flickinger of Somerset Co, Pa/Married same day by Rev Sigler, George Reid to Miss Maria Macname, all of this town

144. MAL Jun 7 1828/Married Thurs evening last by Rev N.B. Little, John Wells, to Miss Elizabeth Robinson, all of this town/Married Wednesday by same, Ashford Parker, of Hampshire Co, Va, to Miss Sarah Wheller, of this co

145. MAL Jun 14 1828/Married Wed 4 inst. in Southampton township, Somerset Co, Pa by Squire Martz, Jonathan Soyster, of this town, to Miss Elizabeth Ann Boyer, of Frederick Co, Md/Died at Cresap-town in this co, Thurs night 1st, James C. Cresap, son of the late Joseph Cresap, Esq. in the 34th year of his age

MARYLAND ADVOCATE (Cumberland)

year of her age, leaving husband and one child and many relatives and friends/Suddenly died at his res about 3 miles from this place Wed 18 inst, William Davidson, in the 59th year of his age, after an illness of about 24 hours; member of Meth Episc church for about 40 years/Married Tues 10 Jun in Harrisburg, Pa, Stephen Duncan, Esq. of Phila, to Miss Louisa P. Pollard, formerly of Cumberland

147. MAL Jul 5 1828/Married in Balt Tues 24 ult by Rev Dr. Wyatt, Lieut. Walter Gwinn of the Engineer Corps, to Miss Elizabeth Bruce, dau of Upton Bruce, Esq./Died after an illness of some days on Mon June 2nd, on Patterson's Creek, Hampshire Co, Va, Rev Ebenezer McNary, preacher of the Regular Baptist Church, about 46 years of age, for a number of years an acceptable minister of the New and Everlasting Covenant/Died at Paddy-town, Va, Tues last, after a short illness, Patrick McCarty, Esq.

148. MAL Jul 12 1828/Married Thurs 3rd inst. by Rev Sigler, John Frost, to Mrs. Harriet Lovett, all of this co/Died Fri 27th ult, at his res, in this co, James Drane, Sen., in the 74th year of his age, husband and father

149. MAL Jul 19 1828/Married Thurs even last by Rev J.J. Jacob, Doct. Jeremiah Berry, to Miss Lavania Cromwell, dau of Thomas Cromwell, Esq. all of this co/On Wed evening 9 inst., between the hours of 10 and 11 o'clock (says the Georgetown, D.C. Columbian), Elie Holtzman, an old and respectable inhabitant of this town arose from his bed in a profund sleep and precipitated himself out of the second story window of his dwelling and so seriously injured himself as to cause his death in a short time afterwards.

150. MAL Jul 26 1828/Died Mon last at the house of Mr. James Black in this town, Robert Armstrong, Esq. in the 62nd year of his age; he was born in the county Down, Ireland, emigrated around 1785; for more than 40 years he was a res of this co; twice represented the co in the state legislature, was at the time of his death, Justice of the Orphans Court/Died Sat morning last, at res of Jacob Hoblitzell, near this town, Miss Matilda Hess, in the 19th year of her age/Died at his res in this co, Mon morning last, Alfred Burgess, aged about 35 years; left a wife and several children/Rev William Chapman died 24 Apr about 10 o'clock (From Christian Advocate and Journal)

151. MAL Aug 2 1828/Died at Western Port in this co, Sun, 20th ult, Rezin Simpson, a Rev soldier, in the 73d year of his age/Died in this Town, Sat morning last, Mrs. Mary Macnamee, wife of Moses Macnamee, in the 49th year of her age, wife and mother; remains interred at Meth Epis burial ground; discourse delivered by Rev Sigler/Ranaway from subscriber, Washington Evans, Martinsburg, va, Mortimore Hasletine, aged about 19 years, apprentice to the Printing bus.

152. MAL Aug 16 1828/Died in this town at the house of her son-in-law, Jacob Fechtig, Mon last, Mrs. Margaret Hilleary, in the 64th year of her age, relict of the late William Hilleary, Esq. of this co; she has left 2 children and several grand children and numerous circle of relations in this, Frederick and Montgomery counties - Civ

153. MAL Sep 13 1828/Married Mon last at Union Town, Pa, by Rev Bascom, Edmund Peale, Esq. of Phila, to Miss Anna B. Searight, dau of James Searight of this co/Frederick, Sep 6 - Died Thurs 4th ins., Mrs. Francina Cheston

MARYLAND ADVOCATE (Cumberland)

Schley, consort of Frederick S. Schley, Esq., and dau of Capt. David Lynn, of Allegany co - Herald

154. MAL Sep 20 1828/Mrs. Mary C. Swearingen, wife of George Swearingen, Sheriff of Wash co, Md, and dau of late James Scott, Esq. of this town, was riding in company with her husband, she was unfortunatley killed on Mon 8 inst, about one mile above Cresap-town, in this co; interred in the family burying ground; left a dau, Mary Catharine. Within the space of little more than 2 years Mary (the decd) has mourned the loss of 8 of her nearest relations (It later develops - see succeeding articles - that she was murdered by her husband).

155. MAL Sep 27 1828/Married in this town Thurs last by Rev Rhoads, John Dickerhoof, to Miss Eliza Deems, dau of Frederick Deems, of this place /Married same evening, by Rev Barns, Jno. Hoaltzman, to Miss Delana Willison, dau of John Willison, of this co/Married Thurs 18th inst. in Moorefield, Hardy Co, Va, by Rev Bowan, Leonard Boward, of this place, to Miss Athaliah Rebecca Hopewell, of the former place/Married recently in Milford at the res of Lowther Layton, Esq., Rev. Smith to Rev. Miss Ellio M. Miller, both Meth preachers/Died at his res on Murleys Branch Wed last, Thomas Stallings, an old citizen of this co

156. MAL Oct 11 1828/Married in this town Thurs evening last by Rev Sigler, Samuel Shockey to Miss Sarah Ann Morrow, dau of Geo. Morrow, all of this place/Died at New Orleans of Yellow Fever, in the month of August last, Mrs. Rebecca Kreps wife of Christian Kreps, late of this town

157. MAL Oct 25 1828/Married in this town Thurs last by Rev Rhodes, Mr. Thomas Jefferson McKaig, to Miss Virlinda Beall, dau of Aza Beall, all of this town/Married in Somerset Co, Pa, on Thurs last by Rev Ryan, John Logsdon, to Miss Eliza Hardy

158. MAL Nov 1 1828/Allegany Co court of equity - William Naylor, adm of William McGuire vs John McDonald, Elizabeth Dangerfield, Edmund T. Dangerfield, John Dangerfield, Mary Dangerfield, John Folk, William Harness, George Bruce and Andrew Bruce - object of bill is to obtain decree for the sale of real est conveyed by John McDonald to Henry Dangerfield, in trust for the benefit of William McGuire, decd; Henry Dangerfield has died intestate leaving widow Elizabeth Dangerfield and children and heirs at law, to wit: Edmund T. Dangerfield, John Dangerfield, and Mary Dangerfield, all under age of 21; the widow and heirs res out of the state

159. MAL Nov 8 1828/Married Thurs evening 30th ult, by Rev N.B. Little, George Shuck to Miss Maria Korn, dau of Capt. Henry Korn, all of this place /Died at his res near town, Tues night last, Francis Madore, aged upwards of 50, for a number of years a respectable citizen of this co

160. MAL Nov 15 1828/Died Tues 28 ult at his res near Western Port, Benjamin Dawson, in the 62d year of his age, member of Meth Ch. a number of years

161. MAL Nov 26 1828/Married Thurs 20th inst. by Rev. Sigler, William Culp, to Miss Eliza Miller

MARYLAND ADVOCATE (Cumberland)

162. MAL Dec 12 1828/Married at Old Town, Tues evening 2nd inst. by Rev James Taylor, Doct. John W. Mountz, of George Town, D.C. to Miss Margarett M. Lantz, of the former place/Married Thurs evening last, by Rev Sigler, Caleb Harvey, to Miss Rebecca McNeill, dau of John McNeill, Esq. of this place/Died Mon last at the house of Wm. Reid Esq. in Frostburg, Doctor Horace Spurrier, of Frederick Co, Md

163. MAL Dec 27 1828/Died in this town Thurs evening last, John Murrell, Jr. in the 46th year of his age, merchant of this place for many years

164. MAL Jan 3 1829/Married Tues 23d ult by Rev N.B. Little, John North to Miss Rosanna Willison, dau of Moses Willison, all of this co/Married Wed morning last, by same, Garrett Blue to Miss Sarah Ann Long, both of Hampshire Co, Va/Married Thurs last by same, James Inskeep to Miss Ruth Hager

165. MAL Jan 10 1829/Married Thurs last by Rev Miller, Abner Ravenscraft of Hamphsire Co, Va, to Miss Ann Corbus, of this co

166. MAL Jan 24 1829/Died in this town Wed morning last, Mrs. Juliana Swan, consort of Robert Swan, Esq, in the 38th year of her age, leaving husband and 3 small children/Married at the house of.... Gaumer in Southampton township, Somerset Co, Pa, Tues 13th inst. by Rev Fought, John Willhelm to Miss Teeny Witt, all of that township/Married Tues 15th inst by Rev Sigler, Hazel Beall to Miss Rachel Philips, all of this co/Married Sun 18th by Jacob Brown, Esq. Jacob Philips to Miss Catharine Rice

167. MAL Jan 30 1829/Married Sun last by Rev Ryan, John Mattingly to Miss Elleanor Winters, both of this co/William Price, Esq., of Western-Port died Sat night last at Annapolis, whither he had gone as a Delegate to the Gen. Assembly from this co; for many years he was a magistrate and member of the Levy Court. He has left a wife and several children. He was not well when he first arrived in Annapolis, and only attended in the House two or three times/Died Mon morning last, aged 7 years, Benjamin, son of George Rizer, near this town/Died 15th inst at his res in Georgetown, in the 66th year of his age, Lieut. Col. Isaac Roberdeau, of the Topographical Bureau in the Department of War, over which he has presided from its creation

168. MAL Feb 7 1829/Died near Selby's-port in this co, on 29th ult, Mrs. Eliza Drane, consort of Washington Drane, leaving 3 small children

169. MAL Feb 14 1829/Died in this town, Sat evening last of apoplexy, Mrs. Elizabeth Clise, relict of the late George Clise; she was well and hearty in the morning and in the evening she was a corpse; she was a mother and obliging neighbor/Henry Miller who res in the South Mountain, about 3 miles from Cavetown has been absent for more than a week, last seen on Sabbath morning, 1st inst., near the house of Robt. Hughes, Esq., 1 miles from Cavetown. He was then returning to his home, from which he was about 2 miles distant. He was a middle aged man, formerly carried on a paper mill near Hagerstown; it is feared that he perished in the snow, which was then very deep.

170. MAL Feb 21 1829/Trustee's sale of lot in Cumberland in the case of equity of Henry Winour and Joseph Everstine vs. George Winour and wife,

MARYLAND ADVOCATE (Cumberland)

Hulda A. Davis, William Simpkins, and wife, William Conner & wife, and George Denine and wife, devisees of Solomon Davis, decd

171. MAL Feb 28 1829/Married Thurs 12 inst by Rev J. Miller, Joseph M'Carty to Miss Susan Singleton, both of Hampshire Co, Va/Married Thurs last by Rev N.B. Little, Samuel H. Gillis to Miss Mazy Robinett, both of Allegany Co /Married Thurs evening 18th inst, by Rev I. Keller, Dr. Samuel H. Rench to Miss Susan Swearingen, dau of John V. Swearingen, Esq. of Washington Co

172. MAL Mar 14 1829/Married Thurs last by Adam Lepley, Esq. Levi Baker of Hampshire Co, Va to Miss Margaret Hardy, of Somerset Co, Pa/Married same evening near Flintstone, William Robinett, to Miss Mazy Wilson dau of Mr. Asias Wilson, all of this co/Died 7th inst at his res in Southampton Township, Somerset Co, Pa, William Hardy, Sr. in the 80th year of his age

173. MAL Mar 21 1829/New Orleans - George Swearingen, who fled from Md last fall in company with his paramour for the murder of his young wife, was arrested on the 17th, near that city. He had assumed the name of Jos. Martin, but on examination before the Mayor, confessed his name to be George Swearingen - he is only 29 years of age/Died in this town Sat evening last after a short illness, Henry Slicer, son of the late Nathaniel Slicer, in the 21st year of his age/Died Sun morning last at his res, near Cresap-town, in this co, Joseph P. Hilleary, in the 37th year of his age, leaving wife and 4 small children/Died 7th inst. near Old-town, in this co, Michael Kimberly, of John, in the 24th year of his age/Died 12th inst. in Old-Town, Mr. George North, Jr., in the 37th year of his age, leaving wife and 7 small children/Died 12th inst. in Springfield, Hampshire Co, Va, Mrs. Sophia Kearn, wife of David Kearn, and dau of Henry Yantz, of this co, in the 24th year of her age, leaving husband and 2 small children/Died Sun night 15th inst about 8 miles below this place, in Hampshire Co, Va, Mrs. Sophia Ward, wife of Jesse Ward; leaving husband and 3 children

174. MAL Mar 28 1829/Feb 18, 1829 - Yesterday George Van Swearingen of Hagerstown, was apprehended by John Ramsey of Pittsburgh, and put in jail on suspicion of killing his wife (Mary Scott) of Cumberland (several newspaper accounts of Swearingen's escape are given. Swearingen had been sheriff of Washington Co)/Married in this Town Thurs evening last by Rev N.B. Little, Charles Heck, Register of Wills for Allegany Co, to Miss Rachel McCleary, dau of the late Andrew McCleary, all of this place/Married in Southampton Township, Somerset Co, Pa, Thurs 12th inst by Rev Voit, Jesse Uhl, to Miss Catharine Shafer, all of said Township/Married in same Township Sun evening last by 'Squire Weller, Ephraim Johnson to Miss Sarah Mumau, both of this place

175. MAL Apr 4 1829/(More about arrest of Swearingen)/Married Thurs last by Rev N.B. Little, George Slicer to Miss Sophia Wilson, dau of John Wilson, all of this co/Married same evening by same, Harrison L. Wyatt to Miss Rosanna Clise, all of this place

176. MAL Apr 11 1829/Married Tues evening last by Rev N.B. Little, Moses Rawlings of this co, to Miss Rebecca McCulloh, dau of George McCulloh, esq. of Frostburg/Died at the mouth of New Creek in Hampshire co, Va, Fri 3d inst., Mrs. Elizabeth McCarty, widow of the late Col. Edward McCarty of that co, in the 72d year of her age, for the last few years a member of the Meth

MARYLAND ADVOCATE (Cumberland)

Society/Died at the res of James Inskeep (his father) in Hampshire Co, Va, Sat last, Abraham Inskeep, about 35 years of age, citizen of Hardy Co, Va /Benoni Davidson, apprentice fo the cabinet making bus., in the 19th year of his age, about 5 ft 7-8 inch, full faced and sore eyes, ran away from Robert McCleary, living in Cumberland

177. MAL Apr 18 1829/Married Thurs evening last, by Rev James Taylor, Rev James Berkley, to Miss Eliza Cromwell, dau of Thomas Cromwell, Esq. of this Co/Married Tues 9th by Rev Sigler, Jacob Rice to Miss Anna Rice, dau of George Rice, all of this co/Died Thurs last John McMahon Sprigg, second son of Joseph Sprigg, Esq. of the Swan Ponds, in Hampshire Co, Va, in the 6th year of his age/Died Tues last near Cresaptown, Mrs. Margaret Athey, at an advanced age/Caution in dealing with my black man Charles Pope and his wife Prissy - M.C. Sprigg

178. MAL Apr 25 1829/Died at his res about 4 miles from Cumberland Sat last, Francis Twigg, Sr., in the 79th year of his age, after a severe affliction of upwards of four years

179. MAL May 2 1829/Married in Hagerstown Tues even last by Rev Fullerton, David C. Newcomer, Esq. to Miss Ellen Grieves, dau of Thomas Grieves, Esq. late Editor of the Hagerstown Herald/Died Mon last after an illness of only a few hours in the 47th year of his age, John Gephart, inhabitant of this town, leaving a widow and a large family of children

180. MAL May 9 1829/Died - Capt. Thomas Post of Hagerstown, on Mon morning last after a few days illness, aged 55 years and 7 months; he was a Captain in the service of the U.S., served during the whole of the last war, retired from the army and elected High Sheriff of Washington Co of which he had been a citizen for more than 20 years; he left a widow and 5 children/Died at his res on Will's creek, near this Town, Wed last, James Moore, an old inhabitant of this co/Allegany Co court of Equity - Robert McClery, complainant vs. Thomas McClery, Andrew McClery, John B. Wright and Polly his wife, Robert McClery, son of John, James McClery son of John, John Clise and Jane his wife, Henry McClery, James McClery, Abraham Dilley and Jane his wife, and Peter Tool and Nancy his wife, defendants - object of bill is to obtain decree for sale of real est of Robert McClery, Sr. late of Allegany Co, who died intestate seized in fee and possessed of lots in town of Cumberland, pt of tract called Distillery; Robert McClery Sr. left following children and grandchildren his heirs at law, Thomas McClery, Andrew McClery, Polly who m John B. Wright, Robert McClery, son of John, James McClery, son of John, and Jane McClery, dau of said John, which said John McClery was one of the sons of said Robert McClery, decd and the said John McClery also died intestate, Henry McClery, James McClery, Jane who m Abraham Dilly, Robert the complainant and Nancy who m Peter Tool and that Jane McClery the dau of John hath m John Clice. Bill also states that Thomas McClery, Andrew McClery, Robert McClery, son of John, James McClery, son of John, Henry McClery, James McClery, son of Robert McClery, Sr, Abraham Dilly and Jane his wife, Peter Tool and Nancy his wife do not res in the state of Md

181. MAL May 16 1829/Died in this town Sun last, John Mummaw, for a number of years a citizen of this place/Married in Southampton Township, Somerset Co, Pa, Sun evening last, by Rev Voight, Charles Uhl, to Miss Eliza Uhl, all of that township

MARYLAND ADVOCATE (Cumberland)

182. MAL May 23 1829/Married Thurs 19th inst by Squire Miller, Hugh Cowens to Miss Druse Huston dau of Andrew Huston, all of Somerset Co, Pa/Hagers-Town, May 21 - Died in this place, this morning, after a few weeks' illness, William Fitzhugh, Jr., Esq. in the 43d year of his age; he was the late Jackson Elector for this dist. - Torch Light

183. MAL May 30 1829/Married Thurs 19th inst, Mathias Frey of Virginia, to Miss Rhody Wentling, of Petersburg, Pa

184. MAL Jun 6 1829/Died at his res in Bedford Co, Pa, Sunday last, Andrew Huston, in the 78th year of his age, for 45 years a res of that co/Andrew Workman, Jr. who res near Frostburg, in this co, put an end to his life on Thurs the 28th ult by shooting himself with a rifle, for several years the subject to fits of mental alienation. On the day preceding his death, he read the Bible attentively, and was much engaged in prayer/Died at his res in Bedford Co, Pa, Sun last, Andrew Huston, in the 78th year of his age, for 45 years a res of that co; raised a large family

185. MAL Jun 13 1829/Married at Moorefield, Va, on Thurs 4 inst, by Rev Scott, John George Minnick, formerly of Cumberland, to Miss Caroline Malcolm, of that place/Married Wed evening last by 'Squire Arnold of Pa, Lewis Lafee, to Miss Elizabeth Hughes, dau of George Hughes, of this place/Died on evening of 28th ult, after a tedious illness, John Cleves Symmes, of the vicinity of Hamilton Butler Co, Ohio; his remains interred with the honors of War on the afternoon of the next day

186. MAL Jun 20 1829/Married 27 ult by Rev Converse, Hon. George M'Duffie, to Miss Mary Rebecca Singleton, dau of Richard Singleton, Esq. of Sumter Distric, South Carolina/Died near Western-port in this co on Fri 12th inst. Mrs. Mary Howell, aged 108 years. She had been a res of this co for upwards of 50 years/Rev Patriot gone - Sat morning last at the res of his son in Roxbury, died, Gen. Henry Dearborn, aged 78 years and 3 months

187. MAL Jul 11 1829/Married at Western Port in this co, Thurs 2d inst. by Rev Miller, Daniel Cleary, to Miss Harriet Layman, dau of George Layman, Esq. of that place

188. MAL Jul 18 1829/Died very suddenly Sun morning last near this town, John Colflesh, aged about 30 years

189. MAL Jul 25 1829/Died Fri last Charles Ridgely of Hampton, late Governor of Md. in the 70th year of his age

190. MAL Aug 1 1829/Married at Urbana, Ohio, 2d June last, Thomas I. McArthur, Esq. to Miss Sarah Ann McMahon, dau of William McMahon, Esq. of this place/Died near Frostburg, in this co, Wed last, Mrs. Anna Combs, consort of Elisha Combs, leaving husband and 6 small children

191. MAL Aug 22 1829/(Trial of Swearingen continues)/Married Sun evening last by Rev N.B. Little, Levi Shaw to Miss Mary Ann Russell dau of Elnathan Russell of this place

192. MAL Aug 29 1829/Swearingen found guilty and sentenced to hang (trial described in detail)

MARYLAND ADVOCATE (Cumberland)

193. MAL Sep 5 1829/Died 31st ult, Miss Louisa, eldest dau of Enoch Moore of this place, in the 21st year of her age, after a lingering and severe illness of 12 months; she became a member of the Meth Episc Ch in her 15th year of age/Died in this town Mon morning last at an advanced age, Mrs. Mary Magdalene Rizer, for many years an inhabitant of this place/Died in this place, yesterday, at an advanced aged, Mrs. Mary Collins, after a severe illness of about 12 months/Bedford Gazette - Died at the house of Humphrey Dillion in this borough Tues night last, Joseph Patterson of Balt, generally known as "Patterson the Gambler."

194. MAL Sep 12 1829/Married Wed evening last by Rev N.B. Little, John Egshaw of this co, to Mrs. Mary Slange, late of Hagers-town/Married in this town on Sun evening last, by Rev Wilson, Elie Wilson, to Miss Naomi Belgg, both of Virginia/We are informed that a young man from this place by the name of Peter Reed, aged about 19 years, was killed by the blowing up of some rock upon the Chesepeake and Ohio Canal, near Georgetown, last week.

195. MAL Sep 26 1829/Died Tues last at her res near Cumberland, in the 69th year of her age, Mrs. Christiana Simpkins, wife of Mr. Disey(?) Simpkins

196. MAL Oct 3 1829/Married Mon last by Rev Marshal, David Logsdon, to Miss Rebecca Uhl/Swearingen hanged yesterday on the west side of Mills creek, near the milldam in this town - approximately 4000-5000 persons were present

197. MAL Oct 10 1829/Married at Cresap-town Tues last by Rev A. Sigler, Emanuel Custer, Esq. to Mrs. Mary Poland, both of that place/Married Thurs last by same, Henry Oswald to Miss Emily Tomlinson/Died at his res in this co, Fri 2d inst, Upton Bruce, Esq. at an advanced age, leaving wife and 7 children, on several occasions elected to the assembly

198. MAL Oct 24 1829/Died at Frederick-town at the house of his son-in-law, Wm. Schley, Esq. on Sun last in the 59th year of his age, Gen. Samuel Ringgold of this co; interred yesterday in the family burial gorund at Fountain Rock - Hagerstown Herald

199. MAL Oct 31 1829/Died Thurs morning last, between 1 and 2 o'clock, Peter Baumward, in the 61st year of his age, upwards of 30 years an inhabitant of this place - Civilian/John Wolf offers reward for apprentice to the boot and shoemaking business, Carleton Belt, in the 17th year of his age, about 4 ft 3-4 inch

200. MAL Nov 7 1829/Testimony in Swearingen case is given in detail, along with Swearingen's confession.

201. MAL Nov 21 1829/Married Tues last by Rev H. Haverstick, Pratt Collins of this place, to Mrs. Mary Kelly of Bedford co, Pa/Died very suddenly in this town Tues morning last, Joseph McCulloh, in the 38th year of his age, leaving wife and 6 small children

202. MAL Nov 28 1829/Reward offered by Elnathan Russell for indented apprentice to the Wheel Right business named Samuel Hughes, in the 19th year of his age, about 5 ft 9 inch, son of George Hughes. Warning given to his father and to his brothers, not to harbour him.

MARYLAND ADVOCATE (Cumberland)

203. MAL Dec 5 1829/Married Tues evening last by Rev Young, James M. Moore, to Miss Ann Shockey, all of this town

204. MAL Dec 19 1829/Body of John Crawford, near Somerset, Pa, was found, after having been missing about 4 weeks, in a corn field, with a bottle drained at his side. Jury of inquest assigned drunkenness as the cause of death/Thomas Freeman found dead in streets of Balt, Sun morning last - death by intemperance

205. MAL Jan 23 1830/A man by the name of Elijah Elliott, residing in Virginia, near Williams-Port, put an end to his existence on Wed last, in a fit of melancholy, by suspension. He was a married man, of about 25 yrs of age

206. MAL Feb 6 1830/Death of Thomas B. Dunn, Esq. the U.S. Superintendant of the Armory at Harpers Ferry, Va, who fell victim to the malice of an assassin on the 29th ult. A man by the name of Coxe, a profligate and intemperate wretch, who had been discharged from employment by Mr. Stubblefield the former Superintendant, had been hovering about the Works for some time, swearing vengence, for no reason, against Mr. Dunn, if he were not again taken into service. (Coxe shot Mr. Dunn with a musket loaded with slugs and shot.) Coxe is now in irons in Charles-town. He is a young man of but 21, of low and degraded character, and was addicted to gambling and intemperance. - Hagers-town Herald/Married in Frederick Co, Mon morning last by Rev John A. Gere, Rev Francis A. M'Neill, formerly of this place, to Miss Mary Cronise, of that co

207. MAL Feb 13 1830/Died at his farm, near Freedom, Balt Co, 5th inst after a severe illness of 12 days, Col. Peter Little, in the 55th year of his age, late member of Congress/Died Sat morning last, Mrs. Rebecca Tilghman, consort of Thomas Tilghman, esq. of Wash Co

208. MAL Feb 20 1830/Married Mon evening 8th inst by Rev Riddle, Rev Benjamin Kurtz, Pastor of the Luth Church in Hagerstown, to Miss Catharine Baker, dau of Henry W. Baker, merchant of Winchester, Va/Died at res of her brother, Moses Rawlings near this town, Wed last, Miss Nancy Rawlings, after a protracted indisposition/Letter from Gen. Samuel Dunn, of Franklin Co, Pa, re the account of the assassination of his brother, Thomas B. Dunn, late Superintendent at Harpers-ferry. (Gives further detail of the event; also states his brother left a wife and 2 children, one of whom was born the morning after its father's funeral)

209. MAL Mar 6 1830/Joseph Evans was tried at a court of Quarter Session for Westmoreland co, Pa, on 8th ult for murder of John Cissler, and found guilty/Married Tues night last by Rev Haverstick, Samuel Charles, Editor of the Civilian, to Miss Margaret Wineow, dau of Henry Wineow, all of this place/Accident - Sun last, a smart and interesting son of George Kearn, of this place, fell into the well, attached to the jail, and was drowned.

210. MAL Apr 3 1830/Died at Bedford, Sat morning last, after a lingering affliction, the Hon. John Tod, of the Supreme Court of Pa

211. MAL Apr 10 1830/Married Sun 28th ult by Rev H. Haverstick, of this place, Jonathan Close to Miss Mary Keller, both of Southampton township,

MARYLAND ADVOCATE (Cumberland)

Somerset co, Pa/Married Thurs evening last by same, Henry W. Ball of Williams-port, Md,to Miss Elizabeth Deems, dau of Frederick Deems, Esq. of this town

212. MAL Apr 17 1830/Died at his res in Somerfield, Pa, 27th ult, Jacob Blocher, after a short illness, at an advanced age. He had been frequently elected Senator to the Legislature of Pa

213. MAL Apr 24 1830/Died at Washington City, Sat last, after a few days illness, Gen. Alexander Smythe, member of Congress from Va; remains interred in the Congress burying ground/Died Tues last at the res of her grandmother (Mrs. Debborah Scott) in this place, Mary Catharine Swearingen, aged about 4 yrs, 6 months

214. MAL May 1 1830/Married Fri 23d ult by Rev H. Haverstock, Matthew T. Wolfe to Miss Sarah H. McMecken, both of Moorefield, Va/Married Tues last by Rev C.B. Young, Isaac Lambert to Miss Agnes McMecken, both of Hardy co, Va

215. MAL May 8 1830/Married Tues evening last by Rev Sigler, John Hendrixon to Miss Ellen Moore, both of this town/Married Thurs 22d ult by John Frey, Esq., Stephen Cuthrie, of Preston co, Va, to Miss Frances Hayslett, dau of Samuel Hayslett of this co/John Magill offers reward for apprentice to the printing business by name of Joshua Ruth, about 19 yrs of age

216. MAL May 22 1830/Married Thurs last by Rev Haverstick, Mr. Levi Uhl of this co to Miss Christiana Beall, dau of late John Beall, of Somerset Co, Pa/Died at his res in Belmont co, Ohio, very suddenly, 17th inst, Henry Neff, formerly of this co/Died in Smythfield, Pa, on 18th inst after a lingering illness, Mrs. Elizabeth Morrow, consort of John Morrow

217. MAL Jun 19 1830/Died at her res on Murley's Branch, in this co, on 10th inst, Mrs. Ruth Robinett, consort of Joseph Robinett, in the 80th year of her age

218. MAL Jun 26 1830/Married Tues evening last by Rev Sigler, James McGill, to Miss Elizabeth Beall, dau of Rezin Beall, Esq., all of this co/Died in this town Thurs night last after a short but severe indisposition, Mrs. Mary Shaw, wife of Levi Shaw, in the 19th year of her age

219. MAL Jul 10 1830/Married Tues evening last by Rev L. H. Johns, Dennis B. Hoblitzell to Miss Sarah Ann Stoddard, dau of James Stoddard, all of this town/Married Thurs 24th ult by Rev Lenox Martin, Jairus Robinett to Miss Jemima Wilson, dau of Asias Wilson, all of this co

220. MAL Jul 17 1830/A man named John Todd, was killed near Benjamin Emmert's on the turnpike Road on Sun 3d inst. When walking by the side of a wagon, he fell under the wheel, which passed on his head, causing instant death. He left a wife and one child - Hagerstown Her.

221. MAL Jul 24 1830/Married Mon last by Rev C.B. Young, William S. Noel to Miss Hetta Miller, both of Rockingham, Va/Married Thurs morning by Rev H. Haverstick, Nimrod Pough to Miss Elizabeth Allen, both of Va

MARYLAND ADVOCATE (Cumberland)

222. MAL Jul 31 1830/Died Tues last at the house of Wm. Heartly, six miles east of Bedford, John McCracken, paper maker, of Skinner's Gap, Franklin co. Mr. McCracken was on his way from the paper mill to Bedford with a two-horse waggon loaded with paper - in attempting to get out of the waggon at the house of Mr. Heartly, he slipped and fell to the ground, the wheels passing over his body, broke several of his ribs, and otherwise so seriously injured him as to cause his death - Bedford Enquirer of July 23.

223. MAL Aug 14 1830/In consequence of the death of his wife, Roderick Dorsey, Esq. who had been placed upon the Jackson Ticket of Frederick Co, declined standing a poll. Madison Nelson, Esq. has been chosen to fill his place on the ticket.

224. MAL Aug 21 1830/Died at Bellefontain, Logan co, Ohio, Thurs 5th inst, after an illness of a few hours, of bilious cholic, Jacob Sides, late of this co/Died Wed last, Miss Sophia Combs, dau of John Combs of this co/Died at the Public Inn of Mr. Zimmer, near Bedford, Pa, Fri last after a short illness, Michael Lane, Esq. of this town, aged about 50 yrs. He will be lamented by those who have many a time and oft been cheered by the music of his voice, his ready wit and good-humoured chat... a noble, generous-hearted son of Erin/Andrew Timmonds was killed a few days since by falling off of an old mill which he was assisting to pull down, near Selby's Port, in this co. He fell from 10 to 15 feet into the tale race upon a bed of stone, and expired in about 10 hours after he fell. He was only about 30 yrs of age. He left a wife and several small children

225. MAL Aug 28 1830/Married Sun evening last by Rev N.B. Little, Jesse Chambers to Miss Margaret Schook, dau of Jacob Schook, all of this town

226. MAL Sep 4 1830/Died in Bedford, suddenly, Wed evening 26th ult, John Lee, formerly of this co, aged about 32 yrs

227. MAL Sep 18 1830/Married Tues evening last by Rev C.B. Young, Jacob Brocius of Hancock, to Miss Lowenso Hoblitzell, dau of Geo. Hoblitzell, Esq. of this place/Died Sat morning last, at his res near Western-port in this co, John Templeman, Esq. aged 76 yrs, of this co

228. MAL Sep 25 1830/Married Sun last by Rev N.B. Little, William F. France to Miss Julian Smouse, dau of Henry Smouse, Esq., all of this co

229. MAL Oct 9 1830/Died in Talbot Co, Md., 27th inst, Gen. James Lloyd, in the 74th year of his age, a soldier of the Rev.

230. MAL Oct 23 1830/Married Tues last by Rev L.H. Johns, William Lewis, of this place, to Miss Eliza Brocius, dau of Jacob Brocius, of Wash Co/Died at her res about 4 miles west of Frostburg, in this co, Fri 17th inst, Mrs. Elizabeth Bromley, in the 65th year of her age/Died at Annapolis, Fri 17th inst, Col. William Done, delegate elect to the Legislature of Md for Somerset Co. Hon Frederick Smith, one of the associate Judges of the Supreme court of the State, died at his res in Reading, Mon evening 4th inst. About midnight he was seized with apoplexy, and died almost immediately

THE MARYLAND HERALD AND HAGERS-TOWN WEEKLY ADVERTISER

231. EAM Jan 4 1820/Married Thurs last by Rev Kurtz, John Baker, to Miss Mary Sprecher

232. EAM Jan 11 1820/Married Thurs last by Rev Kurtz, John Held, to Miss Elizabeth Neikirch/Died Wed morning last, after a short illness, Mrs. Christiana Miller, wife of George Miller, in the 61st year of her age

233. EAM Jan 18 1820/Died Fri last at his res, 3 miles from Hagers-town, in 73d year of his age, John Teisher, after an illness of about 6 weeks

234. EAM Jan 25 1820/Married Thurs last by Rev Kurtz, Daniel Brewer, to Miss Elizabeth West, both of this co/Married same day by same, Thomas Emmerson, to Miss Rachel Stoner, both of this co/Married Sun last by same, Abraham James, to Miss Sarah Stiffler, both of this co/Married same day by same, Jacob Kehler, to Miss Mary Myers, both of Funks-town/Died in this town, Sat morning last, John Julius, in the 43rd year of his age, leaving wife and children; remains interred in burying ground of German Reformed Congregation

235. EAM Feb 8 1820/Married Tues last by Rev George Keedy, Thomas H. Wilson to Miss Harriet Van Peters, both of Boonsborough, Wash Co, Md/Married same day by Rev Kurtz, Thomas Ford, to Mrs. Mary Winters/Married Thurs last by same, John Witmer, junr., to Miss Rosanna Brewer/Married same day by same, Jacob Strause, to Miss Christiana Evy - All the above of this co/Died Tues last at his res near this town, after a lingering illness, Samuel Oster, in the 31st year of his age/Died Wed last Zachariah Beard, in the 71st year of his age

236. EAM Feb 15 1820/Died Sun evening last, after a short illness, Mrs. Catharine Schnebly, wife of Daniel Schnebly, of this town, in the 32d year of her age, leaving husband and 6 young children/Died same evening in this town after a short illness, Mrs. Harriet Hall, wife of John Hall, in the 28th year of her age, leaving husband and 4 small children one of whom is an infant of 12 days; funeral at her late res in North Potomac st/Died yesterday morning, suddenly, at his res on Ringgold's manor, Capt. John Ashbury, leaving wife and large family of children

237. EAM Feb 22 1820/Married Tues last in Adams Co, Pa, about 8 miles from Gettysburg, by Rev Herbst, Daniel Herr, son of John P. Herr, of Hagers-town, to Miss Sarah Gilbert dau of Jacob Gilbert, of Adams Co/Married Thurs last by Rev Kurtz, Martin Newcomer, to Miss Mary Snavely

238. EAM Feb 29 1820/Married Tues last by Rev Kurtz, John Ludy to Miss Susanna Moggins/Married same day by same, Daniel Gerhart to Miss Elizabeth Mong/Married Thurs last by same, Philip Sprecher to Miss Catharine Houer /Married same day by same, Isaac Hanna to Miss Nancy Funk, all of this co /Died Wed last after a tedious illness, Miss Rebecca Ann M'Cardell, dau of Thomas M'Cardell, of this co, in the 15th year of her age/Death of Mrs. Mary Reily, consort of Rev James R. Reily of this place. She died at 3 O'Clock, at the res of her uncle Col. David Schnebly, after a very tedious and lingering pulmonary affection

239. EAM Mar 7 1820/Died last evening in this town after a short illness, George Bower, son of the late Rev George Bower, in the 31st year of his age

THE MARYLAND HERALD AND HAGERS-TOWN WEEKLY ADVERTISER

240. EAM Mar 21 1820/Married Tues 14th inst, by Rev J. C. Clay, James D. Moore, Esq. to Miss Mary Frances Sanders, all of this co/Married Thurs last by Rev Benjamin Kurtz, George Bowman to Miss Dorothy Stoy, all of this place /Married same day by same, David Long to Miss Mary Gletner/Married same day by same, Jacob Miller to Miss Nancy Strite/Married same day by Rev J. R. Reily, Adam Bovy to Miss Elizabeth Reinhart, both of Wash Co/Married Sun last by same, Henry Ohr to Miss Sarah Smith, both of Funks-town/Married same day by Rev Benjamin Kurtz, Jesse F. Davis to Miss Elizabeth Stine/Married same day at Waynesburg, Pa, by Rev Rotraff, John Freaner, of this town, to Mrs. Mary Locher of that place

241. EAM Mar 28 1820/Married Thurs last by Rev Kurtz, William Showecker of this place, to Miss Nancy Slice of this co/Married same day by same, David Brookhart, of the state of Kentucky, to Miss Terace Funk, of this co/Married same day by same, Valentine Alexander, to Miss Rebecca Burgan, of this co /Married Sun last by Rev J. R. Reily, George Moudy, to Miss Margaret Brewa, both of this co/Died Fri last, Peter Conn, of Boonsborough, aged 61 yrs and 8 months

242. EAM Apr 11 1820/Married Tues 4 inst, by Rev B. Kurtz, Joseph Green to Miss Sophia Davis/Married same day by same, Richard Davis to Miss Eliza Downs/Married same day by same, David Brewer to Miss Sarah Snider/Married Sun last by same, George Christonan to Miss Elizabeth Bowers/Married same day by Rev H. A. Kurtz, Baltzer Miller to Miss Rebecca Schriber

243. EAM Apr 25 1820/Married Tues last by Rev B. Kurtz, George Hersh to Miss Sarah Burkhart/Married Thurs last by Rev John Lind, Peter Miller to Miss Elizabeth Brumbaugh, both of this co/Married same day by Rev J. R. Reily, Jacob Crow, of Va, to Miss Sarah Tice dau of John Tice of this co

244. EAM May 2 1820/Married Tues evening last, by Rev J. R. Reily, Jonathan Kershner to Miss Catharine Miller, dau of John Miller, Merchant of this town /Married same evening by Rev. B. Kurtz, Jacob Startzman to Miss Ann Jack, both of Williamsport/Married Thurs evening last by Rev C. Reynolds, Emanuel Holsey of Williams-Port to Miss Maria Reynolds, dau of Col. John Reynolds of this town

245. EAM May 9 1820/Married Thurs last by Rev J. R. Reily, David Cronich to Miss Barbara Wright, both of this place

246. EAM May 30 1820/Married Thurs last by Rev J. R. Reily, George Brandner, merchant, to Miss Eliza Shaffner dau of Matthias Shaffner, esq., both of Boonsborough/Married Sun last by same, Michael Kreps of Williams-Port, to Miss Mary Hoffman/Married yesterday by same, James Harris, to Miss Mary Melven, both of Jefferson Co, Va/Died yesterday in this town of a paralytic attack, Mrs. Ann M'Fall

247. EAM Jun 13 1820/Winchester, June 10. Suicide - A stranger came to this place a few days ago, committed suicide on Mon last by shooting himself, a short distance from town; paper in pocket stated he could not beg and he could not obtain employment. His deportment during his stay at Mr. D. Linn's tavern was decent and orderly. He was a millwright by profession; and it appears has a wife near Hagers-town. His name was James Huston. - Gazette.

THE MARYLAND HERALD AND HAGERS-TOWN WEEKLY ADVERTISER

248. EAM Jun 20 1820/Married Thurs 8th inst by Rev B. Kurtz, Michael Avy to Miss Lydia Moyers, of this co/Married Sun last by same, David Hill of Reading Pa to Miss Sarah Faulkwell of this co/Died Tues morning last at the res of Robert Douglass, Esq., in this town, Mrs. Mary Combs, relict of late Coleman Combs, aged about 80 yrs; remains interred in Presby burying ground

249. EAM Jul 4 1820/Married Thurs evening last by Rev B. Kurtz, Isaac Wells to Miss Elizabeth Herring, of this co

250. EAM Jul 11 1820/Married Tues 4th inst, by Rev J. R. Reily, Daniel Schnebly, Esq. of this town, to Miss Margaret Rench, of this co/Chancery case - Thomas Eaker and Elizabeth his wife, John Needy, George Needy, Margaret Needy & Elizabeth Hose, heirs at law of Isaac Needy, decd, vs Henry Needy, Valentine Wagner and Polly his wife, John Wagely and Catharine his wife, Margaret Hose, and Catharine Hose. The bill states that Isaac Needy on 7 May 1803 made and executed his will and soon after died leaving above named complainants and defendants his children and heirs. In his will he devised all his prop to wife Elizabeth Needy to hold so long as she remained a widow. She died without remarrying in 1819. Henry Needy, Valentine Wagner who m Polly dau of Isaac and Polly his wife and John Wagely who m said Catharine and Catharine his wife, res out of state of Md

251. EAM Jul 18 1820/Married Sun evening last, by Rev B. Kurtz, Noah Carter to Miss Susan Humrickhouse/Equity case - Andrew Heatherington vs Isaac Baker and John Baker, heirs of Isaac Baker, decd. Isaac Baker executed a deed to John Heatherington to tract called Venture, neglected to have deed recorded, dated 1779, and said Isaac removed from this state and hath since died leaving Isaac Baker and John Baker his heirs, who themselves do not res in the state of Md.

252. EAM Jul 25 1820/Died yesterday morning after a short but painful illness, Miss Mary Ann Hoffman Lawrence, eldest dau of Upton Lawrence, Esq. of this place, in the 14th year of her age; remains to be deposited in family vault, 2 miles from town

253. EAM Aug 8 1820/Married Tues last by Rev J. R. Reily, Thomas H. Rench to Miss Jane Hamilton, both of this place/Married Thurs last by Rev B. Kurtz, Abraham Hooper to Miss Mary Stewart, both of this co/Married Sun last by Rev J. R. Reily, David Tschudy to Miss Mary Bovey, both of this place /Married same day by same, Peter Keller, to Miss Rebecca Cobert, both of Wash Co/Married same day by Rev J. C. Clay, Edward M'Coy to Miss Massy Rhoads, both of Sharpsburg

254. EAM Aug 22 1820/Married Thurs last by Rev B. Kurtz, Jacob Hoffman to Miss Polly Bowser/Died this morning about 3 o'clock, of a pulmonary complaint, Mrs. Mary Cooke, wife of David Cooke, of this town, in the 54th year of her age

255. EAM Sep 19 1820/Coroner's inquest at Leitersburg has determined that John M'Gaffin, an Irishman who worked in the neighborhood, was stabbed to death by Hugh O'Donnel, a shoe maker of Leitersburg, in the stomach by a shoemaker's knife/Married at Cumberland Tues evening 12th inst, by Rev J. C. Clay, Jonathan W. Magruder to Miss Mary G. Lynn, dau of David Lynn, Esq/Died Sun 10th inst. in the 19th year of his age, Joseph Crane Saunders, youngest

THE MARYLAND HERALD AND HAGERS-TOWN WEEKLY ADVERTISER

son of major Cyrus Saunders of this co/Died yesterday morning at his res on Conococheague, near Williams Port, Peter Miller, old inhabitant of this co

256. EAM Sep 26 1820/Married at Green-Castle on Sun 17th isnt by Rev Rotraff, James Fleming to Miss Mary Bowman, both of this co/Married Thurs last by Rev Kurtz, Michel Kagerise to Miss Nancy Troup/Married Sat last by same, Joseph Hreckle(?) to Miss Elizabeth Hoffman

257. EAM Oct 3 1820/Died at his res in Mont Co Sun evening, 24th ult, Ludwick Young, formerly an inhabitant of this co/Died Wed last at her mother's res, near this town, after a lingering illness, Miss Elizabeth Oster, in the 24th year of her age; remains committed to the earth in the German Reformed burial ground/Died Thurs last near Hancock, Mrs. Elizabeth Hart, wife of Jacob Hart, in the 25th year of her age/George Brendel offers reward for apprentice to the boot and shoe-making bus., named Thomas Sands, aged 18-19 yrs

258. EAM Oct 31 1820/Married Thurs 19th inst by Rev Kurtz, James Morrison to Miss Nancy Corse/Married same day by same, John Spigler, to Miss Matilda Young/Married same day by same, John Brewer to Miss Elizabeth Fiery/Died Thurs morning 26th inst., Frederick Fechtig, sen., for some yrs a citizen of this place, and for 51 yrs and 8 months an inhabitant of this vale of tears. His complaint was of long duration/Died Fri morning Oct 27 1820 at her res on Conococheague Manor, Mrs. Susanna Swearingen, relict of late Col. Charles Swearingen, in the 82d year of her age, married for upwards of 59 yrs; raised a large family, several of whom and their branches are now to be found in Md, Va, Ky and Ill./Died Fri evening last in 63d year of her age, Mrs. Catharine Brumbaugh, widow of the decd Jacob Brumbaugh, after a short but severe illness; attentive to religious ordinances of German Baptists

259. EAM Nov 7 1820/Died in this town Sat evening last, Mrs. Susanna Funk, relict of late Joseph Funk, in the 58th year of her age, member German Baptist Society

260. EAM Nov 21 1820/Married Thurs 19th ult., by Rev Shull, Jacob Keisacker, of this co, to Miss Mary Ann Lose dau of Conrad Lose of Franklin Co, Pa /Married Thurs last by Rev Kurtz, Daniel Shector to Miss Mary Emmert/Married same day by same, Adam Brewer to Miss Maria Johnson

261. EAM Nov 28 1820/Died Wed last after a short illness, Miss Mary Witmer, dau of Henry Witmer, of this co, aged about 37 yrs

262. EAM Dec 12 1820/Married Sun 26th ult by Rev Kurtz, Daniel Shriver to Miss Elizabeth Grosh, both of Funks-town/Married Tues 28th by same, George Brunner to Miss Elizabeth Faulkwell/Married Thurs 30th by same Nathaniel Webb to Miss Harriet Allender/Married sun last by same, James Kendle to Miss Margaret Wherrett

263. EAM Dec 19 1820/Died Sun morning last at his res about 3 miles from Hagers-town, after a lingering illness, Christopher Trovinger, in the 64th year of his age

264. EAM Dec 26 1820/Married Sun evening 17th inst, by Rev Kurtz, Henry Bowser to Mrs. Christiana Dundore/Died Tues evening last in this town, Mrs.

THE MARYLAND HERALD AND HAGERS-TOWN WEEKLY ADVERTISER

Catharine Tutweiler, wife of Jacob Tutweiler, in the 75th year of her age /Died Wed morning last, at his res, about 9 miles from Hagers-town, Capt Adam Ridenour, son of Martin Ridenour, of this town, in the 43d year of his age

265. EAM Jan 2 1821/Married Thurs last by Rev J. R. Reily, Jonathan Shafer, son of John Shafer, to Miss Susanna Ringer, dau of Robert Ringer, all of this co/Married Sun last by same, Timothy Downing to Miss Christiana Bowser, both of this co

266. EAM Jan 9 1821/Married Tues evening last by Rev John Lind, James O. Carson, merchant, to Miss Rosanna M. White, both of this place/Died Thurs 28th Dec last, at the house of Geo. M. Elliot, near Hagers-Town, in 57th year of his age, Edward Green; formerly engaged in Bay trade from Balt. He stated that he had a dau on the Eastern Shore

267. EAM Jan 16 1821/Married at Frederick-Town, 6th inst, by Rev John Johns, Stuart Gaither to Miss Margaret Schell, all of that place/Married at Cumberland Thurs evening 11th by Rev J. C. Clay, Frederick Augustus Schley, Esq. to Miss Francina C. Lynn, dau of David Lynn, Esq.

268. EAM Jan 23 1821/Died Mon evening 15th inst at the Toll Gate, on the Cumberland road, about 7 miles from Hagers-Town, after a short illness of 8 days, Mrs. Sarah Protzman, wife of Daniel Protzman, in the 63d year of her age, leaving wife and 8 children, 17 grandchildren and many other relatives /Died in William-Port, Sun morning 14th inst, Jemima Hogg, wife of John Hogg/Died Tues night 16th inst, in Williams-Port, Robert T. Friend, Innkeeper, leaving widow and number of small children

269. EAM Jan 30 1821/Married Tues 23d inst by Rev J. C. Clay, Jacob Huyett to Miss Elizabeth Ingram, dau of Joseph Ingram, all of this co/Married same day at Somerset, Pa, by Rev W. R. Harmer, Joseph Smith, Editor of the Western Herald, Cumberland, Md, to Miss Maria L. Boyer, of the former place /Baltimore - Died Thurs afternoon in the 48th year of his age, General Joseph Sterett, of the 3rd Brigade. The 5th Regt in which he had served upwards of 20 yrs and which he commanded in the repulse of the British from our city in 1814, composed the escort; buried at 1st Presby Church/Died at his res in Frederick Co Thurs last, at an advanced age, Thomas Hawkins

270. EAM Feb 13 1821/Married Tues evening last, by Rev Lind, Capt John Johnston of Hancock, Md, to Miss Isabella M'Clanahan, of Franklin Co, Pa

271. EAM Feb 20 1821/Married Tues 13th inst by Rev B. Kurtz, Marmaduke W. Boyd, to Miss Susan Hogmire, dau of Col. Jonas Hogmire, all of this co

272. EAM Feb 27 1821/Married at Flintstone, near Cumberland, Thurs last, by Rev J.C. Clay, David G. Yost, Esq. of this place, to Miss Elizabeth L. Davis, dau of John Davis, Esq/Married near Gettysburg, same day by Rev Hinch, Daniel Middelkauff, of this town, to Miss Julian Middelkauff, of Adams Co, Pa

273. EAM Mar 13 1821/Died Mon morning 5th inst at his father's res, about 3 miles from Hagers-Town, Martin Miller, son of Joseph Miller, in the 24th year of his age; remains interred in Mr. Bachtel's burial ground. Several

THE MARYLAND HERALD AND HAGERS-TOWN WEEKLY ADVERTISER

weeks previous to his death, he attempted to cross the ice at Price's Fording on the Conococheague Creek, but unhappily his horse broke through, and in endeavoring to save his horse, he precipitated himself into the water, where he continued a considerable time. After his fruitless attempt to save his horse he procured another and rode home, a distance of 10 miles, perfectly wet, to which his death is attributed/Married Tues 20th ult, by Rev J.R. Reily, Henry Miller to Miss Nancy Spitznagel/Married Thurs last, by same, John Strite to Miss Elisabeth Summers/Married Sun evening last, by same Samuel Stover to Miss Sarah Schneider, all of this co

274. EAM Mar 20 1821/Died in this town Fri morning last, after a lingering illness, George Reynolds, Teacher, in the 65th year of his age/Equity case - Andrew Heathrington vs Isaac Baker & John Baker, heirs of Isaac Baker, decd. Object of this bill is to obtain decree to have a deed to tract called The Venture, recorded, made by Isaac Baker, decd, to John Heathrington, decd, the father of the complainant. The bill states that Isaac Baker delivered a deed, dated 1779, to Heathrington to be recorded; said Isaac Baker soon after removed from Md, and hath since died, leaving the defendants his heirs

275. EAM Mar 27 1821/Married Thurs 15th inst, by Rev J.R. Reily, Emanuel Brua to Miss Catharine Zacharis/Married Sat 17th inst by same, Jacob Bowers to Miss Mary Kline, both of Va/Married Tues last by same, John Tice to Miss Nancy Newcomer, dau of Henry Newcomer, of this co/Married same day by same, John Hartel to Miss Mary Lecron, both of this co/Married same day by Rev B. Kurtz, George Confer to Miss Elizabeth Bowman/Married same day by same, John Hatsenmiller to Miss Elizabeth Gamble/Married Thurs last by same, John Stemple to Miss Margaret Laughm/Married same day by same, Conrad Watson to Miss Elizabeth Hose/Married Sat last by same, Lewis Stephens to Miss Mary Shepler/Married Sun morning last by Rev J.C. Clay, Charles G. Downes to Miss Sarah Ensminger, both of this co

276. EAM Apr 3 1821/Married Thurs evening 22d ult, by Rev Slator Clay, Charles H. Clay to Miss Maria Evans, both of Evansburg, Mont Co, Pa/Married Tues last by Rev J.R. Reily, Peter Kautz to Miss Catharine Pfautz, both of Franklin Co, Pa/Married Thurs evening last by same, George T. Thornburg to Miss Sarah Oldwine (as corrected in the fol issue)/Died Thurs last at her res about 3 miles from Hagers-Town, Mrs. Elizabeth Kiesecker, relict of late Simon Kiesecker, in the 67th year of her age/Died this morning, in this town, after a short illness, Mrs. Mary Middelkauff, in the 86th year of her age

277. EAM Apr 10 1821/Married Thurs 29th ult by Rev F. Kurtz, Daniel Ridenour to Miss Elizabeth Brewer/Married same day by same, John I. Miller to Mrs. Mary Smith, all of Williams Port/Married Thurs last by Rev J.R. Reily, James M'Alrath to Miss Mary Morris, both of Shepherdstown, Va/Married Sun evening last by same, Archibald Halbert to Miss Catharine M'Laughlin, both of this co/Died at Alexandria Mon 2d inst, in 62nd year of his age, John Winter, Printer, formerly of Frederick-Town, Md

278. EAM Apr 17 1821/From Greensburgh, Pa - Died yesterday morning after a lingering and severe illness, at his res in Unity township, William Findley, hero of the Revolution, for many yrs representative in congress from this district/John Wolford offers reward of 6 cents and a broken awl for appren-

THE MARYLAND HERALD AND HAGERS-TOWN WEEKLY ADVERTISER

tice to boot and shoe-making business named Henry Keefer, about 5 ft, 16-17 yrs old

279. EAM Apr 24 1821/Married Thurs 12th inst by Rev J.R. Reily, Samuel Row to Miss Elizabeth Hint/Married same day by Rev B. Kurtz, Daniel Bragonier to Miss Rosanna Hower/Married same day by same, John Malone, to Miss Mary Nitzle/Married Thurs 19th inst by same, William Power to Miss Mary Rhoades /Married same day by Rev J.R. Reily, Christian Wagoner to Miss Elizabeth Huber/Married Sun 22d inst by same, David Glaze to Miss Elizabeth Furry /Married same day by Rev J.C. Clay, Thomas Robertson to Miss Margaret Albert/Died 7th isnt of a pulmonary indisposition in the 27th year of her age, Rosanna Hawken, wife of Samuel Hawken of Xenia, Ohio, and formerly of this place/Died Tues last after a short but severe illness, Mrs. Ann Landen, wife of Francis Landen of this town, in the 50th year of her age

280. EAM May 1 1821/Married Sun last at Green-Castle by Rev Rothrauff, George B. Pascal to Miss Mary Doyle, both of this place

281. EAM May 8 1821/Married Tues 24th ult by Rev B. Kurtz, Ezra Barnes to Miss Ann Davis/Married Thurs 26th ult by same, Edward Davis to Miss Nancy Smith, both of this place/Married Thurs last by same, Martin Bare to Miss Elizabeth Stahl, both of this co/Married Sun last by same, David Bowers to Miss Rachel Hyland, both of Williams-Port/Died Mon 30th ult, after a short illness, Miss Susanna Harry, dau of John Harry, near this town, in the 13th year of her age/Died Wed last, in this town, after a short illness, Mrs. Mary Protzman, widow of late John Protzman, in the 72d year of her age

282. EAM May 15 1821/Married Tues last by Rev J.R. Reily, Isaac B. ... to Miss Susanna Helser/Died Thurs last in the 65th year of his age, Christian Hawken, old inhabitant of this town; interred in Luth burial ground in this town

283. EAM May 22 1821/Married 24th Apr by Rev Dr. Blythe, Doct. H. Geo. Doyle, of Louisville, to Mary Ann Elizabeth, dau of late Wm. Todd, Esq. of Lexington, Ky/Married Thurs 10th inst by Rev B. Kurtz, Samuel Nonemacker to Miss Elizabeth Bragonier/Married Thurs last by same, Jacob A. Brewer to Miss Harriet Welsh/Died in this town Tues morning 15th inst, after a lingering illness, John W. Miller, son of John Miller, Merchant, in the 28th year of his age

284. EAM Jun 5 1821/Winchester - Caleb Messer had both arms amputated as result of accidental explosion at the new market-house

285. EAM Jun 12 1821/Married Tues evening last, by Rev Buckingham, John Cameron of Shepherd's town, to Miss Maria M'Fall of this place/On Tues evening last, a son of David Barr of this town, about 3 yrs old, fell into a vat in his father's Tan Yard, and was drowned

286. EAM Jun 19 1821/Married Thurs 31st ult by Rev B. Kurtz, Joseph Leidy to Miss Ann Ludy/Married Thurs 7th inst by same, William Lewis to Miss Susanna Miller/Married Mon evening 11th inst by Rev J.R. Reily, Jacob Swope, merchant, to Miss Eliza Leight, dau of Benj. Leight, of this town/Married at Balt on Tues evning, 12th inst, by Rev Nevins, Edward G. Williams, Esq. of this co, to Miss Ann Gilmor, dau of William Gilmor, Esq. of that City/Mar-

THE MARYLAND HERALD AND HAGERS-TOWN WEEKLY ADVERTISER

ried Thurs last by Rev B. Kurtz, John F. Kraber to Miss Mary Hahn, both of this place/Baltimore - Died Mon 11th inst, Alexander Clagett, Esq. in the 77th year of his age, after a long and protracted illness, native of Mont co, Md, settled at an early period in Wash Co; was sheriff of that co for 3 yrs. He removed to this city in the Spring of 1818, where he has since resided

287. EAM Sep 18 1821/Died Thurs night, 30th ult at Phila, in the 64th year of his age, of a lingering disease, Col. John F. Mercer, of West River, Md. At early age he was sent by his native state, Va, as delegate to the Old congress. On his marriage he removed to Md where he commenced practice of law, was soon apptd by legislature of Md a member of the convention which framed our present Constitution. Later chosen member of the House of Rep from Congressional Dist of Md, and elected to Gen. Assembly of Md. His infirmities induced him to visit Phila for purpose of consulting Dr. Physick; remains deposited in Church Yard of St. Peter's/Died in Williams-Port Sat 8th inst in the 32d year of her age, Mrs. Catharine Herr, wife of John Herr, Jr, leaving 6 young children/Died Wed last, after a short illness of a bilious disease, in the 56th year of her age, Mrs. Catharine Hoffman, consort of John Hoffman, residing about 10 miles from this place; remains interred at Firey's meeting house; sermon delivered by Rev Nathan Little

288. EAM Oct 2 1821/Married at Chambersburg, Pa, Sun, 16th ult by Rev Rahauser, John H. Rutter, to Miss Lavinia Kaighn, both of this place/Married Tues 18th ult, by Rev B. Kurtz, Joel Brown to Miss Mary Jolliff, near Winchester, Va/Married Sun 23d ult by same, Henry Grosh to Miss Prudence Ligget, both of Funks-town/Married Tues last by same, John Bragonier to Susanna Cook of this place/Died at Bath, Morgan Co, Va, Sun 23d ult of a typhus fever, Elie Williams Elliot, Esq., youngest son of late Col. Robert Elliot, of this place, in the 29th year of his age, leaving a widow/Died at his res in Mont co, Pa, Tues 25th ult, after an illness of 6 days, Rev Slator Clay, in the 67th year of his age/In consequence of the death of his father, the Rector of the Episc Church, in this place, will be absent for a few weeks /Died in this town, yesterday morning, Mrs. Mary Oldwine, in the 57th year of her age

289. EAM Oct 9 1821/Married Sun morning last by Rev B. Kurtz, Josiah Smith of Canton, Ohio, to Miss Mary Dillman, dau of Henry Dillman, of this place /Died in this town, Thurs last, of a pulmonary complaint, Miss Theresa Gruber, dau of John Gruber, Printer, in the 23d year of her age/Died yesterday morning, Samuel Beecher, merchant, of this town/Died in Woodford Co, Ky, 11 Aug last, after a short illness, Mrs. Elizabeth Hager, wife of Major Christian Hager, formerly of this co, in the 38th year of her age

290. EAM Oct 16 1821/Baltimore, Oct 8 - Death of Miss Ann Hamilton of Baltimore, Friday night aged 15, shot in the head by Joseph Thompson, first mate of the hermaphrodite brig Leopard at the house of her father, John Hamilton. Thompson, who boarded at the house, attempted to kill himself but failed and is in city gaol. Miss Hamilton had rejected him - American

291. EAM Oct 23 1821/Married Thurs 11th inst, by Rev B. Kurtz, George Zigler, to Miss Susan Russell, both of this co/Married Tues 16th inst, by same, David Gilbert to Miss Sarah Young, both of this place/Died Wed morning 10th inst, John Ankeney, of George, in the 23d year of his age/Died Sun

THE MARYLAND HERALD AND HAGERS-TOWN WEEKLY ADVERTISER

morning, at the house of Christian Miller, about 3 1/2 miles from Hagers-Town, Elijah Leisure

292. EAM Oct 30 1821/Died Sat evening last, at his res, about 4 miles from Hagers-Town, after a short illness, David Westenberger, of this co/Died Sun last, in this town, Miss Elizabeth Withney, in the 25th year of her age

293. EAM Nov 6 1821/Married Sun last, by Rev B. Kurtz, Henry Fiery, Jr. to Miss Martha Miller, both of this co/Married evening of same day, by same, at Funks-town, Jacob Geiger of the state of Kentucky, to Miss Eliza Geiger of city of Balt/Died suddenly Sun 28th inst at res of his father, about 3 miles from Hagers-Town, Joseph Kellar, in the 36th year of his age/Died in Williams-Port on Sun morning last, Edmund H. Turner, of that place

294. EAM Nov 13 1821/Married Sun 4th inst by Rev J.R. Reily, Jacob Tutweiler, to Miss Eve Miller, all of this town

295. EAM Nov 20 1821/Married Thurs 8th inst by Rev B. Kurtz, Jacob Friese to Miss Harriot Babb/Married same day by same, Daniel Nyswanger to Miss Susan Slenker/Married Sun evening last by same, Henry Gower to Miss Elizabeth Kelly/Died in this town Mon 5th inst, Mrs. Elizabeth Ebert, mother of John Ebert, Inn-keeper, in the 67th year of her age

296. EAM Dec 4 1821/Married Tues evening last by Rev J.C. Clay, Dr. J.J. Hays, of Sharpsburg, to Miss Sophia B. Pottenger, of this town/Married same day by Rev B. Kurtz, John Fisher to Miss Eliza Conoway/Married Thurs last, by same, Martin Ensminger of William-Port to Miss Margaret Smith of this co/Married Sun last by same, John Daniel to Miss Catharine Hose/Died at his res in Cambridge, Dor Co, Thurs 22nd inst, Benjamin W. Lecompte, in the 85th year of his age, attended in 1804 at age of 18, Washington Academy in Somerset Co, lawyer, politician (long obit.) - Easton Gazette/Died Sun evening last at his res about 7 miles from Hagers-Town, Henry Witmer, old inhabitant of this co

297. EAM Dec 11 1821/Died Tues last, near this place, Daniel Young, in the 60th year of his age, occasioned by a paralytic attack/Died Wed, Mrs. Margaret Cellar, widow of John Cellar and sister of late Martin Kershner, Esq. in the 70th year of her age, also with a stroke of the palsy/Died Thurs last, Frederick Wolfersberger, of this town, in the 44th year of his age, also with a stroke of the palsy/Died suddenly Thurs last at his res about 8 miles from Hagers-Town, Richard Cromwell

298. EAM Dec 18 1821/Equity case - John Miller vs Easter Bargdoll, Samuel Bargdoll, and John Bargdoll, heirs of Peter Bargdoll, Junr, decd. The bill states that John Miller in 1808 entered into articles of agreement with said Peter Bargdoll, for sale and conveyance of parcel of land in Wash Co called Cold Weather, 6 acres. Peter Bargdoll died intestate in Feb 1819, leaving heirs, to wit, Easter Bargdoll of age, Samuel Bargdoll and John Bargdoll minors, all of whom now reside in Pa

299. EAM Dec 25 1821/Married Thurs 18th inst by Rev Kurtz, William W. Allender to Miss Mary Marker/Married Thurs last by same, George W. Kerfoot to Miss Maria Seifert

THE MARYLAND HERALD AND HAGERS-TOWN WEEKLY ADVERTISER

300. EAM Jan 8 1822/Married Tues 4th ult by Rev J.R. Reily, Philip Fox to Miss Catharine Maugins/Married Thurs 20th ult, by same, Samuel Spigler to Miss Nancy Miller/Married Tues 1st inst by same, Josiah Gabriel to Miss Catharine Felker/Died Fri morning last of a consumption at the tavern of Mr. C.C. Fechtig, in this town, James Hervey, in the 24th year of his age; he was from Oron(?) Village, Onondaga Co, N.Y., where his parents yet reside; interred in German Reformed burial ground

301. EAM Jan 15 1822/Married Tues evening last, by Rev J.R. Reily, Christian Betz to Miss Martha Williams/Died 5th ult at Oak Hill, near Kaskaskin, Ill, Joseph Sprigg, in about 62d year of his age, formerly of Wash Co, from whence he emigrated to the Westward nearly 5 yrs ago. He left wife and children

302. EAM Jan 22 1822/Married Thurs last by Rev J.R. Reily, Henry Masters to Miss Sarah Brua, dau of Peter Brua, of this co

303. EAM Feb 5 1822/Married at Long Meadow, Allegany Co, Md, on 26th ult, by Rev Heyer, Jacob Sides, formerly of this place, to Miss Sarah Tomlinson, dau of Jesse Tomlinson, esq./Married Tues evening 29th ult by Rev Buchanan, John Hall to Miss Mary M'Kee, both of Wash Co

304. EAM Feb 19 1822/Married Sun 10th inst by Rev B. Kurtz, Henry Dauble to Miss Barbara Keller, both of Boonsborough/Married Tues 12th inst by same, Michael Crissman to Miss Harriot Davis/Married Thurs last by same, Henry Angle to Miss Susan Fiery/Married same day by same, Jacob Beeler to Miss Elizabeth Shoop/Married Sun last by same, Moses Bowers to Miss Jane Williams, both of Williams-Port

305. EAM Feb 26 1822/John Gibboney, living near Michael Hoffer's mill, 6 miles from Hagers-Town, offers reward for Jonathan Fisher, apprentice to the fulling business, about 19 yrs of age, 5 ft 7-8 inch/Died Sun, 17th inst, Mrs. Mary M'Clannahan, wife of Matthew M'Clannahan, of this co, aged 22 yrs. She joined the Meth Episc Church when about 10 yrs of age. She left husband and 3 small children/Died in this town, Sat last, Mrs. Catharine Carla, aged 109 yrs, 8 months and 23 days, born in Germany, in town of Michelraugh, in Hohenlo, and emigrated to this country in the 48th year of her age. She left one son, 20 grandchildren, 21 great grandchildren, and 2 gr-gr grandchildren.

306. EAM Mar 5 1822/Married Thurs 14th ult, by Rev J.R. Reily, Jacob Brua to Miss Elizabeth Bragonier/Married Tues 19th ult by same, Jacob Hoffman to Miss Magdalena Stauffer/Married same day by same, Thomas Steiner to Miss Catharine Kerns/Married Thurs 28th ult, by same John Schnebly to Miss Lydia Ressly/Married Tues 26th ult, near Shepherds-town, by Rev Hanson, Rev Louis R. Fechtig to Miss Alcinda Harris, dau of Samuel Harris, of Jefferson Co, Va/Died in this town Thurs morning last at 5 o'clock, after a few days illness, William Kreps, Esq. Postmaster, in the 51st year of his age/Equity case - Alexander Grim vs Elias Crampton, John Crampton, Josiah Crampton, Thomas Jackson & Ruth his wife, Mary Wood, Elizabeth Keller, Elisha Crampton, Joseph Crampton, Samuel Rotrock and Mary Anne his wife, Sarah Anne Crampton, Elizabeth Crampton, Abraham Crampton, John Crampton and Ruth Crampton, heirs of Thomas Crampton, late of Wash Co, decd. The bill states that in 1811 Alexander Grim and Thomas Crampton entered into articles of

THE MARYLAND HERALD AND HAGERS-TOWN WEEKLY ADVERTISER

agreement relative to the taking up of a parcel of land. Thomas Crampton died in May 1819, leaving heirs, to wit: his sons Elias Crampton, John Crampton and Josiah Crampton, all of Wash Co, Md; his daus, Ruth Jackson who m Thomas Jackson and now res in Va, his dau Mary Wood who m Joseph Wood, now decd, said Mary res in Kentucky, and his dau Elizabeth Keller, who m Joseph Keller, since decd, said Elizabeth lives in Wash Co, Md – and the following grandchildren, the issue of Joshua Crampton, decd, son of said Thomas Crampton, to wit, Elisha Crampton, living in Ohio and Joseph Crampton, Mary Anne Crampton who m Samuel Rotrock, Sarah Anne Crampton, minor, Abraham Crampton, minor, John Crampton, minor, and Ruth Crampton, minor, all res in Wash Co, Md

307. EAM Mar 12 1822/Married Wed evening, 27th ult in George-town, by Rev Waugh, Henry Protzman, of Dayton, Ohio, to Miss Elizabeth Stembel, dau of Col. Henry Stembel, of the former place/Married Thurs last by Rev J.R. Reily, John Steinmetz to Miss Susan Myers, dau of Martin Myers, both of Wash Co/Died Tues night 5th inst Mrs. Barbara Rohrer, wife of Jacob Rohrer, sen, of this co, in the 70th year of her age

308. EAM Mar 19 1822/Married Thurs evening last, by Rev P.G. Buckingham, John Fechtig to Miss Sarah Beecher, both of this town/Died Sat 9th inst in this town, Bernard Oldwine, Jr. in the 32d year of his age

309. EAM Mar 26 1822/Married Tues 12 inst, by Rev J.R. Reily, Samuel Morgan to Miss Margaret Brunner/Married Thurs 14 inst by Rev B. Kurtz, Solomon Thornburg to Miss Mary Lefeber/Married same day by same, Michael Krissman to Miss Harriet Davis/Married Thurs 21st inst by same, William Smith to Miss Margaret Downey/Married same day by same, John Newcomer to Miss Catharine Knaft/Married same day by Rev J.R. Reily, Jacob W. Mealy to Miss Rebecca Gebhart/Married same day by same, Andrew Shanefeld to Miss Sarah Ann Louisa Branon/Married Sun 24th inst by same, Daniel Miller to Miss Rachel Houser /Married same day by Rev B. Kurtz, Henry Fishaugh to Miss Margaret Flora /Married same day by same, Abijah Smith to Miss Catharine Trovinger

310. EAM Apr 2 1822/Married Thurs last by Rev J.R. Reily, Jacob Good to Miss Sarah Stover, both of Wash Co/Married same day by Rev B. Kurtz, Darius Simpkins to Miss Roena Kadle/Married Sun last by same, Jacob Hawken of St. Louis, to Miss Catharine Allison of this place/Died Sat evening last in this town, Miss Elizabeth Harry, dau of late Jacob Harry, in the 36th year of her age

311. EAM Apr 9 1822/Married Thurs last by Rev B. Kurtz, David Brumbaugh Jun. to Miss Susanna Emorich/Married Sun last, William Davis to Miss Catharine Blentlinger

312. EAM Apr 16 1822/Died Tues evening last at his res about 4 miles from Hagers-Town, Jacob Rohrer, senr, old inhabitant of this co

313. EAM Apr 30 1822/Married 11th inst by Rev J.R. Reily, Peter Bussard to Miss Sarah Reidenour/Married Sun last by same, John D. Keedy to Mrs. Elizabeth Schnebly/Died in this town Sat last, John Eicleberger, aged 69 yrs

314. EAM May 7 1822/Married Tues last by Rev B. Kurtz, James Mackey to Miss Elizabeth Flemming, both of Sharpsburg/Married Wed last by same, William M.

THE MARYLAND HERALD AND HAGERS-TOWN WEEKLY ADVERTISER

Brown, of Franklin Co, Pa, to Miss Mary Bowles, dau of John Bowles, Esq. of this co/Died Tues morning last, after a short illness, at his res, about 3 miles from Williams-Port, James M'Clain, in the 53rd year of his age, leaving widow and 12 children

315. EAM May 14 1822/Married Thus last by Rev B. Kurtz, Peter Shanefelt to Miss Elizabeth Funk/Married Sun last by same, Isaac Rowland to Mrs. Elizabeth Rowland/Married same day by Rev J.R. Reilly, David Beard to Miss Christiana Slick/Died in this town Tues evening last, after a lingering illness, Miss Elizabeth Shimer, in the 27th year of her age/Died Fri last in this town, Christian Hawken, son of late Christian Hawken, decd, in the 30th year of his age

316. EAM May 21 1822/Married Tues evening 7th inst at Green-Castle, Pa, by Rev Strong, of Chambersburg, Rev John Lind, Pastor of the Associate Reformed Church of this town, to Miss Margaretta St. Clair C. Young, dau of late Rev John Young/Married Tues 14th inst, by Rev Shaw, John May to Miss Maria S.W. Kendall, all of this town/Married Thurs last by same, Alexander Kennedy to Miss Susan Booth, dau of John Booth, Esq. of this co

317. EAM May 28 1822/Married Tues 14th inst by Rev B. Kurtz, John Herbert to Miss Sarah Ann Mealy, both of Williams-Port/Married Tues last, by same, David Heffner to Miss Elizabeth Bean/Married 14 inst by Rev J.R. Reily, Andrew Wolgamot to Miss Mary, dau of John Tice

318. EAM Jun 4 1822/Died at his res in Williams-Port Thurs 23d May, after a lingering but painful illness, Capt. Peter Stake, in the 57th year of his age, leaving widow and 3 small children

319. EAM Jul 11 1822/Married Thurs 30th ult by Rev B. Kurtz, Jacob Davis to Miss Sarah Potter/Married Thurs 6 inst, by same, Jacob Gilbert to Miss Elizabeth Ritter

320. EAM Jun 18 1822/Married Thurs evening last, by Rev B. Kurtz, William Miller to Miss Elizabeth Bell, dau of Peter Bell, all of this place

321. EAM Jun 25 1822/Died 17 May last in Lebanon, Tennessee, Mrs. Sarah McGovan, late dau of George Shall, res near this town. She left this neighborhood about 6 yrs ago, to pay a visit to her brothers and sisters in Tennessee, having previously attached herself to the Luth Congregation of this town. Shortly after her arrival in Tennessee she married Mr. McGovan, a wealthy and respectable gentleman residing near Nashville. They had two daus, one of whom is but 2 weeks old/Samuel Gray cautions that his wife Ann Gray has left his bed and board; he will no longer pay any of her debts /Andrew Shanafeld cautions that his wife Sarah Shanafeld has left his bed and board and he will no longer pay her debts

322. EAM Jul 2 1822/Married Tues evening 25th ult, by Rev Samuel B. Shaw, William Robertson, merchant, to Miss Eliza Isabella Gileves, dau of the senior Editor of this paper/Married Thurs evening 27th ult by Rev John Emory, Alexander Mitchell to Miss Amelia Carr, dau of late Col. John Carr

323. EAM Jul 23 1822/Married Sun last by Rev Samuel B. Shaw, John Payden to Miss Elizabeth Lavis, both of the co

THE MARYLAND HERALD AND HAGERS-TOWN WEEKLY ADVERTISER

324. EAM Jul 30 1822/Married Sun last by Rev F. Rahauser, George Lizer to Miss Mary Stottlemeyer, both of this co/Died at Fountain Rock, Sun morning last, after a short illness, in the 16th year of his age, Edward Lloyd Ringgold, son of General Samuel Ringgold, of this co

325. EAM Aug 27 1822/Married in this town Thurs 15th inst by Rev B. Kurtz, George Lorshbaugh to Miss Catharine Albert, dau of John Albert, of this place/Married Sun last by same, Daniel Caufman to Miss Narcissa Davis/Died in this town, Sun morning last, after a short illness, Mrs. Amelia Ragan, relict of late Col. John Ragan, in the 34th year of her age, leaving 3 children

326. EAM Sep 3 1822/Died Wed morning last at the res of his son-in-law, David Cook, Rev Colin M'Farquhar, in the 91st year of his age, born in the highlands of Scotland, in 1732, and had the charge there of 2 congregations for 13-14 yrs; he emigrated to this co in 1774, and accepted a call in Donegal Congregation, Lancaster co, Pa

327. EAM Sep 17 1822/Jacob Hose, living about 10 miles from Hagers-Town, offers reward for apprentice to boot and shoe-making business, named Levi Price, in the 16th year of his age/Died at his res in Boonsborough Sun 8th inst, John Smith, Esq, in the 46th year of his age, leaving wife and several children. On Monday preceding his death, whilst returning home from Williams-Port, his horse took fright, upset the carryall and he was precipitated to the ground and his neck severely injured; remains interred at Funks-town; discourse delivered by Rev Denius/Died at her res in Balt on Fri Last, Eliza Hezlett, 2nd dau of James Hughes, decd, of this co

328. EAM Sep 24 1822/Died at Williams-Port Fri last, Mrs. Ann Eve Crawford, consort of John Crawford, Inn-keeper of that place, in the 29th year of her age/Died Mon morning 9th inst, at an advanced age, at the res of Henry D. Sellers, Esq. in Queen Ann's co, Md, Mrs. Frances Emory, relict of late Robert Emory, Esq. and mother to the Rev John Emory of Hagers-Town, for a number of yrs a member of Meth Episc Church - Easton Star/Annapolis - Died Sun night last, Jehu Chandler, editor of the Md. Rep. in the 38th year of his age, native of Delaware, but resided in this city during the last 13 yrs of his life

329. EAM Oct 1 1822/Married Thurs 19th ult by Rev John Lind, John McFarland to Miss Maria Louisa Rockenbaugh, both of Harpers-Ferry, Va/Married Thurs night last, by Rev J.R. Reily, George Updegraff to Miss Eliza Boyd, dau of Joseph Boyd, all of this place/Married Fri last by Rev John Lind, James Enders of Winchester, Va, to Miss Susanna Parratt, of the same place/Married Sun night last by Rev B. Kurtz, William Crumbaugh to Miss Elizabeth Combs, both of this place/Died Thurs 15th ult, Mrs. Mary Hall, consort of John Hall, of this co, in the 30th year of her age, leaving husband/Died Wed last at her res almost 3 miles from this town, Mrs. Mary Teisher, relict of late John Teisher, in the 55th year of her age, leaving several children/Died Fri night last, after a short illness, at his res about 8 miles from Hagers-Town, John Rentch, Esq. in the 32nd year of his age, leaving wife and 4 children. But a few days ago he was in town, he went several miles to execute his duty as Justice of the Peace - a kind husband and father

THE MARYLAND HERALD AND HAGERS-TOWN WEEKLY ADVERTISER

330. EAM Oct 8 1822/Died Fri last, Adam Leapard, of this place/Died same day, Henry Selser

331. EAM Oct 15 1822/Married Tues last at Harrisburg, Pa, by Rev J.R. Reily, of Hagers-Town, Rev John Weinbrenner, Pastor of the German Reformed Church, to Miss Charlotte Reutter/Died Wed morning last, after a few weeks illness, Mrs. Phebe Grieves, wife of Thomas Grieves, senior editor of the Md. Herald, in the 57th year of her age, wife and mother; funeral at Episc burying ground/Died Sun morning last in this town, Juliann Middelkauff, consort of Daniel Middelkauff

332. EAM Oct 22 1822/Married at Chambersburg, Pa, Sun 18h inst by Rev D. Denny, William Shleigh, of this town, to Miss Elizabeth Spickler, of Wash Co/Married Tues last in this town, by Rev B. Kurtz, Henry Leydy to Mrs. Elizabeth Ridenour, both of this co/Died Thurs night last at the res of David Newcomer, Esq. about 3 miles from this town, of the consumption, George Reynolds, in the 24th year of his age

333. EAM Nov 5 1822/Married Tues evening 22d ult by Rev Redmund, John O'Ferrall of Morgan Co, Va, to Miss Eliza Humrickhouse, dau of Peter Humrickhouse, of this place/Died at Augusta, Georgia, Thurs 17th ult, Oliver Miller, native of Hagers-Town, in the 24th year of his age

334. EAM Nov 12 1822/Married Thurs last by Rev B. Kurtz, Samuel Smith to Miss Mary Howard, both of this co

335. EAM Nov 19 1822/Died Fri night last, Mrs. Elizabeth Wolgamot, consort of Capt. John Wolgamot, in the 49th year of her age, wife, mother; interred in family burial ground, discourse by Rev J.R. Reily

336. EAM Nov 26 1822/Married Thurs 14th inst by Rev Kurtz, Jacob Bare, to Miss Catharine Ringer/Married same day by same, Charles B. Hitchcock, to Miss Mary Ditto/Married Sun 17th inst by Rev Denius, Adam Myers, jr. to Miss Catharine Niebert, all of this co

337. EAM Dec 3 1822/Married Tues lat by Rev J.R. Reily, John Ringer to Miss Mary, dau of John Witmer, all of this co/Died Sat morning last, after a few days illness, in the 28th year of her age, Mrs. Eliza L. Elliott, consort of George M. Elliott, of this co, and dau of Wm. Delahunt, leaving a husband and numerous relatives

338. EAM Dec 10 1822/Married Thurs last, by Rev J.R. Reily, Valentine Wachtel, to Miss Margaret Bovey/Married same day by same, Isaac Hildebrandt to Miss Elizabeth, dau of John Wolfersberger, all of this co/Died Fri evening last, Mary Jane Umbaugh, dau of Michael Umbaugh, of this co, aged 2 yrs, 6 months and 7 days

339. EAM Dec 17 1822/Married Thurs 5th inst by Rev B. Kurtz, John Stuckschlager to Miss Regina Slenker/Married Thurs last by Rev J.R. Reily, John Newcomer (son of Henry) to Miss Catharine, dau of Samuel Newcomer/Died at Hancock on Fri morning 6th inst, Jacob Brosius, in 78th year of his age/Died Thurs morning last, after a short illness, Bartholomew Booth of this co, in the 24th year of his age; interred in family burying ground with Masonic honors

THE MARYLAND HERALD AND HAGERS-TOWN WEEKLY ADVERTISER

340. EAM Dec 24 1822/Married Thurs last by Rev B. Kurtz, Jacob Moats to Miss Catharine Kline/Married same day by same, Christian Palmer to Miss Elizabeth Knode/Married same day by Rev J.R. Riley, David Hershey to Miss Magdalena, dau of David Hershey

341. EAM Dec 31 1822/Died Tues night last, in the 77th year of his age, Christian Stemple, old inhabitant of this place/Died Wed last, David Zeigler, son of George Zeigler, in the 22d year of his age; interred in family burial ground, discourse by Rev Reily/Died at George-town, D.C. on Sun last, at half past 2 o'clock, A.M., Col. Elie Williams in 73d year of his age - patriot of '76, occasioned by long and severe bilious disorder /Died sun morning last, Mrs. Martha Bragonier, wife of Daniel Bragonier, in the 25th year of her age/Died yesterday morning, Mrs. Frances Barr, wife of Capt. Jacob Barr, of this co, leaving husband and 7 children

342. EAM Jan 7 1823/Married Thurs 26th ult by Rev S.K. Denius, Elias Davis of Boonsborough, to Miss Amelia Seibert, dau of Major Peter Seibert, of this co/Died 19th Dec last in Brownsville, Pa, Mrs. Mary Bowman, in the 79th year of her age, leaving 5 children, 35 grandchildren and 37 great grandchildren. The decd was among the earliest settlers of this co and res of Hagers-Town from its foundation until within about 6 yrs since, when she removed to the western country/Died Sun 29 dec last at her mother's, Mrs. Elizabeth Davis, widow of Jesse Davis, and dau of late Henry Stein, in the 33d year of her age, of a lingering consumption/Died in Frederick-town, Md, Tues evening 31st ult, Rev James Redmond, for several yrs past, Pastor of the Roman Cath Congregations of Wash and Allegany counties/Died Wed last in this town, Mrs. Catharine Stover, in the 67th year of her age/Died Thurs last, William Root (stone mason), in the 29th year of his age; interred at Funks-town, address delivered by Rev J.R. Reily

343. EAM Jan 28 1823/Died at his res about 6 miles from Hagers-Town Sat morning last, Nicholas Ridenour, in the 68th year of his age; interred in Luth burial ground at Williams-Port, discourse delivered by Rev Kurtz/Died in city of Lancaster, Pa, Fri morning, 10th inst, William Dickson, Printer, editor of the Lancaster Intelligencer

344. EAM Feb 4 1823/Married Sun last by Rev B. Kurtz, Peter Steffy to Miss Mary Pretzman

345. EAM Feb 11 1823/Died Fri morning last in this town, after a lingering illness, Mrs. Mary Merrick, wife of Joseph I. Merrick, Esq. in the 29th year of her age/Died Sun morning last, Mrs. Ann Hall, wife of Thomas B. Hall of this co, in the 36th year of her age, leaving husband and 7 young children

346. EAM Feb 18 1823/Married Thurs 23rd ult by Rev J.R. Reily, Jonas Knode to Miss Mary Donaldson/Married Thurs 13th inst by same, John Hoffman to Mrs. Mary Weinbrenner/Died Sun 9th inst, Mrs. Mary Betz, widow of Frederick Betz, in the 80th year of her age/Died same day, Samuel, son of Capt Jacob Barr, in the 10th year of his age/Died Wed last, Mrs. Barbara, wife of Samuel M'Cauley, and dau of Henry Landis, in the 23d year of her age; interred in family burial ground at Beaver Creek, leaving husband and infant son/Died Thurs last, Elias Marker, in the 19th year of his age/Died Fri last, at Funks-town, John Shilling, in the 40th year of his age - On all the above occasions, suitable discourses were delivered by Rev J.R. Reily/Died at Balt

THE MARYLAND HERALD AND HAGERS-TOWN WEEKLY ADVERTISER

Tues 11th inst, Mrs. Sarah Lemmon, mother of Rev Lemmon of this place, in the 58th year of her age/Died, Mrs. Mary Ann Harry, consort of John Harry of this place, Tues last about 1 o'clock, P.M., in the 33d year of her age; interred in Luth burial ground

347. EAM Feb 25 1823/Chambersburgh, Feb 18 - Died in this borough, Wed night last, in the 27th year of his age, Peter S. Dechert, Esq. only son of Jacob Dechert, Esq., leaving widow, one child, aged father, 2 sisters. He was a member of the present legislature, formerly Register & Recorder of the co. His disease was the consumption. He was interred in Luth church yard with military honors - Franklin Republican

348. EAM Mar 4 1823/Married Thurs last by Rev J.R. Reily, David Rickenbaugh to Miss Margaret Sprecher, both of this co/Married same day by same, Jacob Cassel of Harrisburg, Pa, to Miss Sophia, dau of Jacob Lambert, of this co

349. EAM Mar 11 1823/Married Thurs 17th inst, by Rev B. Kurtz, Jacob Light, of Pa, to Miss Nancy Ficry, of this co

350. EAM Mar 18 1823/Married Sat 8th inst by Rev J.R. Reily, Jacob Hoffman to Miss Christiana Hoffman/Married Thurs last by same, James Shererd to Miss Anna Smith, both of this co/Married Thurs 7th inst by Rev Keady, Samuel Cunningham, near Zigler's Store, to Miss Mary Ann Wilson, of Pleasant Valley /Died Wed last, on Beaver Creek, Capt. James Walling, in the 34th year of his age; interred in family burial ground, leaving aged mother and number of relatives; discourse by Rev J.R. Reily/Died Tues last, Jacob, son of Andrew Bell, near Leitersburg, in the 24th year of his age; and on Thurs last, Miss Margaret, dau of Andrew Bell, in the 16th year of her age; funeral sermon given by Rev J.R. Reily

351. EAM Mar 25 1823/Married Sun 16th inst by Rev B. Kurtz, William Berry to Miss Susan Winders, both of Funks-town/Married same day by same, Samuel Wolslager to Miss Mary Welsh, both of Funks-town/Married Thurs 20th inst by same, James W. Clarke to Miss Barbara Iseminger/Married same day by Rev J.R. Reily, George Thomas to Miss Sarah Schlosser, both of this co

352. EAM Apr 1 1823/Married Tues evening last by Rev B. Kurtz, Joseph Rowland of this co, to Miss Margaret Hefflybower of Va/Married same day by same, Daniel Middlekauff, of this co, to Miss Catharine Hefflybower of Va

353. EAM Apr 15 1823/Married Sun last by Rev B. Kurtz, John Snyder to Miss Nancy Smith, both of Funks-town

354. EAM Apr 22 1823/Married Thurs night last, by Rev J.R. Reily, George Fechtig to Miss Mary Elizabeth Yoe, dau of Benjamin Yoe, Esq all of this place

355. EAM Apr 29 1823/Died in this town Wed 16th inst, David Alter, in the 32d year of his age/Died Sun last, after a lingering illness, John Leight, in the 77th year of his age

356. EAM May 6 1823/Married Tues 15th ult by Rev B. Kurtz, Peter Renner to Miss Elizabeth Hammaker, both of this co/Married Tues 22d ult by same, Henry

THE MARYLAND HERALD AND HAGERS-TOWN WEEKLY ADVERTISER

Faust, of Berks Co, Pa, to Miss Mary Faulkwell, of this co/Died Tues 29th ult in the 23d year of his age, Washington Price, youngest son of Col. Josiah Price of this co

357. EAM May 13 1823/Died in this town Wed last, in the 64th year of his age, Barney Oldwine, soldier of the Rev; received a pension

358. EAM May 20 1823/Married Tues 6th inst by Rev B. Kurtz, David Hersh to Miss Elizabeth Sheller/Married Thurs last by same, Samuel Middelkauff to Miss Elizabeth Charles

359. EAM Jun 3 1823/Married 1st inst by Rev J.R. Reily, John D. Kieffer to Miss Elizabeth Schmutz/Died Thurs last after a short illness, Miss Susan Scheimer, in the 23d year of her age

360. EAM Jun 10 1823/Married in Shepherds-town, Va, Mon 2d inst by Rev John Matthews, John Weis, sen. of this town, to Mrs. Elizabeth Bishop, of that place

361. EAM Jun 17 1823/Married Thurs morning last, by Rev B. Kurtz, John De Pui, Clerk of the Senate of Pa, to Miss Louisa Amelia Kurtz, dau of Benjamin Kurtz, Esq. all of Harrisburg, Pa/Married same day by Rev J.R. Reily, Samuel Winters to Miss Susan, dau of late Samuel Newcomer/Died in this town Sun night last, Christopher Hilliard, Merchant, in the 52d year of his age, leaving wife and several children

362. EAM Jun 24 1823/Married Thurs last by Rev George Lemmon, James B. Chenoweth to Miss Rachel Payne, both of Frederick Co, Va/Married same day by same, Thorton G. Jordan to Miss Rebecca H. Mullennix, likewise of Frederick Co, Va/Died Thurs evening last, at her res about 7 miles from Hagers-town, Frances Witmer, widow of late Henry Witmer, aged about 56 yrs

363. EAM Jul 1 1823/Married at Woodstock, Va, Tues evening 24th ult by Rev William H. Foote, William Johnston, formerly of this town, to Miss Mary S. Ott, dau of Michael Ott, Merchant, of the former place

364. EAM Jul 8 1823/Married Tues 24th ult by Rev Rothraff, George Hanna to Miss Rebecca Allen, both of this co/Died at Mount Tammany, Sat last after a short illness, Matthew Van Lear, Esq. long a citizen of Wash Co, Md, in the 69th year of his age; had filled many public stations

365. EAM Jul 22 1823/Married Tues morning, 15th inst (at the res of Joseph Van Lear, near Williams-Port) by Rev John Lind, Col. Otho H. Williams, Clerk of Wash Co Court, to Miss Eliza Van Lear, dau of late Major William Van Lear /Died Wed morning last, after a lingering illness, Mrs. Barbara Cellar, wife of George Cellar of this co, in the 65th year of her age/Died on the evening of the same day, at his res near Sharpsburg, Doct. John J. Hays, aged about 25 yrs; interred in Sharpsburg with Masonic honours

366. EAM Aug 5 1823/Died Sat evening last, in this town of a pulmonary complaint, John Crawford, in the 34th year of age, leaving 3 small children /Equity Court case - Alexander Moore vs Frederick Coon & others, heirs of Christian Hartman. Plaintiff paid purchase money for tract, Rural Felicity, to sheriff, the estate of Christian Hartman, decd. Christian Hartman pur-

THE MARYLAND HERALD AND HAGERS-TOWN WEEKLY ADVERTISER

chased said land from Frederick Coon, of Va., but the whole of the purchase money has not been paid to said Coon. Christian Hartman died intestate, leaving his children and heirs: Andrew Hartman, Henry Hartman, Jacob Hartman, and Catharine Hartman, his widow, who all res in Wash Co. And John Deitrick and Elizabeth his wife, which said Elizabeth is the dau of said Christian, reside out of the state of Md

367. EAM Aug 5 1823/Equity case - Leonard Shafer, Thomas C. Brent, John Moyer and Isaac Bachtel vs Barbara Rowland, David Rowland, Addis Linn and Elizabeth his wife, Jacob Rowland, Henry Rowland, Elie David & Christiana his wife, Henry Brewer and Susanna his wife, Jonathan Rowland, John Rowland and Mary Rowland, widow, children and devisees of David Rowland, of Wash Co, decd. Object of bill is to obtain decree to have real estate sold of which said David Rowland died seized, for the payment of his debts. David Rowland devised all his estate to above named defendants, after the payment of his debts, but did not authorise his executors therein named either to sell or convey said real estate. Said David left a widow, above named Barbara Rowland and above named sons and daus, a part of whom do not reside in Md, to wit, David Rowland, Elizabeth who married Addis Linn, Jacob Rowland, Henry Rowland, Christiana who married Elie David and Susanna who married Henry Brewer

368. EAM Aug 5 1823/Samuel Shatt forwarns persons from trusting his wife Christiana on his account, as he is determined to pay no debts of her contracting from this date. "My intention is to leave this county and take up my residence in the south west part of Virginia - my wife has thought proper not to accompany me."

369. EAM Aug 12 1823/Married Thurs last, by Rev B. Kurtz, Peter Fockler to Miss Susanna Yakle/Married Sun last by same, Michael Thomas to Miss Mary Waltz/Died Wed evening last, after a short illness, at Long Meadows about 5 miles from this town, Mrs. Ann Mary Wilson, consort of David T. Wilson, in the 31st year of her age, leaving husband and 4 small children/Died same day at Barton Bean's, at Long Meadows, Mrs. Susanna Tarlton, relict of the late Thomas Tarlton, in the 77th year of her age; she was an inhabitant of this co for more than 20 yrs/Died at Tammany's Mount, near Williams-Port, Thurs evening last, after a short but severe illness, Horatio Nelson Van Lear, son of late Matthew Van Lear, Esq. in the 25th year of his age. It was but a short time since the death of his father was announced/Died in this town Fri last, Thomas Little, in the 24th year of his age/Died same day, John Lawrence, son of Otho Lawrence, Esq. of this town, aged 6 yrs, 10 months/Died Sun morning last, after a short illness, at his res near this town, William Delahunt, aged about 55 yrs, leaving widow and several children

370. EAM Aug 19 1823/Married Sun last by Rev J.R. Reily, Peter Kraus to Miss Susan Winters, dau of John Winters, of this co

371. EAM Aug 26 1823/Died Mon 10th inst in this town, Mrs. Margaret Stemple, wife of John Stemple, Merchant, in the 21st year of her age/Died Tues 19th inst at his res about 4 miles from Hagers-town, John Keckron/Died at Tammany's Mount, near Williams-Port, Thurs afternoon, Aug 21 after a few days sickness, Miss Mary Finley, dau of late Ebenezer Finley, Esq. of Balt

THE MARYLAND HERALD AND HAGERS-TOWN WEEKLY ADVERTISER

372. EAM Sep 2 1823/Died at Middletown, Jefferson Co, Ky, 9 Jul last, of a pulmonary complaint, William Lewis, son of Capt. William Lewis of this town, aged about 33 yrs

373. EAM Sep 9 1823/Married Thurs 21st ult by Rev J.R. Reily, Christian Conrad to Miss Eve Wolf/Married Thurs 28th ult by same, Henry Funk to Miss Harriet Motes, all of this co/Married Fri evening last, by same, Alfred Ball to Miss Matilda Van Horn, both of Winchester, Va/Died Wed morning last, after a short illness, at his res about 6 miles from Hagers-town, John Hyland, in the 47th year of his age, leaving widow and 4 children; interred in family burial ground on his farm/Died at Samuel Slicer's near Hancock, on Thurs evening last, John Conrad Williams, son of late Col. Elie Williams of this co/Died Sat last at his res adjoining this town, George Miller, aged about 65 yrs/Died Sat eveing last, Augustus Riblet, son of Daniel Riblet of this town/Died Sun afternoon last, Mrs. Catharine Wise, dau of John Kausler of this town; and on yesterday morning, Henry Wise, husband of decd. Mr. & Mrs. Wise resided in Brownsville, Pa, which place they left about 2-3 weeks since, for the purpose of paying their friends a visit at this place. They have left 11 children/Died yesterday afternoon, after a short illness, George Smith, merchant

374. EAM Sep 16 1823/Married Thurs last by Rev J.R. Reily, David Stoner to Miss Nancy Teisher, both of this co/Died Sun 7th inst Miss Olivia Boyd, 2nd dau of Walter Boyd, Esq. of this co/Died Sun last, of the dropsy (at the house of her son-in-law Jacob Sturr) in this town, Mrs. Catharine M'Dill, aged about 60 yrs/Christian Middelkauff, living near Hagers-town, offers reward for apprentice to farming business named William Corse, about 4 ft 10-11 inch, 15-16 yrs of age

375. EAM Sep 23 1823/Died Tues last at his res about 5 miles from Hagerstown, John Rice, old inhabitant of this co/Died Wed last, at his farm about 4 miles from Hagers-town, John Petry, in the 46th year of his age/Died Thurs morning last, in Funks-town, Miss Mary Grosh, eldest dau of Frederick Grosh, of that place/Died at Fountain Rock, Sun morning last, after an illness of 48 hrs, Charles Anthony, son of Gen. Samuel Ringgold, about 4 yrs of age

376. EAM Sep 30 1823/Died in Wash City, Thurs last, after an illness of 10 days, Rev Louis/Died, R. Fechtig, son of Christian Fechtig of this place, in the 36th year of his age. He was an Elder in the Meth Episc Church, and at the time of his death Presiding Elder of the Balt Dist./Died Sat last, after a short illness, Mrs. Elizabeth Zeller, wife of Capt. Jacob Zeller, of this co, aged about 57 yrs, leaving husband and 5 children/Died Sun last, in the 5th year of her age, Ann Catharine, only dau of John Buchanan, Esq. of this co/Died yesterday morning, after a short but severe illness, Job Hunt of this place, member of the Meth Episc Church

377. EAM Oct 7 1823/Died at Greensburgh, Pa, of dropsy in the chest, Sun evening 21 Sep at half past 9 o'clock, Frederick Rohrer, Esq. of that place, in the 82d year of his age. He was a native of France, and born 28 July 1742. He came to America during the war between France and Britain. He married Catharine Deemer in 1766 in York co and shortly after removed to Hagers-town. In that year he first visited the Western country, as far as Pittsburgh, then composed of a few Indian huts. He brought a number of cattle with him which he exchanged to General St. Clair for a tract of land

THE MARYLAND HERALD AND HAGERS-TOWN WEEKLY ADVERTISER

in Ligonier Valley. He still left his family at Hagers-town, and in 1767 brought the first wheat over the mountains ever imported into the Western Country. He cultivated it, together with other grain on his farm in the Valley, and prepared for his family, whom he removed there in the following fall. He took out a warrant for all that tract of land on the Connemaugh river, on which the salt is now made, and was the first to discover those immense springs of salt water. In 1771 he returned with his family to Hagers-town, being unable to live any longer amongst the Indians. In 1793 he removed to Greensburgh, from Hagers-town, where he remained until the time of his death. Some time after his removal there, he was appointed a Justice of the Peace by Governor M'Kean. He was interred in the German burying ground. He had 9 children, 42 grand-children and 17 great-grand children - Nat. Intel./Died at Mercersburg, Pa, Mon, 29 ult, Dr. Jesse Magaw/Died Fri last in the 43rd year of her age, Mrs. Mary Grosh, wife of Frederick Grosh, of Funks-town/Died Sat, Mrs. Ann Bowart, wife of Michael Bowart of this town, in the 30th year of her age/Died Sun, in this town, John Smith, mason, in the 33rd year of his age

378. EAM Oct 14 1823/Died in Logan co, Ky, 14 Sep last, Christopher Orndorff (formerly of this co) aged about 72 yrs/Died Tues William M. Reynolds and buried near Mount Aetna Furnace. He was afflicted from his youth; his father, a wealthy farmer of this co, was one of the first purchasers of Kentucky lands; and on his descending the Ohio river with his family, was attacked by the Indians and killed in his boat, his family taken prisoners and carried to Canada, where they suffered a long and rigorous imprisonment, and the loss of a large landed estate in Kentucky. The family at length on their release again settled in this co, where the decd by his industry acquired considerable property, which he lately lost by his disposition to serve others. His widow and 8 small children are now in a situation, claiming that benevolence, he, while in prosperity, so cheerfully bestowed on others/Died at Shepherds-town, Va, same day, after a short illness, James S. Lane, wealthy merchant/Died same day, Henry Landis, old inhabitant of this co

379. EAM Oct 28 1823/Died in Logan Co, Ky, Sat 4th inst, Mrs. Mary Orndorff, relict of late Christian Orndorff (formerly of this co) in the 68th year of her age/Died in Funks-town, on 14 int, Miss Eliza Gaither, dau of Mr. Z. Gaither, in the 16th year of her age/Died in this town, Fri last, after a lingering illness, Michael Kapp, in the 37th year of his age, leaving widow and 7 small children

380. EAM Nov 4 1823/Died Fri night last in the 23d year of her age, Miss Matilda Gruber, dau of John Gruber; interred in German Reformed burying ground; discourse delivered by Rev J.R. Reily

381. EAM Nov 11 1823/Married Thurs 23d ult, by Rev B. Kurtz, Wm. Bridgman to Miss Alcinda Jane Dash, both of Va/Married same day by same, Henry Hersh, to Miss Catharine Summers, both of this co/John T. Lowe died Wed morning 5th inst after a short illness, at the house of his brother. He had been engaged for some time as a clerk in the store of Messrs. Locher and Brandner. Just a few days ago he was the subject of health and hope/Died Sun morning last at his res about 3 miles from this town, Andrew Shanafeld, in the 46th year of his age

THE MARYLAND HERALD AND HAGERS-TOWN WEEKLY ADVERTISER

382. EAM Nov 18 1823/Died in Hancock-town Sat last at an advanced age, Andrew Goulding, Inn-keeper/Died in this town Sun evening last, after a short illness, Mrs. Elizabeth Calder in the 76th year of her age

383. EAM Nov 25 1823/Married Thurs last by Rev B. Kurtz, William H. Miller to Miss Mary M. Park, both of Green-castle, Pa/Died 28 Oct at Williamsburg, Livingston Co, New York, Charles Carroll, Esq., formerly of Belle Vue, Wash Co, Md, after a tedious illness - Nat. Intel./Died Sun 16 inst, Mrs. Elizabeth Calder in the 76th year of her age, of this town. She was born in Scotland, and spent the far greater part of her long life in her native land. During the last summer she was reduced by the prevailing fever to a bed of lanquishing and pain. She recovered from the fever that afflicted her in the summer, and enjoyed her usual health til Sunday the 16th inst, when she was assailed by a malady that terminated her life in 12-14 hrs

384. EAM Dec 2 1823/Married Sun last by Rev Ruthrauff, of Williams-Port, Thomas Davis to Miss Mary Hains both of this co/Died Thurs morning last at his res about 10 miles from Hagers-town, Hugh M'Cauley, in the 39th year of his age/Died Sun morning last at his res, about 3 miles from this town, in the 62d year of his age, John Wolfersberger, Sen., leaving widow and 4 children; interred in family burial ground

385. EAM Dec 9 1823/Married Thurs last by Rev B. Kurtz, John Bower to Miss Elizabeth Wilkes, both of this co/Married same day by same, Samuel Smith to Miss Mary Robison, both of this co/Married same day by same, Jacob Buckwalter to Miss Catharine Stover, both of this co/Married Wed evening last by same, Conrad Miller to Miss Maria Eblehock, both of this place/Died Wed morning last, after a short illness, Mrs. Margaret Cromwell, wife of Joseph Cromwell, youngest dau of Capt Jacob Zeller, of this co/Died at the Globe Tavern in this place Wed evening last 3d inst, Thomas Belt, Esq. in the 83rd year of his age

386. EAM Dec 16 1823/Married Thurs last by Rev George Lemmon, Horatio M'Pherson of Frederick, to Miss Mary S. youngest dau of Thomas Buchanan, Esq. of this co

387. EAM Dec 23 1823/Died Fri 19 inst at the res of Col. Price, ih the 27th year of his age, Josiah Price, Jun. after a very short but severe illness

388. EAM Dec 30 1823/Married Tues last by Rev Lemmon, Christian G. Conradt of Funks-town, to Miss Amelia S. Hughes, of this town

389. EAM Jan 20 1824/Died Thurs 8th inst at an advanced age, Mrs. Martha Towson, wife of Jacob T. Towson, Esq. of Williams-Port/Died Thurs last, Mrs. Susan Wolgamot, wife of John Wolgamot, Jr. and dau of David Martin, of this co, in the 25th year of her age/Died Fri last, in this town, Daniel Geher, in the 61st year of his age

390. EAM Feb 24 1824/Married Thurs 12th inst in Cumberland, by Rev John J. Jacobs, Capt. George Swearingen, of Hagers-town, to Miss Mary Scott, dau of James Scott, Esq. of the former place/Died Sun night 15th inst very suddenly, at his res in Bath, Morgan Co, Va, Ignatius O'Ferrall

THE MARYLAND HERALD AND HAGERS-TOWN WEEKLY ADVERTISER

391. EAM Mar 2 1824/Equity case - Peter River and Elizabeth his wife, and Abraham Troxel and Sarah his wife, vs. Joseph Fiery, Henry Fiery and Lewis Fiery, heirs of Peter Rench, decd/Nicholas Shultz offers reward of 6 cents and a chew of tobacco for apprentice to the tailoring business named George Locher, about 18 years of age

392. EAM Mar 9 1824/Married Thurs 19th ult by Rev B. Kurtz, Jacob Farst to Miss Sarah Hogan, both of this co/Married Thurs 26th ult by Rev Geeting, Joseph Mumma to Miss Elizabeth Shafer, all of this co/Married Thurs last, by Rev B. Kurtz, Jacob Greenawalt to Miss Mary Myers, both of this co/Married same day by same, Jacob Kline to Miss Eliza South, both of Funks-town/Married Sun last by same, Samuel Dussinger to Miss Mary Ann Clarke, both of Funks-town

393. EAM Mar 16 1824/Died Fri night last at Rockland, Mrs. Ann Eliza Tilghman, consort of Geo. Tilghman, Esq. of this co, & dau of Col. Lamar, of Allegany Co. One of her twin infant children was buried in her arms, the other had died about a week before

394. EAM Mar 23 1824/Married 2d inst by Rev J.R. Reily, Henry Shenafelt to Miss Hannah Hartle, both of this co/Married Tues last by same, Henry Funk to Miss Susanna Miller/Married Thurs last by same, Arawine [printed as Erwine in The Torchlight] Miller, of Franklin Co, Pa to Miss Jane Williams, of this co/Died 10 inst at his seat near Bladensburg, Prince George's co, William Bayly, Esq (father of Samuel Bayly, Esq. of this town) in the 83d year of his age, Patriot of the Rev

395. EAM Mar 30 1824/Married Thurs last by Rev J.R. Reily, Peter Wolfersberger to Miss Eliza, dau of Henry Nichodemus, of Franklin co, Pa/Married same day by same, Samuel Welty to Miss Margaret Wolfersberger/Married same day by same, Martin King to Miss Margaret Peiffer, both of this place/Died Mon 22d inst after a short illness, Mrs. Elizabeth Petry, wife of Philip Petry, and dau of Col. Jonas Hogmire of this co, in the 36th year of her age, leaving husband and 7 children

396. EAM Apr 13 1824/Married Thurs evening last, by Rev George Lemmon, Henry H. Gaither, Esq. Attorney at Law, to Miss Catharine [Catharine K. Williams in The Torchlight] Williams, dau of the late Col. Elie Williams /Died in Frederick-town, Saturday morning 3d inst, at the house of her son-in-law, Capt. Ent, in the 71st year of her age, Mrs. Mary Woltz, relict of the late Dr. Peter Woltz, formerly of this town/Died Mon 5th inst, Jonathan Stine, son of Matthias Stine, of this co, in the 27th year of his age

397. EAM Apr 20 1824/Married Tues 6th inst by Rev B. Kurtz, Manly Morrison to Miss Mary Ann Donaldson [of Va., The Torchlight]/Married Thurs 8 inst by same, Samuel Miller to Miss Mary Price [Sarah Price, The Torchlight], both of this town/Married Tues last by same, Jacob Sensenbaugh to Miss Catharine Kline, both of this co/Married Thurs last by Rev J.R. Reily, George Stover to Miss Elizabeth Welty/Married Sun last by same, Nathan Farrow to Miss Mary M'Call/Married at Balt 13th inst by Rev Henshaw, V. [Vachel, Torchlight] W. Randall, Esq. of Hagers-town, to Miss Jane, dau of Elie Clagett of that city/Married at Balt Tues morning 13th inst by Rev George Dashiel, Dr. William D. Maggill, of Hagers-town, to Miss Mary Parron, of that city

51

THE MARYLAND HERALD AND HAGERS-TOWN WEEKLY ADVERTISER

398. EAM Apr 27 1824/Married Tues last by Rev J.R. Reily, George Fight to Miss Sophia, dau of Henry Ankeney

399. EAM May 11 1824/Married Tues last by Rev B. Kurtz, George Dean, to Miss Mary Snyder, both of this town/Married Thurs last by same, Daniel Carver to Miss Amelia S. Heflich, both of this place/Married Thurs 29th ult by Rev J. Reily, Jacob Garlinger to Mrs. Rachel M'Vitty, both of this co /Married Thurs last by same, Andrew Krick to Miss Amelia Castle/Died Thurs last at his res about 8 miles from Hagers-town, Joseph Cromwell, in the 32d year of his age

400. EAM Jan 3 1826/Married Thurs 22d ult by Rev Rothrauf, Jacob Stine to Miss Mary Hanes, both of this co/Married Thurs last by Rev Isaac Kellar, Jacob Miller to Miss Mary Hoffer, both of this co

401. EAM Jan 10 1826/Married Thurs evening 29 Dec by Rev Dr. Jennings, Wilson L. George of Wash Co, to Miss Elizabeth B., dau of John E. Stans... of Balt co/Died Wed last at his res on Beaver Creek, 3 miles from Boonsborough, Rev Peter Newcomer, aged about 73 yrs/Died Fri last at his res 1 mile from town, John Moyer, in the 71st year of his age --- remainder of column missing/Died in Hampshire co 19 inst, John Haines, from a blow received in an encounter about 2 months previously, with two men named Slater and John Davy who have been apprehended - Winchester Republican

THE TORCHLIGHT AND PUBLIC ADVERTISER

402. TLM Jan 25 1820/Died at his res near this place on 14th inst in the 73d year of his age, John Teisher, long a res of this co/Died 5th inst at an advanced age, Mrs. Christiana Miller, wife of George Miller, of the neighbourhood of this town, wife and mother

403. TLM Feb 1 1820/Died Sat last, after a short illness, Mrs. Barbara Gill, wife of John Gill, near this town, leaving 2 small children and husband; remains interred in Episc burial ground

404. TLM Feb 8 1820/Married Sat last, by Rev Kurtz, Samuel Harrison to Miss Elizabeth French, both of Winchester, Va

405. TLM Mar 21 1820/Married Sun 12th inst by Rev Keedy, Daniel Bell, to Miss Polly Warner, both of this co/Married Tues 14th inst by Rev J. Clay, James D. Moore, Esq. to Miss Mary Francis Saunders, all of this co/Married Thurs last, by Rev Kurtz, George Bowman of the neighbourhood of Funks-town, to Miss Dorothy Stoye, of this place

406. TLM Apr 25 1820/Married Sun 16th inst by Rev Myers, Josiah Curtis, to Miss Esther Ernsberger, both of this co/Married same day by same, Jacob Moates, to Miss Sarah Beckley, both of this co/Married same day by Rev Keedy, Jacob Fisher, to Miss Rosanna Gloss, both of this co

407. TLM May 2 1820/Married in Washington, Pa, 20th ult, by Rev Wheeler, Michael S. Johns, merchant of this place to Miss Margaret Haslett/Married Tues 25th ult by Rev Keedy, John Spealman to Miss Mary Sigler, both of this co/Married Tues 18th ult by Rev Kurtz, George Hersh, to Miss Sarah Burkhart

THE TORCHLIGHT AND PUBLIC ADVERTISER

408. TLM May 16 1820/Died in Boonsborough, Sat last, in the 78th year of his age, Abraham Lemaster, long a inhabitant of that place; remains interred with Masonic honors; discourse delivered by Rev Clay

409. TLM Jun 6 1820/Died 30th ult in the 19th year of her age, Miss Louisa Johnson, dau of captain John Johnson, of this place. Her complaint was pulmonary

410. TLM Jun 27 1820/Died Tues 13th inst, at the res of Robert Douglass, esq. in this town, Mrs. Mary Combs, relict of the late Coleman Combs, aged about 80 yrs

411. TLM Jul 4 1820/Married Sun 18th ult by Rev Keedy, Rev John Clapper, to Miss Susanna Longman, both of Pleasant Valley

412. TLM Aug 1 1820/Died very suddenly at Mt. Aetna Furnace, in this co, about 10 o'clock yesterday morning, John H. Hughes, in the 30th year of his age/Married Sun morning 23d ult by Rev Kurtz, Christopher Seigman Zipperer, to Mrs. Margaret Welsh, all of this place/Married Tues last by same, Nelson Stattlemyer, to Miss Hannah Pryor, of Frederick Co/Married Sun evening last, by same, Nicholas Shultz, to Miss Elizabeth Shank, all of this place

413. TLM Jan 16 1821/Married Thurs evening 11th inst at Cumberland by Rev J.C. Clay, Frederick Augustus Schley, Esq. of Ft to Miss Francina C. Lynn, dau of Capt David Lynn, of that place/Married Tues evening 2d inst by Rev Addison, Henry Addison, Esq. Merchant, to Miss Martha E. Claggett, both of Georgetown, D. C.//Married in Beverly, Mass., Larkin Moore, travelling preacher, physician, poet, trader, &c. to Mrs. Nancy Cook/Married Tues 9th ult by Rev Herley, Henry Lawman to Miss Mary Poffinberger, dau of Henry Poffinberger, all of this co

414. TLM Jan 23 1821/Died Thurs Thurs last in Balt in 48th year of his age, General Joseph Sterrett, soldier

415. TLM Jan 30 1821/Married Tues 16th inst at Green Castle, John Murphy, Jr., of Gettysburg, to Miss Ann Pears, formerly of this place/Married same day by Rev J. R. Reily, Daniel Thomas to Miss Margaret Carpenter, both of this co/Married Tues last by Rev J. C. Clay, Jacob Hewett to Miss Elizabeth Ingram, dau of Joseph Ingram, of this co/Died yesterday morning, Mrs. Catharine Hartman, relict of the late Dr. John Hartman, at Sharpsburg, in the 84th year of her age; discourse delivered by Rev. B. Allen/Died Fri night 26th inst at res of his father, John Knode, in Sharpsburg, after a short but severe illness, William Knode, in the 29th(?) year of his age, an only son

416. TLM Feb 6 1821/Married Sun 28th ult in M'Connellsburg, Pa, by Rev Shultz, Joseph Little, of this place, to Miss Catharine Fore, of the former place/Died Wed last, after a lingering pulmonary indisposition, at his res near this place, in the 31st year of his age, Jacob Young

417. TLM Feb 13 1821/Married Sun evening by Rev Sockman, Jacob Hutter, Jr. to Miss Margaret Doomer, all of Pleasant Valley/Married Thurs 1st ins, William Duffield, to Miss Elizabeth Bowen, all of Franklin co, Pa/Married 30th ult, John Knode of Funks-town, to Miss Lydia Hoffman, of Balt co

THE TORCHLIGHT AND PUBLIC ADVERTISER (Hagerstown)

418. TLM Feb 27 1821/Married Thurs last by Rev J.C. Clay, David G. Yost, Esq. of this place, to Miss Elizabeth L. Davis, dau of John Davis, Esq. of Allegany co/Married same day by Rev George Keedy, Benjamin Wagner, to Miss Mary T. Hamm, dau of Peter Hamm, of Winchester, Va

419. TLM Mar 6 1821/Married Wed morning last, by Rev B. Kurtz, Rev Samuel Schmucker, of Newmarket, Va, to Miss Eleanora Geiger of this place/Married 22d ult, near Gettysburg, Pa, by Rev Hinch, Daniel Middelkauff of this town, to Miss Julian Middelkauff, of Adams co, Pa

420. TLM Mar 27 1821/Married 1st inst by Rev R. Finnell, Alexander Finnell, to Mrs. Catharine Mitchell, relict of J. Mitchell, decd, and dau of Samuel Hanson, Esq. formerly of Md., but now of Ky, all of Clover Hill, Shenandoah co, Va

421. TLM Apr 10 1821/Married Thurs evening, 22 ult by Rev Slator Clay, Charles H. Clay, to Miss Maria Evans, both of Evansburg, Mont co, Pa/Married Tues 27th ult, by Rev J.R. Reily, Peter Kuntz to Miss Catharine Pfautz, both of Franklin co, Pa/Married Thurs 26th by same, Thomas T. Thornburg, to Miss Sarah Oldwine/Married Thurs 29th by Rev B. Kurtz, John I. Miller, to Miss Mary Smith/Died Tues morning last, in this town, after a short illness, in the 86th year of her age, Mrs. Mary Middelkauff

422. TLM Apr 17 1821/Married Thurs evening last at Oakage, res of Saml. D. Price, Esq. by Rev J. Matthews, John Wilson, Esq. of Jefferson co, Va, to Miss Susan N. Chapline, dau of Jeremiah Chapline, Esq. late of this co/Married Tues last, near Park Head Forge, by Rev J. Mason, George Moore, to Miss Ann Bryan, all of this co/Winchester, Va, Apr 14 - George Kreps and family, of this town, emigrated last fall to Alabama. In crossing a river in the Indian nation, they mistook the ford, and the wagon and horses, with the contents, were suddenly immersed in the stream! In the agitation of the moment, Mrs. Kreps parted from her infant child, which was rapidly carried down the current. At this instant a large dog, which had joined the family a few days before, sprung after the babe, overtook it just as it was sinking, and conveyed it safety to the shore. The horses also regained a footing and the whole party were saved. (The dog rejoined them later and remained with them.)

423. TLM Apr 24 1821/Married Thurs 12th inst by Rev J. R. Reiley, Samuel Row, to Miss Elizabeth Hinty

424. TLM May 1 1821/Died Fri evening 20th inst at Jacob Moots, near Hagers Town, John King. From papers found on him, it would appear that he was from New Brunswick, New Jersey, and had a family in that place, consisting of a wife and 3 children. He was a pedlar of Essences, and came to Mr. Moots' on Wed previous to his decease; while there he appeared to be delirious till his death

425. TLM May 8 1821/Died Wed morning lat, in the 72d year of her age, Mrs. Ann Maria Protzman, relict of the late John Protzman, inhabitant of this place for a long time, leaving 3 children; sermon preached by Rev Kurtz/Died Mon 30th ult, Martha Susan Harry, aged about 12 yrs, dau of John Harry of this place; interred in Luth burial ground; sermon given by Rev Kurtz

THE TORCHLIGHT AND PUBLIC ADVERTISER (Hagerstown)

426. TLM May 15 1821/Married 3d inst by Mr. Brutie, at Mount St. Mary's Seminary, George Foreman, of Waynesburg, to Miss Jane Radford, 2d dau of Thomas Radford, of Emmittsburg/Married Sun 6th inst by Rev Powles, Christian Snider to Miss Elizabeth Glaze, both of this co

427. TLM Jun 12 1821/George youngest son of Capt. David Barr, on Tues afternoon last, drowned in one of his father's tan vats

428. TLM Jun 26 1821/Married Thurs 11th inst by Rev Jacob Powlus, John Mumma, to Miss Mary Schnebly, both of this co

429. TLM Jul 17 1821/Died Fri 6th inst, Mrs. Sarah McPherson, wife of Co. John McPherson, of Frederick-town, in the 55th year of her age, leaving husband and numerous children

430. TLM Jul 31 1821/Married Thurs last by Rev B. Kurtz, Elias Lyttle, of Gettysburg, to Miss Mary Bernhiser, of this co

431. TLM Aug 7 1821/Married Thurs 19th ult by Rev D. Holmouth, Rev George Schmucker, of York, Pa, president of the German Luth Synod, to Mrs. Ann Weinert, of Phila/Died 8th ult at his res near Sharpsburg, after a short illness, in the 76th year of his age, Jacob Myers/Died 15th ult at his res near Sharpsburg, after a painful confinement of upwards of 2 yrs, in the 85th year of his age, Leonard Kretzer/Died Sat 21st ult at his res about 9 miles from Hagers Town, John Johnston/Died Sat 28th ult, in Hancock, Benjamin Bean, inn-keeper/Died Fri last in this town, at an advanced age, Jacob Kinkle, Sen

432. TLM Aug 14 1821/Married Mon 6th inst by Rev Buchanan, Mr. Harlet of Balt, to Miss Eliza Hughes, of this town

433. TLM Aug 21 1821/Died on this place, Tues 14th inst, Miss Mary Pottenger, dau of Dr. Pottenger, decd, and formerly of Prince George's co, Md/Died Sat last in the 75th year of his age, after a lingering illness, Capt Martin Ridenour, old inhabitant of this town/Died Sun last at her res in this place, after a lingering illness, in the 42d year of her age, Mrs. Magdalena Hefleich, widow of the late John Hefleich, decd/Shepherds-town, Aug 15. On Thurs morning last, the hero and sage of '76, Col. Joseph Swearingen, died in the 68th year of his age; interred in family burial ground. In 1775 he was among the first who offered his services. He continued in the army of his country till 4 July 1776. After a short lapse of time he re-entered the service in the capacity of lieutenant, later promoted to Captain at an early age - Virginia Monitor.

434. TLM Aug 28 1821/Married at Green Castle, 15th inst by Rev Rothrauff, George Strause, of this place, to Miss Ellen Cromwell of Balt/Married Thurs 16th by Rev Kurtz, George W. Sands to Miss Ann Maria Crouise, all of this place/Married Thurs last by same, Jeremiah Leggett to Miss Mary Easterday, both of this co/Died Wed morning last at his res (Walkin's Ferry, Va), Peter Light, Sen., in the 64th year of his age; remains interred in public burying ground, Williams-Port/The only son of Joseph Strach(?), aged about 9 yrs, was killed Thurs 16th inst, by the fall of a log from a building erecting near this town

THE TORCHLIGHT AND PUBLIC ADVERTISER (Hagerstown)

435. TLM Sep 4 1821/Married Tues last by Rev B. Kurtz, James M. Welsh, of this place, to Miss Elizabeth H. Smith, dau of Nicholas Smith of this co

436. TLM Sep 11 1821/Married Tues evening last at Frederick by Rev Helfenstine, Charles Humrickhouse of this place, to Miss Maria C. Levy, of the former place/Married Thurs last by Rev Buckingham, Jacob Chrest, to Miss Amelia Snider, all of this town/Died at Mount Pleasant, his seat, near Sharpsburg, in this co, Fri morning 31st Aug, Capt Joseph Chapline, in the 75th year of his age. He was a soldier of the rev. He assembled an unusually large company of volunteers and led them on to the American Camp at the north/Died Sat last in Williams Port, in the 32d year of her age, Mrs. Catharine Herr, wife of John Herr, Jr., leaving 6 young children/Died Sun night last at his res near this town, Nicholas Smith, farmer of this co

437. TLM Sep 18 1821/Died Sun evening last, at Shepherds-town, Va, in the 20th year of his age, Samuel Bell, youngest brother of the editor of this paper

438. TLM Oct 9 1821/Married at Chambersburg, Pa, Sun 16th ult by Rev Rahauser, John H. Rutter, to Miss Lavinia Kaighn, both of this place/Married Tues 18th ult, by Rev B. Kurtz, Joel Brown, to Miss Mary Jolliff, near Winchester, Va/Died at Bath, Morgan co, Va, Sun 23d ult of a typhus fever, Elie Williams Elliot, Esq., youngest son of late Col. Robert Elliott, of this place, in the 29th year of his age, leaving widow/Died in this town Mon 2d of Oct, Mrs. Mary Oldwine, in the 57th year of her age/Died Thurs last in the 23d year of her age, Miss Theresa Gruber, dau of John Gruber, printer, of this town, after a tedious and painful pulmonary indisposition; remains interred in German Presby burying ground

439. TLM Oct 23 1821/Married Thurs 11th inst by Rev B. Kurtz, George Zeigler, to Miss Susanna Russell, both of this co

440. TLM Oct 30 1821/Died Wed morning 10th inst, John Ankeney of George, in the 23d year of his age/Died Mon 15th inst after a short illness, Mrs. Amelia Boteler, wife of Hezekiah Boteler, of Pleasant Valley/Died Sun 21st inst, Abraham Rowland, old inhabitant of this place/Died Mon 22d inst, at the house of Christian Miller, about 3 1/2 miles from Hagers Town, Elijah Leisure/Died Sun last, Miss Elizabeth Withney, dau of late Arthur Withney, of this place/Died Sun afternoon last at the res of his father near this town, Joseph Kellar, Esq. formerly a practising attorney at the Hagers Town Bar

441. TLM Nov 6 1821/Died Sun morning last, Mrs. Reidenour, widow of late Jacob Reidenhour, of this co/Died yesterday afternoon, Mrs. Ebert, wife of John Ebert, of this place/Died 31st ult Mr. Mittoe(?), aged 87, soldier of the Rev/Died at his res at Carey's Cross Roads, Wed 31st ult, Francis Davis

442. TLM Nov 20 1821/Died Sat morning 10th inst, in New-Market, Francis Deakins Wayman, in the 24th year of his age, res of Maryland tract, near New Town (Trap), a young mechanic

443. TLM Dec 4 1821/Married Thurs last by Rev J. C. Clay, Dr. John J. Hays, of Wash Co, to Miss Sophia B. Pottenger, 2d dau of Dr. Robert Pottenger, late of Prince Georges' Co, Md/Died in Cahawba, Alabama, on 14th ult, Mrs. Eveline Kreps, wife of Geo. Kreps, formerly of this place

THE TORCHLIGHT AND PUBLIC ADVERTISER (Hagerstown)

444. TLM Dec 11 1821/Died Sat last, at Green-Castle, in the 24th year of her age, Mrs. Ann Miller, wife of William Miller, formerly of this co

445. TLM Dec 25 1821/Died at his res near Harper's ferry, Jefferson co, Va, on 18 Oct last, with the prevailing fever, Charles W. Ogden (long obit)

446. TLM Jan 1 1822/Married Thurs 13th inst by Rev Kurtz, William W. Allender, to Miss Mary Marker/Married Thurs 20th ult, Reily, Jacob Tutweiler to by same, George W. Kerfoot, to Miss Maria Seifort /Married Tues last by same, Jonathan Reidenauer, to Miss Eleanora Reidenauer/Married Sun last by same, George Bowman, of this place, to Miss Mary E. Fiery, dau of Joseph Fiery, of this co/Died Sat morning 29th ult at the house of Dr. John Reynolds, in this place, of a pulmonary complaint, in the 18th year of his age, Edward Burd Yeates Shippen, son of late John Shippen, Esq. of Shippensburg, Pa

447. TLM Jan 15 1822/Married at Canton, Ohio, Sun 2d ult, George Binkly, son of Jacob Binkly, formerly of this place, to Miss Frances Sterling, dau of John Sterling, merchant, of the former place/Married Tues 4th ult by Rev J. R. Reily, Philip Fox to Miss Catharine Maugins/Married Thurs 20th ult by same, Samuel Spiglar to Miss Nancy Miller/Married Tues 1st inst by same, Josiah Gabriel, to Miss Catharine Felker

448. TLM Jan 22 1822/Married Thurs last near Myersville, Henry Masters to Miss Sally, dau of Peter Bruer, of this co/Chambersburg - Died in this borough, Thurs last, John Colhoun, Senior, aged 70 yrs - Repository./Died Fri 11th inst, Mrs. Anna Maria Margaretta Shryock, widow of Leonard Shryock, formerly of Hagers Town. She past 4 score yrs, through this vale of tears, only once confined to the sick bed, except during her last illness. Great grandmother; had at least 100 offspring; remains buried in Meth burying ground

449. TLM Feb 12 1822/Married in Lancaster, 10th ult by Rev Antris, Samuel Lantz, of this co, to Miss Elizabeth Fail, dau of Maj. Jacob Fail, of Lancaster Co, Pa

450. TLM Feb 19 1822/Married Sun last by Rev Benjamin Kurtz, George Neikirck, to Miss Elizabeth Bowser, both of this co

451. TLM Mar 5 1822/Died near Connersville, Fayette co, Indiana, 29 Dec 1821, Otho Rench, about 30 yrs of age, late of Wash Co, Md

452. TLM Mar 12 1822/Married Thurs last by Rev Elliot, John Bradley to Miss Jane M'Curdy, all of Franklin co, Pa/Married in Somerset Co, Md, on 26 Feb, Edward North, aged 21, to Mrs. Russel Dun, aged 70, both of said co/Died Tues morning last, in Sharpsburg, at an advanced age, James Leggett, Sen.; remains interred with Masonic honors/Died Wed evening last, at her res 1 mile from Hess' mill, Mrs. Elizabeth Hamman, widow of Philip Hamman, Sen., dec'd, aged 81 yrs, 11 months, 7 days/Died same evening, in Pleasant Valley, at an advanced age, John Showman/Died Sat last in this town, very suddenly, Barney B. Oldwine, Jr.

453. TLM Mar 19 1822/Married Sun 10th inst by Rev M'Cawley, Samuel Rohrer to Miss Elizabeth Crampton, dau of Elias Crampton, both of Pleasant Valley

THE TORCHLIGHT AND PUBLIC ADVERTISER (Hagerstown)

/Married same day by Rev Sockman, William Cunningham to Miss Rosanna Warner, both of this co/Married Sun 17th inst by Rev Geo. Keedy, Andrew Double, to Miss Susanna Glaize, both of Wash Co

454. TLM Mar 26 1822/Married Thurs 7th inst by Rev J.R. Reily, John Steinmetz, to Miss Susan Myers/Married Tues 12th by same, Samuel Murcan to Miss Margaret Brunner/Married Thurs 21st by same, Jacob W. Mealy, to Miss Rebecca Gerhart/Married same day by same Andrew Shenefelt, to Miss Sarah A. Luiza Brannan/Married Thurs 14th by Rev Kurtz, Michael Crissman, to Miss Harriet Davis/Married Thurs last by Rev Kurtz, John Newcomer to Miss Catharine Knafe

455. TLM Apr 2 1822/Married Thurs last, by Rev Geo. Keedy, Joseph Eakle to Miss Catharine Kauffman, all of this co/Died in this town Sun evening 24th ult, Jacob Kinkade, in the 30th year of his age. As it is believed his parents live in the neighborhood of Lancaster, Pa, the Lancaster papers will please copy this notice/Died Fri morning last, at his res in this co, Edward Boteler, Esq

456. TLM Apr 9 1822/Lawrenceburgh, March 23 - Accident - On night of 18th inst, the house occupied by William Duncan, in Manchester township in thic co, was consumed by fire, along with 4 of his children. Mr. Duncan & his wife had gone out on a visit to neighbors, leaving their 7 children in the house, between 10 and 11 o'clock at night

457. TLM Apr 16 1822/Married Sun 7th inst by Rev Dennis, Samuel Nikirk to Miss Susan Bealer, both of the neighbourhood of Boonsborough/Died 9th inst at his res, 4 miles from this town, Jacob Rohrer, in the 76th year of his age. He was born on the farm on which he died/Died at his res in Kent Co, Md, William Spencer - Federal Gazette.

458. TLM Apr 30 1822/Married Thurs 4th inst by Rev B. Kurtz, David Brumbaugh, to Miss Susan Emrich/Married Sun 7th by same, Wm. Davis to Catharine Blentlinger/Married Thurs 18th by same, Samuel Stickel, to Miss Sarah Miller, both of Winchester, Va/Married same day by same, Isaac Bare to Miss Rosanna Rowland/Died Sun evening last in the 15th year of her age, Miss Eliza Seibert, dau of Major Peter Seibert, of this co, occasioned by the breaking of a blood vessel

459. TLM May 7 1822/Married 28th inst by Rev Kraught, Jesse Myers of Sharpsburg, Md., to Miss Elizabeth, dau of Peter Grove, of Berkely co, Va/Married Thurs last, by Rev Keedy, Jacob Staups, to Miss Elizabeth Middlekauff, dau of Christian Middlekauff, all of this co/From the Winchester Gazette - Died at his country seat, Mon last, John Holker, Esq., long a res of this co. He was born in England in 1745. His father was the proprietor of an extensive manufacturing establishment. He joined himself to the exiled Charles in his attempt to place himself and family upon the British throne, and his fortunes fell with those of the Pretender. He was compelled to seek an asylum in France, whither his family with his son John, then an infant, soon followed. He remained in France until the United States raised their arms against the government of England. Mr. Holker entered into a prvate contract with Dr. Franklin, who was at Paris, to supply the United States with a large quantity of clothing and arms. He embarked for the U.S. in 1776... (long and detailed account)

THE TORCHLIGHT AND PUBLIC ADVERTISER (Hagerstown)

460. TLM May 14 1822/Married Sun last by Rev J. R. Reily, David Beard, to Miss Christiana Slice

461. TLM May 28 1822/Married Tues 14th inst by Rev B. Kurtz, John Herbert to Mrs. Sarah Ann Mealy/Married Tues last, by same, Andrew Heffner to Miss Elizabeth Bean

462. TLM Jul 9 1822/Married Tues last by Rev Lind, Joshua Murray to Miss Mary Ann Schleigh, dau of John Schleigh, all of this place/Chancery case - John J. Hays, vs Henry Barkman, Peter and Jacob Barkman & others. Object of bill to obtain decree for sale of tract in Wash Co called Resurvey on well done, which had been sold by Joseph Chapline to Frederick Barkman in 1799. Henry, Peter and Jacob Barkman do not res in Md

463. TLM Jul 16 1822/Died in New Orleans 11th ult., after a severe attack of the bilious fever, which lasted 6 weeks, Mrs. Jemima Nichols, late Miss Jemima Kinsell, of this place. She had for many yrs previouse to her death, a member of Meth Episc Church

464. TLM Aug 6 1822/Married at Sharpsburg, Md., Sun 21st ult by Rev E. Matthews, Edward Johnson, to Miss Elizabeth M'Crae, both of that town/Married Thurs evening last, by Rev Kurtz, Captain Daniel Donnelly, merchant, of Sharpsburg, Md., to Miss Elizabeth, dau of Michael Moler, of Jefferson co, Va/Died Sat last, after a short illness, in the 22d year of her age, Miss Eliza M'Fall, of this town

465. TLM Aug 13 1822/Died Sun evening last, at the home of George Lowe, in this co, after a short illness, in the 26th year of his age, Cyrus Saunders, Jr., printer, son of Cyrus Saunders, Sen., of Williams Port

466. TLM Sep 3 1822/Died Mon morning last, in the 18th year of his age, Jacob Cordiman. And about the same time and age, John Leypold, both of this town

467. TLM Sep 10 1822/Married in Frederick-Town 3d inst, by Rev Johns, Maj. Daniel Hughes, to Miss Elizabeth Potts, of that place/Williams-Port - Died at the house of Milton H. Sackett, Esq., James Hemphill, merchant of this place, after a short illness

468. TLM Sep 17 1822/Died at Washington City, 11th inst in 74th year of his age, after a few days' severe illness, Leonard Harbaugh, who had been, for upwards of 50 yrs, an inhabitant of the cities of Balt and Wash, in which places, with a few others, he lived to see expended, immediately under his own superintendance, in public and private buildings of various kinds, including the internal navigation of the rivers Potomac and Shenandoah, upwards of $600,000, principally by contract

469. TLM Oct 1 1822/Died 20th inst, Jacob Myers, Esq. in the 64th year of his age, third member of his family, who, in the short space of 3 weeks, have died by bilious remittent fever. He was for more than 40 yrs past engaged in a mercantile business in this city - Balt. Federal Gaz.

THE TORCHLIGHT AND PUBLIC ADVERTISER (Hagerstown)

470. TLM Oct 15 1822/Died Sun evening 15th Sep at Nashville Tenn, after a short illness of fever, in the 47th year of his age, Ephraim Pritchet, formerly of this place/Died Fri 4th inst, Adam Leapard, in habitant of this place/Died same day, Henry Selser, of this place/Died Sat 5th inst in Essex co, Va, Dr. Geo. Clarke, of Georgetown, formerly of Green-Castle, Pa

471. TLM Oct 22 1822/Married Sun 13th inst at Chambersburg, by Rev Denny, William Schleigh, of this town, to Miss Elizabeth Spigler, of this co/Died Fri morning 4th inst, at his res in Pleasant Valley, in 62d year of his age, Abraham Grim, native of Wash co/John E. Howard, Jr., Esq. of Balt, died Fri evening last, in Mercersburg, Pa, to which place he had gone but a short time previous for the purpose of waiting on a sick relative/John M'Henry of Balt, died about the time Mr. Howard was taken sick, was on his way home from the Bedford Springs

472. TLM Oct 29 1822/Died of the prevailing fever, near the Merryland Tract, Frederick Co, John Slifer, Sen., aged 79 yrs, 5 months, 3 days

473. TLM Nov 5 1822/Married Thues 29th ult by Rev J. R. Reily, George Coler, to Miss Catharine Martin, both of this co/Died Wed night last, after a short illness in the 20th year of her age, Mrs. Catharine Houser, wife of Jacob Houser and dau of John Brown, all of Pleasant Valley

474. TLM Nov 26 1822/Died Sun 17th inst in Balt, in the 35th year of his age, William E. Williams, Esq. of Frederick co, son of the late Gen. Otho H. Williams

475. TLM Dec 3 1822/Married in Fleming co, Ky, 12th inst, Joseph Glass to Miss Elizabeth Wire/Married Sun evening last, by Rev John Emory, William Shepherd to Miss Eliza Dick, both of Winchester, Va/Died at Williams-Port on the morning of 28th ult, Cyrus Saunders, at an advanced age/Died Thurs last, Mrs. Mary Thornburg, wife of Solomon Thornburg, of this town

476. TLM Dec 17 1822/Died Tues morning 7th inst in Hancock, Jacob Brossius in the 78th year of his age; discourse delivered by Rev Jeremiah Mason/Died Thurs morning last, after a short illness, at an early period of life, at the res of Alex'r Kennedy, near Boonsborough, Bartholomew Booth, son of John Booth; remains interrred in family burial ground with Masonic honors, of Ureka Lodge, of Boonsborrough, of which he was a highly esteemed officer

477. TLM Dec 24 1822/Married Thurs last by Rev B. Kurtz, Christian Palmer to Miss Elizabeth Knodle.

478. TLM Dec 31 1822/Married Thurs last by Rev Benj. Kurtz, Jacob Fritz, of this co, to Miss Catharine Cook, of this town/Married same day by same, John Eberhart to Miss Juliana Harbaugh/Died Sun last, at his res in this co, Andrew Hershey, old inhabitant of this co/Died yesterday morning, in Williams-Port, Peter Ardinger, long an inhabitant of that place

479. TLM Jan 7 1823/Married Thurs last, Dr. John Ridout, of this place, to Miss Prudence Owings, of Anne Arundel Co/Died after a protracted and severe indisposition, James W. Steele, recently of this town; he died at his bro-

THE TORCHLIGHT AND PUBLIC ADVERTISER (Hagerstown)

ther's on the 10th ult. near Lake Champlain, state of New York, in the enjoyment of this mental powers/Died 10 Dec at Brownsville, Pa, Mrs. Mary Bowman, in the 79th year of her age, leaving 5 children, 35 grandchildren and 37 gr-grand children; she was among the earliest settlers of this co, and a res of Hagers-town from its foundation until within about 6 yrs since, when she removed to the western country/Died in Fredericktown on 31st ult, Rev James Redmond, aged 47 yrs, for several yrs past Pastor of the Roman Catholic congregations of Wash and Allegany cos.

480. TLM Jan 14 1823/Married Sun evening last, by Rev J. R. Reily, David Morrison, to Miss Amelia Dillman, dau of Henry Dillman, all of this place

481. TLM Jan 21 1823/Married Tues last by Rev J. Mason, George Faughwell, to Miss Rebecca Friend/Married same day by Rev J. R. Reily, Henry Wolford, to Miss Susan Knodle/Married Thurs last by Rev Lemmon, Samuel T. Fitzhugh, of Ky, to Miss Eliza M. Fitzhugh, of Balt/Died near Sharpsburg on Thurs 16th inst, Mrs. Mary Ann Abigail Chapline, relict of Capt. Joseph Chapline, lately decd, in the 74th year of her age. Although for many yrs past in a delicate state of health, her departure from this vale of tears was sudden and unexpected; active member of Prot Episc church, contributed liberally to the erection of St. Pauls Church in Sharpsburg

482. TLM Jan 28 1823/An arrival at Charleston in a short passage from Liverpool, brings news of the death of Hon. William Lowndes of S.C. at sea on 27 Nov, on his way to Europe as the last hope of benefiting his health

483. TLM Feb 4 1823/Married Thurs evening, 23d inst by Rev Helfenstein, Nathaniel Mitchell, Editor of Virginia Monitor, to Miss Elizabeth, dau of Capt. John L. Tabb, all of Shepherd's town/Died some time since in Dublin co, N.C., Jacob Mathies, aged 111, to Mrs. Sellars aged 119.

484. TLM Feb 11 1823/Equity court - Augustus Ferguson, Charles Ferguson, William Ferguson and Joseph Ferguson, vs. Joseph Dayton and George Dayton. Object is to obtain sale of house and lot in Sharpsburg, prop of late John W. Ferguson, decd. The complainants state that their father, John W. Ferguson, died intestate, seized of a lot of ground in Sharpsburg, leaving the complainants and defendants his heirs. The defendants are infants living out of the state of Md/Equity case - Isaac Hiester, William Hiester, Daniel J. Hiester, Catharine Hiester, Rebecca Hiester, Edward Climer, and Maria his wife, vs. John Hiester and Juliana Miller. Object of the complainants' bill is to obtain sale of real estate of late William Hiester, decd. The bill states that William Hiester, decd, at time of his death was seized of real estate in Frederick and Wash Co, died intestate, leaving said complainants and the defendants, John Hiester and Juliana Miller, his heirs. Said defendants are both under age of 21 and do not res in state of Md

485. TLM Feb 18 1823/Married 23d ult by Rev J. R. Reily, Jonas Knode to Miss Mary Donaldson/Died Tues last about 1 o'clock, Mrs. Mary Ann Harry, consort of John Harry, of this place, in the 33d year of her age; interred in Luth burial ground. She had been in delicate state of health for 2-3 yrs but confined to her bed only about 3 weeks. She left a husband and two small children, one only three weeks old/Died Sun night last, after a

THE TORCHLIGHT AND PUBLIC ADVERTISER (Hagerstown)

lingering illness, in the 71st year of his age, Jonathan Hager, sen. He resided in the neighborhood when the ground on which it stands was a "howling wilderness" - soldier of the rev and participated in many of the hard fought battles/Died Fri last, at Funks-town, John Shilling, in the 40th year of his age, leaving wife and 5 small children/Died Fri last in this place, Mrs. Christiana Weis, wife of John Weis, Senr. in the 62d year of her age

486. TLM Mar 11 1823/Married Thurs the 27th (sic) by Rev Benj. Kurtz, Jacob Light of Franklin co, Pa, to Miss Nancy Fiery, dau of Joseph Fiery of this co

487. TLM Mar 18 1823/Married Sat 8th inst by Rev J. R. Reily, Jacob Hoffman of Va, to Miss Christina Hoffman, of this co/Married Thurs last by same, James Sherrard (sic), to Miss Anna Smith, both of this co/Died Sat evening last, Joseph, infant son of John Spielman, of this town

488. TLM Apr 8 1823/Equity Case - Sam'l Ringgold, William Gabby, O. H. Williams, William Heyser, Henry Lewis and David T. Wilson, vs. the heirs and devisees of Christian Winebrenner, decd. Object of bill is to obtain decree compelling defendants to convey to the plaintiffs a lot of ground on South West corner of Franklin and Jonathan streets, Hagers-town. The defendants, Christian Winebrenner, David Winebrenner and Mary Daush, heirs of Sebastian Winebrenner, Christian Winebrenner, Peter Winebrenner, Matthias Barnhiser and Christiana his wife, and John Snyder and Catharine his wife, reside out of the state of Md

489. TLM Apr 15 1823/Married in Williams-Port by Rev F. Ruthrauff, Thurs 3d inst, Charles Morrow, to Miss Francis Payton Christian, both of Martinsburg, Va/Died at his res in Montgomery township, Franklin co, Pa, Sun night, William Huston, farmer and native of that co. He was the last member of a family of 6 persons, who died within a very short period.

490. TLM Apr 22 1823/Married Sun 13th inst, by Rev Benj. Kurtz, John Snyder, to Miss Nancy Smith, both of Funks-town/Married Tues last by same, Peter Renner, to Miss Elizabeth Hamaker/Died James M'Lenahan of this vicinity on morning of Thurs last, at age of 87 yrs and 6 months/Equity case - Samuel Hawken, Jacob Hawken, George Hawken & William Hawken, vs. Juliana Hawken, Nancy Hawken, Christ'n Hawken, David Hawken, Nancy Hawken, Jr., Robert Miller and Juliana Miller, widow and heir at law of Christian Hawken, late of Wash Co, decd

491. TLM Apr 29 1823/Married Thurs 3d inst by Rev T. Hitt, Samuel M. Hitt, to Miss Barbara Hershey, dau of late Andrew Hershey, all of this co/Died 13th inst in 43d year of her age, Mrs. Buckwalter, wife of Gerhart Buckwalter, of this vicinity

492. TLM May 13 1823/Died yesterday morning, John Buckwalter, son of Gearhart Buckwalter, near this place

493. TLM May 20 1823/Married Tues 5th inst by Rev Benj. Kurtz, David Hersh, to Miss Elizabeth Sheller, both of this co

THE TORCHLIGHT AND PUBLIC ADVERTISER (Hagerstown)

494. TLM May 27 1823/Married 6th inst by Rev J. R. Reily, Elic M'Clain to Mrs. Elizabeth Barnett/Married Thurs last by same, David Troup to Miss Elizabeth dau of David Cushwa/Died in this town on 23d inst, Archibald M. Waugh, Esq. in the 46th year of his age, inhabitant of this place/Died Sat last at the res of his father in this co, after an illness of a few weeks, occasioned by the breaking of a blood vessel, Jesse Kellar, a worthy young man/Died Sun morning last, at an advanced age, Mrs. Christiana Kausler, wife of John Kausler, of this town/Died same day Baltzar Bowman, old inhabitant of this town

495. TLM Jun 10 1823/Married at Chambersburg, Tues 27th ult, by Rev David Denny, Otho Williams, of this co, to Miss Ann M'Dowell, of that place/Died John Oliver, after a very short illness, native of Ireland - Balt., Fed. Repub./Married Thurs 12th inst, by Rev B. Kurtz, Dr. John De Pui, clerk of the Senate of Pa, to Miss Louisa Amelia Kurtz, dau of Benj. Kurtz, Esq. all of Harrisburg, Pa/Married Thurs last by same, Andrew Swartz to Miss Rebecca M'Daniel, both of this place/Married Tues 17th inst by Rev Wilson, Theodore Malott to Mrs. Mary Bartlett, both of this co/Married Thurs last by Rev G. Lemon, Thornton G. Jordan to Miss Rebecca H. Mullannix, both of Frederick co, Va/Died Thurs 5th inst near York, Pa, Frederick Eichelberger, at age of 81 yrs

496. TLM Jul 8 1823/Died Matthew Van Lear, Esq. Sat afternoon, after an illness of 24 hrs, at his res near Williams-Port, aged about 68 yrs

497. TLM Jul 15 1823/Died on 3d inst in New Market, Va, after a protracted illness of several months, in the 24th year of her age, Mrs. Eleanora Schmucker (formerly Miss Eleanora Geiger of this place) wife of Rev. Samuel S. Schmucker, of the former place

498. TLM Jul 22 1823/Married 15th inst by Rev Lind, at "Marven," the res of Joseph Van Lear, Col. Otho Holland Williams, Clerk of Wash co Court, to Miss Eliza England Van Lear, dau of late Col. William Van Lear

499. TLM Jul 29 1823/Died Sun last at his res in 64th year of his age, John Long, for many yrs a inhabitant of this co

500. TLM Aug 12 1823/Married Thurs last by Rev Keedy, Jonas Middelkauff to Miss Nancy Zuck, all of this co/Died Thurs 7th inst at Long Meadows, Mrs. Tarlton, in the 73d year of her age/Died Sun morning last, near this town, William Dillehunt, for many yrs an inhabitant of this co/Died Thomas Lytle Fri last in 24th year of his age, after a short illness at the house of John Robertson, in this place, in whose store he had been for some time engaged as a clerk/Died at Tammany's Mount, near Williams-Port, Thurs evening last, after a short but severe illness, Horatio Nelson Van Lear, son of the late Matthew Van Lear, Esq., in the 25th year of his age

501. TLM Aug 19 1823/Died at his res near Williams-Port, Sun morning last, Matthias Miller, at an advanced age/Married Thurs 7th inst by Rev Kurtz, Peter Feckler to Miss Susanna Yakle/Married Sun 10th by same, Michael Thomas to Miss Mary Waltz/Died Fri last, Joseph Kershner of this co, in the 40th year of his age, leaving wife and 2 small children/Died Sat last after a

THE TORCHLIGHT AND PUBLIC ADVERTISER (Hagerstown)

short illness, whilst on a visit to a sick dau, Mrs. Ann Ashbury, relict of Capt. John Ashbury, late of Wash Co, decd, aged about 46 yrs/Death of Samuel Shuman on last Tues evening about 9 o'clock, after a short illness; buried in Luth burial ground. His age was 27 yrs and 4 months

502. TLM Aug 26 1823/Married Thurs last, by Rev Benj. Kurtz, Daniel Slenker, to Miss Sarah Poffenberger, both of this co

503. TLM Sep 9 1823/Died Thurs last, near Williams-Port, at about 30 yrs of age, Dennis M'Cafferty, the only support of a wife and 3 very young children /Died at his res near Boonsborough, on 28th ult, Joseph Wagner, in the 34th year of his age/Died Sun morning last, Augustus Riblet, of this town, aged about 23 yrs

504. TLM Sep 16 1823/Died Mon 8th inst William Hogg, son of John Hogg, of this place, in the 18th year of his age/Died at Hancock Thurs evening 11th inst Michael Garaghty, aged 21/Died at Boonsborough Sun last, Elijah Collins, aged about 35

505. TLM Sep 23 1823/Died Thurs night last, in Funks-Town, in the 23d year of her age, Miss Polly Grosh, eldest dau of Frederick Grosh/Died Sun morning last, at Fountain Rock, after an illness of 48 hrs, Master Charles Anthony, son of Gen. S. Ringgold, about 4 yrs of age

506. TLM Sep 30 1823/Married Sun evening last, by Rev Dennies, Samuel G. Harbaugh to Miss Catharine Bentz, all of Boonsborough/Died at Washington City, Fri last, after an illness of 10 days, Rev Louis R. Fechtig, Elder in the Meth Episc Church and at time of his death Presiding elder of the Baltimore District.

507. TLM Oct 7 1823/Died Wed morning last, after a severe illness of 4 days, in 7th year of his age, master Henry, only child of Mich'l Oyler, of this co/Died Sat last in the 28th year of her age, Mrs. Nancy Boward, wife of Michael Boward, of this town

508. TLM Oct 14 1823/Married Thurs last, by Rev Ruthrauff, Jno. Hoffman to Miss Susan Boyer, all of Williams-Port

509. TLM Oct 21 1823/Married at Georgetown, D. C. Wed evening last, by Rev M'Ilvaine, John Harry, Merchant of this town, to Miss Harriet Eliza Williams, of that city

510. TLM Oct 28 1823/Died Fri last, in this town, after a lingering illness, in the 36th (sic) year of his age, Michael Kapp

511. TLM Nov 4 1823/Died 15th ult at his res near Boonsborough, in the 43d year of his age, Gabriel Thomas/Died at Carlisle, Pa, Tues, 21st ult of bilious fever, Mrs. Mary Duncan Lee, wife of Richard H. Lee, Esq., of Leesburg, Va/Died at his res in this co on Sun last, after an illness of about 6 weeks, George Eakle, in the 34th of his age; remains interred with Masonic honors, at Baker's Cross Roads' burying ground.

THE TORCHLIGHT AND PUBLIC ADVERTISER (Hagerstown)

512. TLM Nov 18 1823/Married Sun evening last, by Rev Dennies, John Adams, to Miss Mary Wentlinger, both of Boonsborough

513. TLM Nov 25 1823/Married Thurs last by Rev B. Kurtz, William M. Miller to Miss Mary M. Park, both of Green-Castle, Pa

514. TLM Dec 16 1823/Married Thurs 4th inst by Rev B. Kurtz, Samuel Smith to Miss Mary Robinson, both of this co/Married Thurs 1st by same, Daniel Kershner to Miss Nancy Westenberger, both of this co/Married Thurs last, by same, Jacob Shoop to Miss Catharine Dooble, both of this co/Married Sun last by same, Samuel Kline to Miss Maria Senseman, both of this co/Married at Frederick-town Tues evening last, by Rev Johns, Capt. John McPherson, Jr. to Miss Fanny Johnson, all of that town/Died Wed morning 4th inst, after a short illness, Mrs. Margaret Cromwell, wife of Joseph Cromwell, and youngest dau of Capt. Jacob Zellar, of this co

515. TLM Dec 30 1823/Married Sun 14th inst by Rev Keedy, Daniel Tompson, to Miss Sarah Cross, all of this co/Married Tues 16th inst by Rev Schnee, Richard Hurdle, of Boonsborough, to Miss Anna Maria Shriner, of Frederick c'ty /Married Mon 22d inst by Rev G. Lemon, Christian Singhars to Miss Rozanna Baker, both of Winchester, Va

516. TLM Jan 20 1824/The house of Andrew Kershner burned to the ground; most of the furniture was saved/Married 28 Dec last by Rev F. Ruthrauff, William Kirby to Miss Elizabeth Murry, both of Frederick Co/Married 11 inst by same, Michael Hiegel to Mrs. Mary Mittag, both of this co/Died, Mrs. Susanna Wolgamot, wife of John Wolgamot, Jr., and dau of David Martin of this co, Thurs last, in 26th year of her age, after a lingering illness; remains interred in family burial ground on farm of Jacob Bostater

517. TLM Jan 27 1824/The house of Henry Stitzel burned down except for the stone walls, on his farm about 2 miles from this town/Married Thurs last by Rev Moore, Hezekiah Boteler to Miss Elizabeth Easton, all of Pleasant Valley /Died Wed last in this town, Frederick Worster, in the 46th year of his age

518. TLM Feb 3 1824/Married Sun last by Rev Kurtz, William Kendle to Miss Elizabeth Burrell, all of this co/Married same day by same, William Bowers to Miss Susanna Nunemacher, all of this place/Married same day by Rev Ruthrauff, Simon Watson to Miss Rachel Friend, all of Williams-Port

519. TLM Feb 10 1824/The barn on the farm of Josiah Price, occupied by John Barnett, was burned down Fri last. The barn adjoining the jail also burned down Fri night last - property of Job Hunt, decd/Died Wed 28 ult after a lingering illness, Mrs. Maria Cameron, wife of John Cameron, of Shepherdstown, formerly Miss Maria M'Fall of this place

520. TLM Feb 17 1824/Married Tues last by Rev J. R. Reily, Abraham Herr to Miss Nancy Herr, dau of Rudolph Herr, all of this co/Married Thurs last by same, William Howard to Miss Mary Cristman, both of this co/Married same day by Rev Jeremiah Mason, William M. Herly, merchant, to Miss Ann Eliza Lowe, dau of George Lowe, all of Clear Spring/Married last week at res of Thomas C. Brent, Esq. near Hancock, George M. Swan, Esq. of Alleghany Co to Miss

THE TORCHLIGHT AND PUBLIC ADVERTISER (Hagerstown)

Louisa L. Graham/Died in this town Sat last, James Chapline, an old inhabitant of this co

521. TLM Feb 24 1824/Married at Shawneetown, Illinois, Thurs 15 ult, Alex'r Kirkpatrick, merchant, to Miss Elizabeth Marshall, both of that place/Died Thurs 5th inst, Henry Welty of this co, in 52nd year of his age/Died Thurs last at an advanced age, Philip Kriegh, farmer of this co/Died Fri last, Michael Tice, at an advanced age

522. TLM Mar 2 1824/Married Thurs last by Rev J. R. Reily, Joseph Emmert to Miss Elizabeth, dau of William Reynolds/Died 27 Jan near Newmans Town in Lebanon Co, Henry E. Shulz, brother of governor of Pa/Died 9 ult at Wammelsdorf, Berks co, Michael Egy, brother-in-law of governor of Pa/Died 13 ult, Mrs. Mary, wife of Frederick A. Shulse and dau of Gabriel Hester, Esq. and sister-in-law of governor of Pa

523. TLM Mar 9 1824/Married Thurs last in Balt by Rev Lee, Samuel Pinor of that city, aged 70 yrs, to Mrs. Hannah Selby of Snow Hill, aged 80 yrs/Died about a fortnight since, at his res in this co, at an advanced age, Isaac Houser, Sen. of this co

524. TLM Mar 16 1824/Married Thurs last by Rev B. Kurtz, Jacob Funk to Miss Susana Myers, both of this co/Married Thurs 4th inst by Rev F. Ruthrauff, David Boyer to Miss Martha Brua, both of this co/Married Sun last by same, John Palmer to Miss Elizabeth Welty, both of this co

525. TLM Apr 6 1824/Married Thurs last by Rev J. R. Reily, John Herman to Miss Rebecca Goodman, both of Frederick Co/Died Tues night last in this town in the 45th year of his age, Upton Lawrence, Esq.; interred in family vault on his farm, about 2 miles from town, with Masonic honors

526. TLM Apr 13 1824/Married Thurs 25 ult by Rev Kurtz, Emanuel Rowland to Miss Nancy Stouffer, both of this co

527. TLM Apr 20 1824/Married at Mercersburg, Pa, by Rev Elliott, John Skinner of Flint Hill to Miss Nancy Sterett of Cony Hall

528. TLM Apr 27 1824/Married Thurs last by Rev Keedy, George Leggett to Miss Holly Davis/Died 15 inst, James Jewett, son of Albert Humrickhous of Shepherds-town, Va

529. TLM May 4 1824/Married Tues evening 20 ult by Rev James Buchanan, Dr. Thomas Walker to Miss Harriet Coskery of Waynesburg/Married 24 ult by Hon. Mr. Rolin of Pa, James Meryman of Balt to Miss Sarah Wiles of this co

530. TLM May 11 1824/Married Thurs evening last by Rev B. Kurtz, Daniel Carver to Miss Amelia S. Haeflinch, both of this town/Married Thurs last by Rev J. R. Reily, Philip Krick to Miss Amelia Castle

531. TLM May 18 1824/Married Thurs last by Rev Lemmon, Thomas Neill of Frederick Co to Miss Rebecca, dau of A. Neill, Esq. of this place/Married Tues last by Rev Reily, Jacob Hartel to Miss Nancy Kuhns/Died Mon 10th inst

THE TORCHLIGHT AND PUBLIC ADVERTISER (Hagerstown)

at house of Mr. B. Leight in this place in 77th year of her age, Mrs. Susanna Gordon of Frederick co/Died Tues morning last in this town, in 36th year of his age, James M'Cauley, inn-keeper/Died Sat morning last in Williams-Port, Benjamin Brown; interred with Masonic honors

532. TLM May 25 1824/Died Tues morning last after a lingering illness, Mrs. Mary Lowe, aged 46, consort of George Lowe of Clear Spring in this co

533. TLM Jun 8 1824/Married Thurs last by Rev Lind, James Little of Williams-Port to Miss Eleonora, dau of C. Burckhartt, Esq. of Leitersburg/Married same day by same, Samuel Anderson to Miss Elizabeth Bratton, all of this co /Married Tues 25th ult by Rev J. R. Reily, Jacob Myers of Va, to Miss Mary Ann Myers of this co/Married Fri last by same, George Strickler to Miss Barbara Bruebaker (Brucbaker?), both of Shanandoah Co, Va/Died Fri night 28 ult in 22d year of her age, Miss Amelia Marteney, dau of George Marteney of this place/Died Mon 31st ult at Boonsboro', in 31st year of her age, Mrs. Rosanna Spielman, wife of David Spielman

534. TLM Jun 15 1824/Died Thurs evening last, Thomas Wilkinson of this town, in 68th year of his age/Died at his farm near Hagers-town Sat afternoon, David Cooke, Esq., formerly of Marietta, Pa, where he was the founder, aged about 74 years. By the sudden changes in times he lost a princely fortune. He leaves his sons a good name; interred in Presby burial ground

535. TLM Jul 6 1824/Married Thurs 10 ult by Rev F. Ruthrauff, Joseph Smith to Miss Maria Louisa Merideth, both of Frederick Co, Va/Married Tues 29 ult by same, Joseph Firey to Miss Mary M. Beard, both of this co/Married Thurs 10 ult by Rev B. Kurtz, Samuel Sturr to Miss Letitia Webb, both of Cavetown /Married Thurs 24 ult by same, Daniel Weise of this town to Miss Mary Steffey, of this co

536. TLM Jul 13 1824/Married Tues last by Rev Isaac Keller, John Hershberger to Miss Margaret Ruthrauff/Married Thurs last by Rev J. R. Reily, David C. Devenny to Miss Mary Light, both of Berkeley co, Va/Died Sat 26 ult at his res in this co, after an illness of a few hrs, in the 59th year of his age, Daniel Keedy, farmer and miller of this co/Died 5th inst in the 45th year of her age, after a lingering illness, Mrs. Agness Friend, wife of late Robert T. Friend, of Williams-Port/Died Thurs morning last in 46th year of her age, Miss Mary Maffitt of this town

537. TLM Jul 20 1824/Married Sun 11 inst by Rev Keedy, George Marteney of this town to Miss Catharine Lider of Frederick Co/Married Sun last by Rev Ruthrauff, Stephen Murray of this place to Miss Maria Sensil, of this co /Died Thurs last, Mrs. Margaret Knode, wife of Jacob Knode of this place, in 75th year of her age

538. TLM Jul 27 1824/Married Tues evening last by Rev F. Ruthrauff, Francis Dorsey to Miss Eliza Crow, both of this co/George W. Sands, Hagers-town, offers reward for apprentice to shoemaking business, Jonathan Neill, about 15 yrs of age, 4 ft 8-10 inch, impudent, worthless fellow

THE TORCHLIGHT AND PUBLIC ADVERTISER (Hagerstown)

539. TLM Aug 3 1824/Died in Hancock Fri lasst, Hon. John Johnston, Chancellor of Md., on his way to join the Board of Commissioners for fixing the line between Maryland and Virginia

540. TLM Aug 10 1824/Died 3d inst at the house of Samuel Martin, in this town, Mrs. Mary Martin, in the 88th year of her age/Died Fri last in 68th year of her age, Mrs. Anna Hager, relict of late Jonathan Hager, decd, of this town/Reward offered for John Bragden, about 18 yrs of age, 5 ft 5-6 inch, who left my employ on 24th ult and may have taken $9.00 of subscriber, Jabez Kenney, 2 miles below Funks-town

541. TLM Aug 17 1824/Married Thurs last by Rev J. R. Reily, Josiah M'Clain to Miss Eliza Coss/Married same day by same, Jacob Wethknecht to Miss Mary Ossier, all of this co/Died suddenly at Frederick-town on his way home from Balt, by the rupture of a blood vessel, Sat evening 7th inst, L. H. Johns, Esq., in the 46th year of his age, of George-town; he left a wife and large family of children/Died in this town Sun last, Mrs. Christiana Zwisler, wife of James Zwisler, Sen.

542. TLM Aug 24 1824/Married at Carlisle Thurs evening, 12th inst, by Rev R. S. Vinton, Jacob Spangler, to Mrs. Elizabeth Waterberry, all of Carlisle /Married same day in Sharpsburg, Robert P. McWilliams to Miss Sarah Ground, all of that place/Died Fri last in 34th year of her age, Mrs. Mary Cromwell, wife of Nathan Cromwell, of this co and dau of Capt. Jacob Zellar/Died same day at his res in Funkstown in 74th year of his age, Henry Shroeder/Died at his res in this place Wed last, William Feigley in 45th year of his age/Died at the res of Dr. Macgill, her nephew, in this place, Wed last, Miss Mary Macgill aged 77 yrs, formerly of Balt/Died at res of J. I. Merrick, Esq. in this place, yesterday evening, Col. Samuel Hughes, of Mount Pleasant, Harford Co, in the 75th year of his age/Miss Nancy Light died at the res of her brother on south bank of the Potomac near Williams-Port early in morning of 16th ult, after an illness of 4 days, in the 20th year of her age/Harpers Ferry Free Press - died in Harpers ferry 12th inst, Capt. Smith Slaughter, of Shanendoah Co, in the 61st year of his age, for many yrs a magistrate, several times elected to Legislature of that state/Died - D. (Dr.?) Charles Brown; buried near Jefferson's Rock by Masonic and military procession. He left most of his estate to medical hospital of Phila

543. TLM Aug 31 1824/Married Tues last by Rev B. Kurtz, Christian Smith to Miss Cath. Sensebaugh/Married Thurs last by same, Jacob Schmutz to Miss Mary Schlenker, all of this co

544. TLM Sep 7 1824/Died Mon night 23d at his res about 5 miles from this place, Daniel Brumbaugh, aged 52 yrs/Died Sun 22nd ult in Shepherdstown, Va, Peter Smith, long an inhabitant of this place/Died Fri morning last at her res in this co, in 38th year of her age, Mrs. Elizabeth Swingley/Died Sat morning last at res of her father, Elisha Hyland in this co, Miss Ann Hyland, in 18th year of her age/Died - Franklin Republican editor, John Sloan

545. TLM Sep 14 1824/Married 30 ult by Rev J. Ruthrauff, John Craven, to Miss Mary Heiskill, both of this co/Married 31st ult by same, Jacob Kuhns to Miss Barbara Spitznagel, both of this co/Married 2d inst by Rev Kurtz, John Beckley to Miss Nancy Byers/Married Thurs last, by same, George Kline to

THE TORCHLIGHT AND PUBLIC ADVERTISER (Hagerstown)

Miss Cath. Miller/Married 2d inst by Rev J. R. Reily, David Neff to Miss Susanna Weidman/Married 7th inst by same, William Bender to Miss Elizabeth Sietenstick, all of this co/Married 9th isnt by same, John Beachly to Miss Catharine Leinbach, both of Frederick Co/Died 2d inst in Balt of a short but severe illness, Michael Kimmel, in the 42d year of his age, for many yrs, merchant of Balt/Died 3d inst at his farm, near Reading, Pa, of a bilious remitent fever, Gabriel Hiester, Esq. in the 76th year of his age

546. TLM Sep 21 1824/Married in Front Royal, Va, Thurs 9 inst, by Rev Dorsey, Jon. Hager Ragan of this town to Miss Selonary W. Jacobs, dau of Thomas Jacobs, Esq. of this former place/Died at his res in Green Castle, Pa, Tues morning last, Rev John X. Clarke/Died Fri morning last at res of John Harry in this town, Samuel Harry/Died yesterday morning, Mrs. Anna Newcomer, wife of Christian Newcomer, Jr. of this co/Died yesterday afternoon, at his res in this place, after an illness of about 2 weeks, Rev John Lind, Pastor of one of the English Presby Congregations of Green Castle and that of Hagers-town; to be interred at Green Castle/Died Mon 23d inst, in 40th year of his age, James Kirkpatrick, Esq., for many yrs merchant of this place, and formerly a citizen of Wash Co, Md - Shawnee town Gazette.

547. TLM Sep 28 1824/Married Thurs 9th inst by Rev B. Kurtz, George Kline to Miss Cath'ne Miller, both of this co/Married 16th last by same, John D. Ridenour to Miss Sarah Protzman, of this co/Married same day by same, Lewis Moyer to Miss Susanna Bergman, both of this co/Equity case - Samuel B. M'Clenahan and Christopher Flory vs Christopher Smith, Elizabeth Logan, Henry Kagey, Solomon Lower, David Bashore, George Meyer, James Meyer, Cathrine, James, Mary, Nancy, John and Edward Carr, heirs of Edward Carr. The object of the bill is to foreclose a mortgage executed by defendant, Christopher Smith to complainant, Samuel B. M'Clanahan and assigned by M'Clanahan to Christopher Flory. After mortgage was executed Smith sold part of premises and laid out residue in a town called Smithsburg and defendants are owners of lots in said town. Elizabeth Logan, Henry Kagey, Solomon Lower, David Bashore, George Meyer, James Meyer, and heirs of Edward Carr, decd, all res out of Md.

548. TLM Oct 5 1824/Married at Fountain Rock, near Hagers-town, Tues evening last, by Rev Lemmon, William Schley, Esq. of Frederick to Miss Ann Cadwalader, 3d dau of Gen. Samuel Ringgold/Died Sun evening last at his res near this place, Capt Christian Orndorff, in 67th year of his age, veteran of Rev. He entered the army in '76 as a Lieutenant; advanced to Capt in 6th Regt, Md. Line, which he held until close of the war. He was captured at Fort Washington; after exchange of prisoners he joined the army at the South under Gen. Green - Martinsburgh Gaz. of Sep 30

549. TLM Oct 12 1824/Married 23d ult by Rev B. Kurtz, Marcus Alder of Va to Mrs. Mary Page of this co/Married at Sharpsburg Thurs last by Rev J. R. Riely, Thomas O. Sheets to Miss Elizabeth Hamm/Married at Bellvin near Mercersburg, Pa, Thurs last, by Rev D Elliott, Alexander Sellars to Miss Mary dau of D'd Rankin, all of Montgomery township, Franklin Co/Married in Chambersburg, Pa, on 30th ult by Rev David Kenny, Kenton Harper, editor of the Staunton Spectator, to Miss Eleanor, dau of Capt. Samuel Colhoun of that borough

THE TORCHLIGHT AND PUBLIC ADVERTISER (Hagerstown)

550. TLM Oct 19 1824/Married Thurs last by Rev J. R. Reily, Daniel Rulet to Miss Elizbeth Piper/Married same day by Rev D. Elliott, Major J. Bahn, to Miss Matilda S. Beall, both of Mercersburg, Pa/Died Sat 9 inst after an illness of a few days, Rev Patrick Davidson, minister of English Presby Congregation of this town. Mr. Davidson had attended the funeral of a dau, who died after an illness of only a few hours - Fredk. Exam.

551. TLM Oct 26 1824/Married Thurs last by Rev B. Kurtz, Stephen Carpenter to Miss Mary Summers/John Surghnor, Leesburg, Va, offers reward for apprentice to boot and shoemaking business, James Ryen, about 18 yrs of age, 5 ft 6 inch, dark complexion, square built

552. TLM Nov 2 1824/Married Thurs 21st ult by Rev John Brown, John O. King, of this place, to Miss Catharine Bowman, of Franklin Co, Pa/Married Wed last, at Sharpsburg, by Rev J. R. Reily, James M'Clure to Miss Mary Bell, both of Va/Married Thurs last by same, James S. Stanly to Miss Sarah Ann Feigley

553. TLM Nov 9 1824/Died this morning at 2 o'clock at the Globe Tavern in this town, George L. Chenoweth/Married Thurs last by Rev B. Kurtz, Benjamin Buckwalter to Miss Catharine Miller, both of this co

554. TLM Nov 16 1824/Married Thurs last by Rev J. R. Riely, George Marker, to Miss Mary Moats, all of this co/Died early yesterday morning at house of John Gruber, senior, editor of the German paper in this town, Mrs. Christiana Gruber, in the 87th year of her age

555. TLM Nov 23 1824/Married Thurs last by Rev B. Kurtz, John Huber to Miss Nancy Shenk, all of this co/Died Sun last at his res in this town, Samuel Bayly, Esq. in the 50th year of his age

556. TLM Nov 30 1824/Died at his res in New town (Trap), Frederick Co, Thurs last 25th inst at 2 o'clock in the morning, Basil Murray, formerly of this place, in the 35th year of his age, leaving wife and 2 children/Equity case - Daniel Piper vs Henry Kephart & Elizabeth his wife, John Eckhart & Margaret his wife, John Stone & Mary his wife, Ros'na Brown, George Miller & Mary his wife, Adam Snyder & Elizabeth his wife, Vincent Davis & Susanna his wife, Jacob Piper, Jacob Johnson, Elizabeth Johnson, John Johnson, Henry Johnson, Susan Johnson, & Eleanor Johnson - For the sale of real estate of John Piper and Jacob Piper, both decd. Jacob Piper devised considerable estate to John Piper and encumbered said real estate with payment of 450 pounds to other children of Jacob Piper. Henry Kephart & Elizabeth his wife, John Eckhart & Margaret his wife, John Stone & Mary his wife, Ros'na Brown, George Miller & Mary his wife, all reside out of state of Md.

557. TLM Dec 7 1824/Married Tues last by Rev J. R. Reily, George Shafer to Miss Martha B. Swearingen, dau of J. V. Swearingen, Esq., all of this place/Married Sun evening 28 ult by Rev B. Kurtz, Henry Snider to Miss Catharine Aubert, all of this place/Married Thurs last by same, Henry Rice to Miss Nancy Mauggins, all of this co/Married Sun last by same, William Harvin to Miss Mary E. Holliday, both of Va/Married same day by Rev Ruthrauff, Samuel Huffer to Miss Elizabeth Welty, both of this co/Married same

THE TORCHLIGHT AND PUBLIC ADVERTISER (Hagerstown)

day by same, Richard Tigner to Miss Sarah Smith, both of Va/Married same day by same, Henry H. Porter to Miss Elizabeth Little, both of this place

558. TLM Dec 14 1824/Married Thurs evening last by Rev John Davis, Rev Samuel Clark to Miss Elizabeth dau of Colonel John Reynolds of this place /Died Tues last after a lingering illness, Seth Lane, Esq., of this town /Died at his seat at Montpelier, in this co, 10 inst, John Thomson Mason, Esq. in 60th year of his age

559. TLM Dec 21 1824/Married at Washington, Pa, 25th ult, by Rev C. Wheeler, Lucius W. Stockton of Balt, to Miss Rebecca, dau of Daniel Moore of that place/Died at his res Sat evening last, after a lingering illness, George Klink, in 48th year of his age, native of Germany. The last 10-14 yrs he was an inhabitant of this place

560. TLM Dec 28 1824/Married 9 inst by Rev F. Ruthrauff, Joseph Pollick to Miss Sarah Collins, both of Berkley Co, Va/Married Sat last by same, James C. Pollick to Miss Jane N. Bowen, of Greenbrier, Va/Married Sun last by same, George Snider to Miss Nancy Davis, both of this co/Married 14 inst by Rev B. Kurtz, Henry Leisure of Bedford, Pa, to Miss Sophia Shane of this co/Married 16 inst by same, Matthew West to Miss Prudence Hathorn, all of this co/Married Thurs last by Rev J. R. Reily, Samuel Deitrick to Mrs. Elizabeth Rietz, dau of Capt. Adam Myers of this co

561. TLM Jan 4 1825/Washington, Pa, Dec. 27 - On Tues morning last, between 1 and 2 o'clock, the alarm of fire was raised, by a blaze proceeding from the roof of a small frame building on the back street, east of the courthouse, in this borough. The bodies of Francis Henry, an old revolutionary pensioner and his wife were discovered and interred. Cause of the fire is matter of conjecture, but is generally supposed to be by the carelessness of those two unfortunate old people, who sometimes partook too freely of ardent spirits/Married 23d ult by Rev N. B. Little, Jacob Whetstone to Miss Sarah Armstrong, both of Martinsburg, Va

562. TLM Jan 11 1825/Married in Williams-Port 30th ult by Rev R. Kennedy, Samuel Craig, Esq. of Wetmoreland co, Pa, to Miss Sarah Ann, dau of John Hogg of the former place/Married Thurs last by Rev Deneas, Michael Beard to Miss Eliza Tylor, both of this co/Married Sun last by Rev J. M'Cauley, Capt. Lewis Fletcher to Miss Delila Shafer, both of Boonsborough/Died at his res in Williams-Port, 30th Dec, after a distressing and protracted illness, William S. Compton, Esq. in the 67th year of his age

563. TLM Jan 18 1825/Married 4th inst by Rev Keedy, John Hays, aged 19, to Mrs. Catharine Eakle, aged 45, all of this co/Married same day in Wash Co, Pa, by Rev. H. Weinandt, Rev Charles Zwisler to Miss Barbara Stacher/Married same day by Rev Kurtz, John Koontz to Miss Susan Bowman, all of this co /Married Thurs last, by same, Christian Newcomer to Miss Sarah Keller, all of this co/Equity case - John Harbaugh, vs. Barbara Potter, Daniel Potter, Daniel Beshore and Mary his wife, Jno. Nichodemus and Margaret his wife, John Baker, Abraham Baker, Elizabeth Baker, Catharine Baker, Justina Baker, Barbara Baker, Henry Leady & Barbara his wife, and Daniel Baker. Object is to obtain decree for sale of real estate of John Potter, later of Franklin

THE TORCHLIGHT AND PUBLIC ADVERTISER (Hagerstown)

co, Pa, decd, in Wash Co, Md, for payment of debts of decd. John Potter died in Pa, seized of real estate in Wash Co, Md. The following devisees and heirs of said Potter, namely, Daniel Potter, Daniel Beshore and Mary his wife, John Nichodemus and Margaret his wife and the children of Catharine Baker, who are under age of 21, namely, John, Abraham, Elizabeth, Catharine, Justina and Barbara Baker, grand children of said Potter, reside out of the state of Md

564. TLM Feb 1 1825/Married 20th inst by Rev B. Kurtz, John Peltz to Miss Nancy Feigley/Married Thurs last by same, Peter Hammer to Miss Catharine Brendel, dau of Geo. Brendel, all of this place/Married Thurs last, by Rev G. Keedy, Christian Farver to Miss Sarah Stokes, both of Sharpsburg

565. TLM Feb 8 1825/Married Thurs last by Rev Keller, Jacob Knode, Jr. to Miss Mary Cheney/Married same day by same David Brewer to Miss Elizabeth Cushwa/Died 28th ult at Winchester, Va, Hon. Hugh Holmes, after a severe stroke of paralysis/Died same day, Dr. Zachariah Clagett, of Pleasant Valley, Wash Co, in the 65th year of his age

566. TLM Feb 15 1825/Married Thurs 3d inst by Rev B. Kurtz, John Miller to Miss Elizabeth Needy, all of this co/Married same day by Rev Keys, Rev James H. Hanson to Miss Sarah Burnett, of Jefferson co, Va/Married Thurs last by Rev N. B. Little, John H. Morrison to Miss Isabella W. Dickey, of Loudon, Pa

567. TLM Feb 22 1825/Married Thurs last, by Rev H. A. Kurtz, Elias O'Neal to Miss Sophia Alter, both of this co/Married same day by Rev J. R. Reily, Dietrich Cobaugh to Miss Sarah Shanefelt/Died Sat last, of a lingering pulmonary affection, Mrs. Nancy Kurtz, wife of Rev. Benj. Kurtz, of this town; remains interred in Luth grave yard

568. TLM Mar 1 1825/Married 13th ult at Freederick-town, by Rev D. F. Schaeffer, William D. Sterrett to Mrs. Lydia S. M'Cauley, both of this place/Married Tues last by Rev Isaac Kellar, Daniel Zeiler (Zeller?) to Miss Elizabeth B. Foulke, both of this co/Married same day, at Boonsboro', by Rev Hanson, Rev John L. Gibbons to Miss Ellenora Carr, dau of late Col. Carr, of this co /Married Thurs last by same, John Dillon to Miss Maria Riblett, both of this place/Death of Mrs. Ann Kurtz, late consort of the Rev B. Kurtz, Pastor of the Evang. Luth. Church of this town, on 19th ult at 10 o'clock, A.M., aged 26 yrs, 2 months, leaving husband and 2 small children (very long obit.) /Died suddenly Thurs evening last, Mrs. Mary Myers, consort of John Myers, living near Sharpsburg, aged 76 yrs and 13 days

569. TLM Mar 8 1825/Married Thurs 3d inst by Rev Dennies, Samuel Shafer, to Miss Elizabeth Petry, both of this co/Married Tues last by Rev Miller, Jacob Fechtig to Miss Matilda Hillery, of Allegany co, Md/Married Sun last by Rev N. B. Little, Jacob Roland to Miss Elizabeth Stover, both of this co/Married Sun last by Rev Ruthrauff, Owen B. Frazer to Mrs. Kitturah Hooper, both of this place

570. TLM Mar 22 1825/Married Tues evening last by Rev J. R. Reily, Mr. A. Wotring, merchant of Washington, Pa, to Miss Mary Elizabeth Rahauser, 2d dau of late Rev Jona. Rahauser, of this place/Married Thurs last, by same, Jona-

THE TORCHLIGHT AND PUBLIC ADVERTISER (Hagerstown)

than Ridenour, to Miss Sarah Reed, both of this co/Married same day, by same, John Sprecher to Miss Sarah Bowser, both of this co/Married same day by Rev N. B. Little, Jacob Shaneberger to Miss Sophia Grosh, all of this co

571. TLM Mar 29 1825/Distressing Accident! - A child about 13 months old, was burnt to death, on Sun last, at Cap. Caspar Schnebly's near Sharpsburg. The mother, Mrs. Varner, had left the room and during her absence the clothes of the child took fire at the fire-place in the room, and so burnt it before she returned, that it survived but 4 hours!/John M'Afee, was tried at a late term of the court of Common Pleas of Montgomery co, Ohio, for the murder of his wife; found guilty and sentenced to be hanged on 28 March (yesterday) /Died at her res in Williams-Port Thurs 10th inst, Mrs. Mary Ann Sharer/Died Tues 15th inst at his res about 3 miles from this town, Christian Landis, in the 30th year of his age

572. TLM Apr 5 1825/Married 8th ult by Rev Isaac Keller, John Barr to Miss Nancy Winders/Married 24th ult by same, George Ankeny to Miss Catharine Troup /Married same day by Rev N. B. Little, Frederick Moudy to Miss Mary Snyder /Married same day by same, Jacob Palmer to Miss Catharine Knodle, all of this co/Married 22d ult at Sharpsburg, by Rev J. R. Reily, John Sturr to Miss Elizabeth Hess, both of that place/Married Thurs last by same, John Hoover to Miss Catharine Steffy, both of this co/Married Fri last by Rev I. Keller, Anthony Wayne Lewis to Miss Ann Hawken, both of this place/Married same day by same, Alexander G. Herron to Miss Eliza Donalson, both of this place/Married Sun last by Rev N. B. Little, Jacob Rohrer, to Miss Elizabeth Hill, all of this co/Died Mon evening 28th ult in Berkely co, Va, Richard Clagett, Esq. of that co; remains deposited in Epis burying ground with Masonic Honors/Died Mon morning 28th ult in Boonsborough, Wm. Carroll

573. TLM Apr 12 1825/Married Tues last by Rev Wilson, Matthew M'Clanahan to Miss Eliza Byers, dau of John Byers, all of this co/Married Thurs evening last, by Rev J. R. Reily, Charles Levis to Miss Mary Keller, both of this place /Married same evening by Rev I. Keller, Richard Weise to Miss Sarah Kline, both of this place/Died Sun last at his res in this place, Francis Landen /Died yesterday morning at her res in this place, in the 49th year of her age, Mrs. Catharine Lane, wife of late Seth Lane, Esq./Suicide! - A man named Stephen Fry, of Waynesburg, Franklkin co, Pa, lately put an end to his life, by cutting his throat with a drawing knife, a sober, industrious man, left a wife and 6 children

574. TLM Apr 19 1825/From Shepherds-Town Journal of Thurs last - We understand that a child of Mr. E. B. Kinsell of Hagers-town, Md. aged about 4-5 yrs, was trod to death by a horse on the 9th inst - Mr. Fleming is misinformed. Mr. Kinsell's child was thrown from the horse and seriously injured, but is on the recovery/Married Thurs 7th inst by Rev Kurtz, Daniel Traubinger to Miss Sarah Ridenouer, both of this co/Married Thurs last by same, David Shelleberger to Miss Christiana Newcomer, dau of Christian Newcomer, Jun. of this co/Married same day by same, William Hause to Miss Mary Lillich, both of this place/Married Tues last by Rev Little, George W. Black to Miss Catharine Graeff, both of this town/Died Sun last, Mrs. Barbara Horine, wife of John Horine, Esq. of this co

THE TORCHLIGHT AND PUBLIC ADVERTISER (Hagerstown)

575. TLM May 3 1825/Married 21st ult by Rev Geo. Lemon, Thomas Turner, Esq. of Georgetown, D. C. to Miss Ellenor T. Pratt, dau of Thomas Pratt, Esq. of Alleghany co/Married Thurs last by Rev J. Brown, Rev Daniel S. Middlekauff to Miss Mary Thomas of Frederick co, Md/Died 17th ult in Smithsburg, after a few week's illness, Mrs. Margaret Oswald, in the 85th year of her age/Died in this town Thurs last, at an advanced age, Mrs. Mary Bean, wife of George Bean, of this place

576. TLM May 10 1825/Married 28th ult by Rev Isaac Kellar, Geo. Brown to Miss Julian Scott, both of this co/Married same day by Rev. B. Kurtz, George Steffy to Miss Ann Mary Winter/Died at Elizabeth-town, Tenn, 29th March last, Thos. B. Evans, formerly of Franklin co, Pa, and of Washington co, Md /Died Sat last at his res in this town, in the 56th year of his age, Christopher Kealhofer

577. TLM May 17 1825/Married Tues last, by Rev Buchanan, John M. Buchanan, editor of the Cumberland Advocate, to Miss Mary S. Grieves, dau of Thomas Grieves, editor of the Md. Herald, of this place/Married Sun last, Hugh McAteer, of Funkstown, to Miss Margaret S. Smith, of this place/Died Thurs evening 5th inst, Mrs. Elizabeth Downs, wife of William Downs, Sen. in the 54th year of her age/Died Fri evening 6th, Mrs. Henrietta Downs, wife of William Downs, Jr. in the 30th year of her age/Died Wed morning 11th inst at his res, Henry Zuck, in the 46th year of his age/Died same day in Berkley co, Va, John H. Zuck, in the 29th year of his age

578. TLM May 24 1825/Married at York, Pa, Tues 3d inst, Jacob Eisenhart, son of Dr. George Eisenhart, of West Manchester township to Miss Eliza Schumcker, dau of Rev J. G. Schmucker, all of the former place/Died in this town Sat 14th inst, Mrs. Barbara Middelkauff, wife of Henry Middelkauff, in the 64th year of her age/Died at his res in this co, Mon 14th inst, William Downes, Sen.in the 64th year of his age/Died in Williams-Port, on Thurs 19th inst, after an illness of 30 hrs, by bilious colick, Daniel Weisel, in the 61st year of his age, inhabitant of Williams-Port for last 30 yrs, leaving 7 children

579. TLM May 31 1825/Married Sun 22d by Rev B. Kurtz, John B. Lynch to Miss Pamelia Watts, both of this co/Married Thurs last, at Leitersb'g, by Rev Buchanan, William Fields, of Waynesburg, to Miss Elizabeth Hays, of the former place /Died Thurs last, after a lingering illness, Mrs. Elizabeth Mendenhall, wife of Mr. E. B. Mendenhall, of this co

580. TLM Jun 7 1825/Married by Rev N. B. Little Sun 22d ult, Daniel Piper to Miss Eliza Kitsmiller, all of this co/Married Wed 25th ult by Rev Dr. Hill, Samuel Ott, merchant of Woodstock to Miss Sidney I. Heiskell, dau of the Editor of the Winchester Gaz.

581. TLM Jun 14 1825/Married Tues morning last, by Rev Kellar, Thomas J. Clagett, of Balt, to Miss Elizabeth B., eldest dau of Col. O. H. Williams, of this place /Married 19th ult Henry Wade to Miss Nancy Crampton - and on Thurs last, John Stitzel to Miss Catharine Hoffman - all of this co/Married Thurs last by Rev Reed, Gilbert Nowell of Williams-Port, to Miss Maria Riblet, of this place/Died at res of her son-on-law, Jacob Firey, about 4 miles

THE TORCHLIGHT AND PUBLIC ADVERTISER (Hagerstown)

from Hagerstown, Tues 7th inst, Mrs. Eve Startzman, relict of late Henry Startzman, in the 83d year of her age, mother of 9 children, of whom four are dead and five living; lived to see 64 great children and 8 great-grand children; remains interred in Luth burial ground/Died Sat 11th inst in this place, Mrs. Sophia Duckett, in the 54th year of her age, after a severe and distressing illness of 4 months

582. TLM Jun 21 1825/Married Thurs 9th inst by Rev Hanson, Charles Nourse of Sharpsburg, to Miss Susan Cameron, dau of Mrs. Susanna Cameron, of Shepherds-town, Va/Married Tues last, by Rev Kurtz, John S. Hamilton of Funkstown, to Miss Hannah McCauley of this co/Married Sun last by Rev Denies, Benjamin Grim, to Miss Catharine Rohrback, all of this co

583. TLM Jun 28 1825/Died in this place Fri last, of a pulmonary affection in the 26th year of his age, John Reynolds, Jr. of the firm of John Reynolds & Son

584. TLM Jul 5 1825/Died Fri 24th ult, at Fairhill, Md., Otho Blackford, aged about 17 yrs, eldest son of Col. Blackford, of Wash Co, Md. We understand his death was occasioned by a mortification in one of his arms, produced by a hurt he received while engaged in some of the exerceses common to all institutions of learning - Shepherdstown Journal

585. TLM Jul 26 1825/Married in Green-Castle, Sun 17th inst by Rev Shull, John Thomas to Mrs. Rosanna Smith, both of this co/Died Thurs evening last, at his res in this co, after a short illness, Ignatius Drury, Es. in the 36th year of his age, one of the Delegates from Wash co, in the Legislature of Md. during the session 1822-23/Died Fri last at her res in this place, after a protracted illness, Miss Eleanora M'Dannell

586. TLM Aug 2 1825/Married Thurs last, by Rev N. B. Little, Jacob Forman to Miss Eliza Locke, both of Jefferson co, Va

587. TLM Aug 9 1825/Married Tues last, by Rev N. B. Little, Nathan C. Baker to Miss Mary Ann Roberts, both of Winchester, Va

588. TLM Aug 16 1825/Married Mon 8th inst by Rev Buchanan, William Murray to Miss Susan Jackson, both of this town/Frederick - On Mon night last, a free black man, the well known Tom Graham, of Hagers-town, put a period to his existence by drowning himself in Carroll's Creek

589. TLM Aug 23 1825/Married Thurs 28th ult by Rev B. Kurtz, John Smith to Miss Nancy Rowe, all of this co/Married Sun last, by same, Daniel Lowman to Miss Elizabeth Robinson/Died Tues last in the 64th year of her age, Mrs. Mary Walling, wife of the late col. James Walling, of this co/Died Sat morning last, at the res of her son-in-law, Martin Showaker, in this town, Mrs. Barbara Rigler, at the age of 95 yrs, wanting 11 days

590. TLM Aug 30 1825/George Alter of this co, was thrown from his horse and killed on Fri last, between his res and Funks-town, from which place he was returning with his wagon; he was in the 42d year of his age - And on Sat a laboring man, named Thomas Steiner, was killed in a well near the new jail,

THE TORCHLIGHT AND PUBLIC ADVERTISER (Hagerstown)

by the falling of a stone/Married Thurs last, near Cave-town, by Rev B. Kurtz, David Steffy to Miss Anna Ridenour, all of this co/Died in this town, Thurs last, Mrs. Catharine Lorshbaugh, wife of George Lorshbaugh, and dau of John Albert/Died Sun last, at an advanced age, Mrs. Ann Boyd, wife of Walter Boyd, Esq. of this co/Died yesterday evening at her res in this place, Mrs. Ann Hughes, widow of the late Col. Daniel Hughes

591. TLM Sep 6 1825/Married in Frederick-town, Sun 28th ult by Rev D. F. Schaeffer, William Little, of this place, to Miss Wilhelmina Stenger, dau of Chs. Stenger, of the former place/Died in Frederick 17th ult in the 45th year of his age, George Duffield, of Ohio; remains interred in Presby graveyard/Died in Pleasant Valley, Sun 28th ult in 86th year of her age, Mrs. Ann Mary Maria Crampton, relict of late Thomas Crampton, one of the earliest inhabitants of the Valley/Died at last at res of Elie Beatty, Esq. in this town, Miss Nancy Hoye, dau of late Paul Hoye, Esq. of this co

592. TLM Sep 13 1825/Married at Columbian Inn, in this place, Sun last by Rev G. Lemon, Jacob Keesecker to Miss Elizabeth Criswell/Married same time and place, by same, George Houke to Miss Catharine Harrison, all of Berkeley co, Va /Death of Freeland Dorsey Fri last in 16th year of his age, after a short illness, 2d son of Dr. Frederick Dorsey

593. TLM Sep 20 1825/Married 23d Aug by Rev Isaac Kellar, James Bowen to Miss Margaret Mowser/Married 6th inst by same, John Yakle to Miss Catharine Eustachieus/Married 8th inst by Rev William Clingen, in Pleasant Valley, Benjamin Potter to Miss Sophia Grim, all of this co/Married at Green-Castle Sun 11th inst, by Rev Ruthrauff, Rudolph Tanner to Miss Elizabeth Bancord, both of Clear-Spring, Md/Died at Cumberland 12th inst, Mrs. Catharine Boose, wife of John Boose, and dau of Matthias Shaffner of Hagers-town

594. TLM Sep 27 1825/Married at Carlisle, Pa, Tues last by Rev George Duffield, Dr. Joseph Martin to Miss Rebecca L. Hughes, dau of late Col. Daniel Hughes, both of this place/Married same day by Rev J. Reid, William Hathorn to Miss Margaret Hilliard, all of this town

595. TLM Oct 4 1825/Married Thurs last by Rev James Reid, Robert Buckley to Miss Elizabeth Lutz, both of this co/Chambersburg - Sep 27. Died Wed morning last, William M. M'Dowell, Esq. Attorney and Counsellor at law, of this place, in the 32d year of his age

596. TLM Oct 11 1825/Married Tues evening last by Rev Geo. Lemmon, George Bean to Miss Henrietta Cox, all of this place/Married Sun last by same, David H. Petman to Miss Amelia S. Ritenour, both of Rockingham co, Va/Died 4th inst, John Donovan, aged 85, for more 60 yrs, a res of Hancock/Died at his res in Pleasant Valley, Thurs 6th inst, Elias Crampton, in the 64th year of his age/Died at Williams-Port, Wash Co, Md., on his journey homewards from the Springs, Dun, Oct 2d, Colonel Samuel Chapman, of Charles co, in the 59th year of his age; his son Henry, of 13 yrs of age, watched over the death-bed of his father. He was buried at Williams-Port on the banks of the Potomac /Died at Springfield, near Williams-Port, Tues morning last, Miss Sophia Davis, dau of late Amos Davis, of this co/Died Wed 28th ult in the 54th year of his age, James Wood, Esq. of Green-Castle. About a week before

THE TORCHLIGHT AND PUBLIC ADVERTISER (Hagerstown)

his death, he received a severe contusion in the head and was otherwise much injured, by being thrown out of a dearborn, his horse having run off. He was in the battle in which Gen. Wayne defeated the Indians in 1794. During the late war with Great Britain, he marched as a Major of a battalion of volunteers and militia ordered from this county into Canada, and was in the Battles of Chippawa and Bridgewater, in the latter of which he received a severe wound; after the war he was appointed Justice of the Peace. He left a large family of children. - Franklin Repository

597. TLM Oct 18 1825/Married Tues last in Berkeley co, Va by Rev Krauth, David Hess, of Wash co, Md. to Miss Ann Grove, dau of late Peter Grove, of Berkeley co/Died Thurs morning last, after a painful illness of a few weeks in the 35th year of her age, Mrs. Elizabeth Murray, wife of Matthew Murray of this place, leaving husband and several small children, one of whom is but an infant/Thomas Leggett son of Jas. Leggett, Esq. of Sharpsburg, was recently killed near Waynesburg, Franklin co, Pa, by the accidental discharge of a gun, in attempting to cross a fence with the gun in his hand, the top rail broke; he endeavored to guard against a fall by throwing out the butt end of the gun, at which instant the load was discharged. He survived about 30 yrs. His remains conveyed to Sharpsburg and there interred.

598. TLM Oct 25 1825/Married Tues 4th inst by Rev B. Kurtz, George Thumb to Miss Margaret Waughtle, all of this co/Married Thurs 6th by same, Josephus Reed, of Pa, to Miss Arabella Eliza M'Clelland of this co/Married Tues last by same, Michael Hinds to Miss Elizabeth School, both of this place/Married same day by same, at the house of Col. Schnebly, Dr. Meredith Helm of George-town, D. C. to Miss Elizabeth Orndorff, of this co/Married at Mount Airy, Va, Wed 12th, by Rev Moyerhaffer, Rev Samuel S. Schmucker of New Market, to Miss Mary Catharine, dau of William Steenbergen, Esq./Married at Chambersburg Thurs 13th by Rev Rauhouser, Joseph Pritts to Mrs. Nancy Sloan, proprietress of the Frankin Republican/Married at same place, on same day, by Rev Denny, William Gilmore to Miss Martha Kirby, all of that place/Married Sun last by Rev Kurtz, Henry R. Richards to Miss Elvina Brison, both of Frederick co, Va/Died in this place, Thurs last, John Miller (baker) in the 77th year of his age/Died Sat last at his res about 5 miles from this place, Beal Gaither, in the 70th year fo his age/Died yesterday morning, Miss Maria Artz, dau of Peter Artz, of this place, in the 17th year of her age/Died in Chambersburg, Thurs 13th, Mr. W. F. Schoepflin, editor of the German "Redliche Registrator," in the 48th year of his age/Died Mon 17 Oct about 10 o'clock in the evening, Rev Daniel Hitt, in the 58th year of his age, about the 35th year of his itinerant ministry (Meth Episc). He preached his last sermon at a Camp Meeting near Green Castle, Pa. He was taken from the ground ill of a bilious fever, and died of the same at his nephew's, Samuel M. Hitt, of Wash Co. He preached from New York to Virginia, and from the Chesapeake to the Ohio/Died 14 inst, Miss Melrora(?) Ridout, formerly of this city, and late of Prince-George's co, at the Lodge, res of her father, after a short illness - Annapolis Gazette

599. TLM Nov 1 1825/Married Thurs morning 27th ult in City of Balt, Singleton Du Val, esq. of Frederick, to Miss Eleanor Clagett, dau of Hezekiah Clagett, of the former place/Henry Grosh, Jr., Williams-Port, offers reward

THE TORCHLIGHT AND PUBLIC ADVERTISER (Hagerstown)

for apprentice to boot and shoe making business, named George W. Grosh, between 19 and 20 yrs of age, 5 ft 7-8 inch, of dark complexion, light hair

600. TLM Nov 8 1825/Married Thurs 27th ult by Rev B. Kurtz, Jacob Winders to Miss Sarah Landis, all of this co/Married same day by same, David Hubbard to Miss Margaret Shriver, all of this co/Died Thurs evening 27th ult at the house of her sister, Mrs. Rahauser, in this place, Mrs. Catharine Young, widow of the late Ludwick Young, formerly of this co, in the 58th year of her age

601. TLM Nov 15 1825/Married Thurs last, by Rev N. B. Little, John Palmer to Miss Ann Cnodle, all of this co/Married same day by Rev B. Kurtz, John Deaver to Miss Caroine, dau of Dan'l Boerstler, of Funks-town

602. TLM Nov 22 1825/Married Sun last by Rev B. Kurtz, Daniel Magee to Miss Catharine Staunton, both of Funks-town/Another Rev Hero gone! Died at his res in Liberty-Town, Mon evening 14th inst, Maj. General Robert Cumming, commander of the second division of Md. Militia, in the 72d year of his age

603. TLM Nov 29 1825/Married 15th inst by Rev James Reid, John Buzzard to Miss Charlotte Ridenour, all of this co/Equity case - John Miller, vs. Andrew Beck and Susanna his wife, Thomas Binkley, William Binkley, Louisa Binkley, George Binkley, Ferdinand Binkley & Jacob Binkley. Object of the bill is to obtain decree for sale of real estate of John Miller, late of Wash co, decd. John Miller died intestate, seized of real estate which is vested by descent in his heirs above named. William Binkley, Louisa Binkley, George Binkley, and Ferdinand Binkley, the defendants, are under age of 21 and resided out of state of Md. The remainder of the said defendants reside in Wash Co

604. TLM Dec 6 1825/Married Thurs 24th ult, by Rev Metart, Philip Neibert to Miss Elizab. Householder, both of this co/Married at Balt Fri evening, 18th ult by Most Rev Archibishop Mareschal, Robert Coleman Brien, Esq. of Frederick co, to Miss Ann Elizabeth, dau of Luke Tiernan, Esq. of that city /Married 17th ult by Rev Martin, John Keedy, of this co, to Miss Elizabeth Kenege, of Frederick Co/Died Thurs evening last, at the house of her son, Dr. Frederick Dorsey, Mrs. Lucy Sprigg of Frederick co, in the 74th year of her age/Equity case of David Newcomer, vs. Rebecca Adams, and others, heirs of Henry Adams, decd - sale of house/Equity case - George Cronise vs. Richard Moore & Mary his wife & others, heirs of Jac. Beckly. Sale of property made/Equity case - Nicholas Baker, complainant vs Elizabeth Baker, Catharine Baker, Alexander Baker, William Webb & Mary Webb, his wife, Jno. Baker, Richard Baker, James Murray & Margaret Murray his wife. Object of bill is to procure a foreclosure of a mortgage from Maurice Baker, late of Wash co, decd, to complainant, of a tract called Baker's Rest, 130 acres. Maruice Baker died intestate, leaving a widow, Elizabeth Baker, and following children and heirs at law, Catharine Baker, Alexander Baker, Mary Webb, wife of William Webb, John Baker, Richard Baker, and Margaret Murray, wife of James Murray. John Baker, Richard Baker, James Murray and Margaret Murray, his wife are not residents of state of Md

THE TORCHLIGHT AND PUBLIC ADVERTISER (Hagerstown)

605. TLM Dec 13 1825/Married Thurs 24th ult by Rev B. Kurtz, John M'Coy to Miss Sarah Bond, both of this co/Married Thurs last, by same, David Hatter to Miss Elizabeth Kuntz, all of this co

606. TLM Dec 20 1825/Married 20th ult by Rev Denius, Rev Clingin, formerly of Montgomery co, and now of Boonsborough, to Mrs. Sarah Guyton, of this co/Married 1st inst in Montgomery co, by Rev Jones, Alfred Clagett, of this co, to Miss Susan Wilson, dau of Joseph Clagett, of the former co/Married 11th inst in Balt by Rev Ulhorn, Ferdinand Bodmann, of this place, to Miss C. Popplein, of that city/Married Thurs evening last, by Rev Bryan, Dr. Jos. C. Hays, to Miss Lavinia, 2d dau of Philip Grove, Esq. of Sharpsburg/Died Sat morning last at an advanced age, at his res in this co, Col. Josiah Price/Died Sat last, Miss Christiana Little, dau of Joseph Little, sen. of this place

607. TLM Jan 3 1826/Married Sun 4th ult by Rev G. L. Geeting, Henry Miller to Miss Catharine Glaze, both of Pleasant Valley/Married Thurs 8th by same Andrew Zeigler to Miss Sarah Marker, both of this co/Married Thurs 15th by same, John Myers, Jr. to Miss Mary Russell, both of this co/Married Tues 20th by Rev Kurtz, Samuel Gehr to Miss Elizabeth Miller, both of this co /Married Thurs 22d by same, Henry Snyder to Miss Catharine Lahm, both of this co/Married same day by same, John Gray to Miss Mary Clam, both of this co/Died Thurs 22d ult at res of her son Mr. Isaac Kershner, about 3 miles from Hagers-town, Mrs. Christiana Kershner, wife of Philip Kershner, aged 69 yrs/Died Thurs morning last, Mrs. --- Wolfersperger, wife of Mr. J. P. Wolfersperger of this co/In memory of Miss Christiana Little ---

608. TLM Jan 10 1826/Married 13th Dec last, by Rev F. Ruthrauff, Joseph Beard to Miss Darcus Ranes, both of Va/Married 26th by same, Jacob Stine to Miss Mary Hanes, both of this co/Married 1st inst by same, Jacob M. Rohrer, to Miss Mary Smith, both of this co/Married same day by same, Aaron Walker to Miss Mary Horsenest, both of this co/Married Thurs 29th Dec by Rev Dr. Jennings, Wilson L. George of this place, to Miss Elizabeth B. 3d dau of John E. Stansbury of Balt co/Lamentable occurrence - a fatal quarrel took place on Christmas day, at Mr. Hughes' Mount Alto Iron Works, between a white man named Pennell, and a black man, slave of Mr. Hughes. The former attempted to strike the latter with a shovel, and he evading the blow, seized what is termed a ravel, and gave stroke upon the head of Pennell, which fractured his skull. He lingered until the Fri morning following. He has left a wife and 6 children. The black fellow was committed to the jail of Franklin co, Fri last. - Adams Centinel, Jan 4.

609. TLM Jan 17 1826/Married Sun last by Rev Medtart, George Lorshbaugh to Miss Maria Renner, both of this place/Died 15th ult in Shippensburg, Pa, Rev Daniel Stevens, itinerant preacher of the Meth Episc Church, aged 67 yrs /Died 4th inst at his res on Bever Creek, Rev Peter Newcomer, aged about 73 yrs/Died 6th inst at his res near town, John Moyer, in the 71st year of his age, of this co/Died in this place Sun night last, in the 85th year of his age, George Bradshaw, a rev soldier

610. TLM Jan 24 1826/Married 19th ult by Rev Snow, Samuel Baker to Miss Mary Leighter, both of this co/Married 10th inst by Rev F. Ruthrauff, Jona-

THE TORCHLIGHT AND PUBLIC ADVERTISER (Hagerstown)

than Wachtel to Miss Pamelia Baxton/Died Sun afternoon last in the 69th year of her age, Mrs. Isabella Neill, mother of Alexander Neill, Esq. of this place/Died - Notly M. Ball, in Williams-Port Wed last, for some time previous engaged in the store of Thomas W. Hoffman, a young man of mild and conciliatory disposition/John Clippinger offers reward for apprentice to the wagon making business, Abraham Rockafield, 19-20 yrs of age, 5 ft 6-7 inch

611. TLM Jan 31 1826/Died Sat morning last at Newcomer's Hotel in this place, in the 65th year of his age, John Rohrer, Sen. of Pleasant Valley, in this co, for the last 30 yrs much affected by the stone in his bladder and came to town about a fortnight since, for the purpose of being operated on. On Saturday week last, Dr. Macgill performed the operation and extracted the stone which was nearly 2 inches in length by about 1 1/8 inches in width and 3/4 in thickness. The operation was performed in 5 minutes and general aspect considered quite favorable/Died in Boonsborough 25th inst, Michael Stonebraker, aged 40 yrs, 1 month, 13 days

612. TLM Feb 7 1826/Married Thurs 26th ult by Rev B. Kurtz, Jacob Poffenberger to Miss Amelia Stoufer, all of this co/Died Thurs last in the 24th year of her age, Miss Elizabeth Newcomer, dau of David Newcomer, of this co/Died Sun last, Mrs. Nunamacher, wife of Mr. Nunamacher, of the vicinity of Hagers-town

613. TLM Feb 14 1826/Died at his res near Mount Vernon, Ohio, Nov last in the 73d year of his age, Frederick Brentlinger, formerly of this place, rev soldier, present at the fall of Montgomery at Quebeck/Died in Balt Wed morning last, aged 88, James Inglis

614. TLM Feb 21 1826/On Wed 8th inst Thomas Kennedy and Mrs. Dorothea Kennedy, his wife, of Perry co, Pa, in attempting to cross the Conodoguinnet creek, on the ice, broke through and lost their lives/Married Tues 7th inst, by Rev Kellar, John Shaw to Miss Julian Coon, both of Winchester, Va/Died Mon 13th inst, at his res in this co, Charles Bean, son of George Bean, of this town/Died Tues night 15th inst in the 32d year of her age, Mrs. Mary Dechert, widow of the late Peter S. Dechert, Esq. of Chambersburg, and dau of David Harry of this place, after an illness of more than 3 yrs/Died a few days since, after a short illness, at Poplar Springs, Benjamin Kershner, of this co. The decd was on his road home from Balt, where he had been with his wagon

615. TLM Feb 28 1826/Married Thurs 17th inst by Rev Geo. Schmucker, John F. Bryan of this co to Miss Sarah B., dau of Thomas Sappington, of Jefferson co, Va/Married Tues last by Rev Kurtz, Rev N. B. Little to Miss Ann Fouke, dau of Henry Fouke of this co/Married Sun last by same, William M'Dade, to Miss Catharine Burns/Died Thurs last in 26(?)th year of her age, after a lingering pulmonary indisposition, Miss Mary Ann Reynolds, dau of Maj. John Reynolds, of this place

616. TLM Mar 7 1826/Married Thurs 23d ult by Rev Jon. Ruthrauff, John Witmer to Miss Elizabeth Shank/Married same day by same, Jacob Smith to Miss Mary Snider, all of Green-Castle, Franklin co, Pa/Died Fri last, Daniel Hughes Esq. of this place

THE TORCHLIGHT AND PUBLIC ADVERTISER (Hagerstown)

617. TLM Mar 14 1826/Married at Steubenville, Ohio, 1 inst by Rev James Morrow, Joseph Ashbury, formerly of this co, to Miss Elizabeth Jones of Pittsburg, Pa/Married in Balt on 21 Feb by Rev Joseph Frye, Rev Robert S. Vinton of Washington City, to Miss Juliet Matilda Berry of Balt Co/Married in Balt 1st inst by Rev Davis, Levin Mills to Mrs. Elizabeth Brown/Married in Georgetown, D. C. Tues evening by Rev Balch, Dr. R. H. Beatty of Hancock, Md. to Miss Mary C. Ott, dau of late Dr. John Ott of the former place/Married Thurs 1st by Rev B. Kurtz, Charles Frick to Miss Martha Elliott, both of this place

618. TLM Mar 21 1826/Married 6th inst by Rev F. Ruthrauff, William Lilly to Miss Jane Fleming/Married 9th inst by same, Samuel Baker to Miss Elizabeth Martin/Married same day by Rev Medtart, Jacob Poorman to Miss Nancy M'Clain /Married same day by same, Daniel Housley to Miss Elizabeth Shenafelt/Married Tues evening last by Rev Clarke, John G. Beard to Miss Ann M. Lane, both of this place

619. TLM Mar 28 1826/Married Thurs 9th inst by Rev A. M'Candlass, James Noble Nesbit, merchant, of Stewartsville, Westmoreland co, formerly of M'Connell's burgh, to Miss Mary Logan of Westmoreland co, Pa/Married Tues last, by Rev Lemmon, Mark Giles to Miss Harriet Rewlett/Married Thurs last by Rev Medtart, George Baer to Miss Elizabeth Todd/Married same day by Rev Ruthrauff, Daniel Startzman to Miss Ann Stahl/Married same day by same, James M'Coy to Mrs. Mary Withney/Married Sun last by Rev Keedy, Peter Benner to Miss Sophia Stoner/Died after a long and severe illness Fri 17th inst at her late res on West River, Mrs. Mary Galloway/Died in this place at an advanced age, Thurs last, Mrs. Catharine Shank, wife of George Shank

620. TLM Apr 4 1826/Married in Balt Thurs morning last by Rev Ulhurn, Samuel Rohrer, of this place, to Miss Elizabeth Schultz, of the former place /Married same day by Rev Medtart, William Boren, to Miss Sarah Hamilton, both of Funks-town/Married Sun last by Rev George Lemmon, George Gower, to Miss Mary Ann Bond, all of this co/Died Thurs evening last, at res of John Weis, of this place, Mrs. Ann Margaret Keller, in the 79th year of her age /Equity case - Robert Clagett, John Grim and Agnes his wife, vs. Peter Sigler and Lydia his wife, John Heastand & Abby his wife, Wm. Shilling and Hannah his wife, Matthias Sly and Sophia his wife, David Martin and Samuel Martin. Object of bill is to obtain decree for sale of real estate of David Martin, late of Wash co for the payment of debts and balance to be divided among the heirs. David Martin died intestate, indebted to a large amount to Robert Clagett. The following are heirs at law: Agnes who m John Grim, Lydia who m Peter Sigler, Abby who m John Heastand, Hannah who m William Shilling, Sophia who m Matthia Sly, David Martin and Samuel Martin. All defendants res out of the state of Md

621. TLM Tues Apr 11 1826/Married in Hampton, Sat evening 1st inst by Rev Richard Gilliam, Capt. William Whitfield, aged 21 years, to Miss Mary Allmand, aged 95 yrs, all of Hampton/Married in Frederick Thurs last by Rev Jonathan Helfenstein, Charles Nagle, editor of the Republican Gazette and Political Intelligencer, to Miss Sophia Rollington, all of that city/Died in this place Sat evening last, in the 75th year of age, William Bomgardner, soldier of the rev

THE TORCHLIGHT AND PUBLIC ADVERTISER (Hagerstown)

622. TLM Thurs Apr 20 1826/Married 9th inst, Jacob Kershner to Mrs. Catharine Albert, both of this co/Married Sun last, in Green-Castle, Jacob Seuter to Miss Rebecca Creager, both of this town

623. TLM Apr 27 1826/Married Thurs 13th inst by Rev George Geeting, John J. Keedy to Miss Mary Ann Middlekauff, dau of Christian Middlekauff, all of this co/Married Thurs last by Rev Medtart, Solomon Praime to Miss Orphit Taylor/Died near Norris-town, Montgomery co, Pa, 16 Apr inst, Mrs. Margaret Clay, wife of Rev J. C. Clay, aged 28 yrs, after a long illness, taking with her a little infant son, William Annan Clay, born but a few hrs before her death, and after a sickly existence of 48 hrs, consigned to the same coffin and same grave with the mother

624. TLM May 4 1826/Married Tues 25th ult by Rev N. B. Little, John Boose, of Cumberland to Mrs. Elizabeth Wengert, of Alleghany co/Married same day by same, George Tilghman, of this co, to Miss Anna Lynn, dau of Capt. D. Lynn, of Cumberland/Died at Harpers-Ferry, Va, 23 ult, Mrs. Margaret Hawken, formerly of this place

625. TLM May 11 1826/Married Thurs 27th ult by Rev Isaac Kellar, John T. Miller, to Miss Susan Ankeny, dau of Henry Ankeny, all of this co/Died Tues morning 2d inst at her res in Pleasant Valley, Wash Co, in theh 45th year of her age, Mrs. Elizabeth Keller, widow of late Joseph C. Keller, of this co /Died Thurs 4th inst, Mrs. Ann Gibbony, wife of John Gibbony, of this co, in the 39th year of her age/Died Sat 6th inst in this town, Elias Couter, in the 52d year of his age

626. TLM May 18 1826/Married 2d inst by Rev Geo. Lemmon, James Hanagan of Va, to Miss Catharine Wherrit of this co/Married Thurs evening last by Rev Isaac Kellar, David Zeller, to Miss Theresa Rench, all of this co/Married same evening in Winchester, Va, by Rev Dr. Hill, Samuel Johnston, formerly of this place, to Miss Jane Hoye, of the former place

627. TLM May 25 1826/Married Tues evening last, by Rev I. Kellar, Greenberry Barker Wilson of Balt, to Miss Louisiana Orndorff, of this co/Married Wed evening last by Rev Medtart, Samuel Bentz, to Miss Maria Stonebraker/Married Thurs morning by same, Isaac Miller, to Miss Eliza Fisher/Died Mon last, Samuel Middelkaff, son of Leonard Middelkaff, of this co

628. TLM Jun 1 1826/Died Sun last, Daniel Gelwicks of this town/Shepherd's-town, May 24. Yesterday evening a young man of this neighborhood, John Lickliter, after disengaging his horse from the plough, and mounting, for the purpose of coming home, from an alarm in the animal, was thrown from its back, and being entangled in the gears, was dreadfully mangled and killed

629. TLM Jun 8 1826/Edward Hughes, a young man in the employ of Mr. Lloyd, was very much injured on Thurs last, by an accidental explosion in a stone quarry in this vicinity, in which he was working. By this accident he was much mangled, and deprived of one eye with little hope of the other one being saved. He was in the habit of appropriating part of his hard earnings to the support of his mother, a poor woman living in Chambersburg/Married in this co Sun 28 May by Rev Barnes, Joseph Menghinne, to Miss Joida E. A.

THE TORCHLIGHT AND PUBLIC ADVERTISER (Hagerstown)

Flagg, dau of Joseph Flagg, all of Berkeley co, Va/Married Tues evening May 30, by Most Rev Archibishop Mareshal, Francis E. Rozer, of Notley Hall, Prince Georges co, Md. to Miss Harriet E. Brooke of Balt, dau of late Richard Brooke, Esq. of Frederick-town/Married Thurs evening May 25, by Rev Matthews, Daniel Kretzer of Jefferson co, Va, to Miss Maria Ann Miller of this co/Married same day by same, David Kretzer of Jefferson co, Va to Miss Rosanna Poffenberger of this co/Died Sun 28 ult after a most painfully protracted illness, Mrs. Sarah Galloway, relict of the late John Galloway, Esq. of Tulip Hill, Anne Arundel co, Md. and dau of late Benjamin Chew, Esq. of Phila, formerly chief justice of the state of Pa, at the advanced age of 73/Died in city of Balt Mon evening 5th inst, William C. Inglis, in the 23rd year of his age/John Newcomer, on Beaver creek, offers 6 1/2 cents reward for apprentice to the milling business, named Henry Lizar, 19-20 yrs of age

630. TLM Jun 15 1826/Married Thurs last by Rev F. Ruthrauff, Daniel M'Fee to Miss Catharine Brown, both of Frederick Co/Married same day by same, Martin Dieffenbacher to Miss Nancy Schweitzer, both of this co/Married Tues 30th ult by Rev Isaac Kellar, Matthew Spear to Miss Martha Anderson/Married Thurs 1st inst by same, Jacob Emswiler to Miss Elizabeth Newby/Died Fri last a little before 3 o'clock, P.M. at her res in Washington City, Mary A. Ringgold, consort of Tench Ringgold, Esq. Marshal for the District of Columbia, in the 32d year of her age

631. TLM Jun 22 1826/Married Thurs 8th inst by Rev Buchanan, Daniel Miller of this co to Miss Eleanor B. Miller, dau of Daniel Miller of Franklin co, Pa/Married Sun 11th inst by Rev Walsh, at the res of the hon. John Lee, in Frederick co, Dennis O'Byrne(?), Esq. to Miss Amelia Cooper, both of this co/Married Thurs last by Rev J. Reid, John Dorby of Williams-Port, to Miss Margaret Walker, of this place/Died 9th inst at New Haven, Rev Jedediah Morse, D.D.L.L.D. aged 65 yrs/Died same day near Green-Castle, Pa, in the 28th year of her age, Mrs. Mary G. McLanahan, consort of William McLanahan, after 14 yrs of illness - Frankin Repository/Died Mon night 12th inst, John Randall, Esq. Collector of the Port of Annapolis, after a short illness, one of the oldest citizens of that place/Died Fri morning last in this place, Joseph M'Ilhenny, in the 42d year of his age

632. TLM Jun 29 1826/Married Tues 27th inst by Rev Ruthrauff, Isaac C. Lutz, to Miss Matilda Calbert, both of this co/Died Mon 26 inst at his res near Clear Spring, in this co, George Mish, formerly of Cumberland co, Pa, in the 55th year of his age

633. TLM Jul 6 1826/Death of Samuel Martin Fri night last in the 62d year of his age; interred Presby grave yard. He was the humane and faithful jailer the co. In exerting himself during a recent cold and rainy night to overtake and apprehend a prisoner who had made his escape from the jail, which he succeeded in doing, he contracted the disease that terminated, after a few days continuance, his unobtusive but useful life

634. TLM Jul 13 1826/Married Thurs last by Rev Buchanan, Dr. Samuel Duffield of McConnellsburg, to Miss Matilda McDowell, of Green-Castle/Died 12th inst after a protracted illness, in the 54th year of his age, George C. Smoot, Esq. Register of Wills for Wash co/Died on night of 12 inst in 50th

83

THE TORCHLIGHT AND PUBLIC ADVERTISER (Hagerstown)

year of her age, Mrs. Margaret Bender, wife of George Bender of this place /Died 2d inst at Lancaster, Pa, in the 32d year of his age, Colin Cooke, Esq. formerly of this place/F. & E. B. Kinsell, Hagers-town, offer reward 1 cent reward for indented apprentice to the Hair Dressing business, Hughes Walkinghood, about 18 yrs of age, 5 ft 7-8 inch, dark complexion, down look when spoken to/Isaac Roland cautions persons against trusting his wife Elizabeth, as he is determined to pay no debts contracted by her/Equity case - Jacob Baker & others vs William W. Evans & others, heirs at law of Jere. Chapline, decd. This supplementary bill states that since the exhibition of the original bill William Wilson the infant defendant has died. William W. Evans and Sarah his wife have put in their answers to the original. Susanna Chapline after she attained age of 21 yrs and before her marriage with John K. Wilson received a portion of the purchase of her interest in said land from said Jacob Baker. William W. Evans and Sarah his wife reside out of the State of Md.

635. TLM Jul 27 1826/Died at Tammany Mount, res of Mrs. Van Lear, Wash Co, Tues morning last, Matthew Van Lear Ramsay, son of Col. John Ramsay, of Pittsburg, in the 21st year of his age; he had an affectionate brother at his side; remains interred in grave yard at Williams-Port

636. TLM Aug 3 1826/Died in this town, Sun morning last, George F. Kreps, in the 28th year of his age

637. TLM Aug 10 1826/Married Thurs 27 Jul by Rev Charles Helfenstein, Levi H. Swigart of this place, and formerly of Berlin, Adams Co, to Miss Catharine B. Noel of York, Pa/Married 3d inst by Rev Ruthrauff, John Miller, to Miss Mary Lechrone/Married Tues last by same, William D. Brown to Miss Mary Thomas/Married same day by Rev Medtart, Rev Leonard H. Johns of Georgetown, D. C. to Miss Henrietta Geiger, of this place/Died Sat morning last, at his res in Boonsboro', Matthias Shaffner, formerly Sheriff of this co, and for many yrs an inhabitant of this town

638. TLM Aug 17 1826/Married in Mercersburg, Pa, Thurs last by Rev David Elliott, Thomas Grubb, merchant, to Miss Eliza V. L. Cowan, all of that place/Married Tues morning last, by Rev Reid, Thomas M. Waugh to Miss Eliza M. Kealhofer, dau of John Kealhofer, all of this place/Married same day, by Rev Ruthrauff, Mr. Van S. Brashear to Miss Mary Lynch/Married same day by same, John Spitzel to Miss Hannah Grove

639. TLM Aug 24 1826/Married Thurs 14th inst by Rev Geo. Geeting, John Grim to Miss Susan Rohrer/Married Tues 15th by same, John Domer to Miss Sarah Myers, both of this co/Married Thurs 17th by same, George Hoffmaster to Miss Elizabeth Eakle, both of Pleasant Valley/Died at her res in Prince George's Co, Md., Mon 14th inst in the 45th year of her age, Mrs. Eleanor Lee Kent, consort of Hon. Joseph Kent, Gov. of Md/Died same day in city of Balt, Mrs. Elizabeth Kemp, consort of Right Rev James Kemp/Died 14th inst at res of her father in Allegany co, in the 5th year of her age, Margaret, eldest dau of Michael C. Sprigg, Esq./Died in Georgetown, Wed 16th inst, Mrs. Prudence H. Stull, consort of J. I. Stull, Esq. She had lived near to the completion of her 45th year/Death of Paul Allen, writer, after a short illness, this morning - Balt Gazette, Aug 19.

THE TORCHLIGHT AND PUBLIC ADVERTISER (Hagerstown)

640. TLM Aug 31 1826/Married Thurs last by Rev Ruthrauff, Solomon Patterson to Miss Susanna Panell/Married Sun last by same, John Fogler to Miss Catharine Meisner/Married same day by Rev Medtart, Isaac Wikes to Miss Eliza Tritch/Married Sun 20th inst by Rev George Geeting, Jacob Lop to Miss Susanna Kretzzinger/Died on his farm in Wash co, 24th inst, of a bilious fever, Geo. Lowe, in the 63d year of his age, born and raised in Prince George's Co/Died early in this month at the Sulphur Springs, Monroe Co, Va, Addison Ridout, Esq., Attorney at Law, of Annapolis, aged about 31, elected at last election a Delegate to the Legislature from his native City/Died at Fort Wayne, Indiana, 8th inst of bilious fever, James Shriver, Esq. of Union town, Pa. He was attending to his duties as U.S. Engineer in the neighborhood of Brookville

641. TLM Sep 7 1826/Married Thurs last by Rev Ruthrauff, Josiah Kershner to Miss Susanna Snider/Married Sun last by Rev Medtart, John Glass to Miss Lydia Stiffler/Married Fri last by same, Daniel Winders to Miss Catharine M. Knode/Married same day by Rev Lemon, Peter Koontz of Winchester, to Mrs. Mary Miller of this place/Died Mon last in this town, Mrs. Mary Dean, in the 28th year of her age/John Dillon, Hagers-town, offers reward for apprentice to the boot & shoe making business, by name of Joseph Gletner, 19 yrs of age, 5 ft 5-6 inch, has stiff knee and a failure in one of his eyes, remarkably lazy

642. TLM Sep 14 1826/Married Wed 6th inst by Rev Clingen, Samuel Cunningham to Miss Elizabeth Macken, both of Pleasant Valley/Married Thurs 7th, by Rev Isaac Kellar, Daniel Washabaugh, of Chambersburg, Pa, to Miss Sarah M'Laughlin, dau of Henry M'Laughlin, of this co/Married same day in Prince William co, Va, Jacob Snively, of Hancock, to Miss Harriet Blackwell, dau of D. Blackwell, Esq./Married Thurs last, by Rev Medtart, John Lantz to Miss Catharine Roads/Married Tues evening last, by same, Samuel L. Hesser to Miss Ann Maria Slagle, both of Winchester, Va/Married same evening by same, Samuel Bender, formerly of this place, to Miss Mary Effenger, of Woodstock, Va /Married same evening by same, J. F. Haines to Miss Harriet Fry, both of this same place/Married same evening by Rev Ryan, Dr. George L. Hardey, to Miss Editha Edwards, dau of Thomas Edwards, all of Boonsborough/Died 6th inst at his res in Loudoun co, Va, Samuel Clapham, Esq./Died in Green-Castle, Aug 26th, after a few days illness, William Young Campbell Lind, youngest son of late Rev John Lind, aged 3 yrs, 3 months

643. TLM Sep 21 1826/Married Sun last by Rev F. Ruthrauff, Michael Boward to Mrs. Catharine Kershner/Died in Hancock Mon evening 11th inst, Joshua B. Miles/Died Wed 13th inst at his res in Williams-Port, John Hogg, aged about 70 yrs, oldest inhabitant of that place

644. TLM Sep 28 1826/Married Tues last by Rev Kroh, Edward Smith to Miss Elizabeth Justice, both of this co/Married same day by Rev Ruthrauff, Henry Lutz to Miss Frances Mowdy, both of this co/Died at Sulphur Spring, Va, in the early part of the present month, Miss Harriet Ridout, dau of Samuel Ridout, Esq. of Annapolis/Died Fri last after a short illness, Mrs. Susanna Shafer, consort of Jonathan Shafer, Esq. of Boonsborough, in the 27th year of her age/Poem to Dr. Smith from Williams-Port, Sep 25 1826 - "The scene of life with him is ended ... etc."

THE TORCHLIGHT AND PUBLIC ADVERTISER (Hagerstown)

645. TLM Oct 5 1826/Married Thurs evening last by Rev Isaac Kellar, Kennedy T. Friend, of Williams-Port, to Miss Sevilla S., eldest dau of Charles Shaffner, of this place/Married same day by Rev Medtart, Robert Hanna to Miss Catharine Billmire/Died Sun last by same, Henry Davis to Miss Frances Shirley/Died yesterday, Mrs. Tarlton, wife of Mr. Tarlton of this co

646. TLM Oct 12 1826/Married Thurs evening last by Rev Ruthrauff, John Baumgartner, to Miss Charlotte Wilks, all of this town/Died Thurs last, at Harper's Ferry, of bilious fever, Edward Wager, leaving husband and 4 children/Died Thurs last at Clear Spring, Samuel Neill, Merchant, aged about 26 yrs, interred in Episc burial ground/Died Tues morning last in same place, Adam Neill, in the 18th year of his age, brother of Samuel Neill

647. TLM Oct 19 1826/Married Thurs evening last by Rev Lemmon, Jacob S. Smith, to Miss Sarah Ann, dau of Benjamin Yoe, Esq. all of this town/Married same evening by Rev Geo. Geeting, Jacob Grice to Miss Elizabeth Myers, all of this co

648. TLM Oct 26 1826/Married Sun last by Rev Geo. Geeting, John Mullen, to Miss Barbara Ann Lorshbaugh, all of this co/Married Thurs 12th inst by Rev Ruthrauff, Solomon Davis to Miss Mary Zuck/Married Thurs 19th by same, John Finfrock to Mrs. Margaret Beatty/Died 19 inst at his res in Pleasant Valley, John Crampton, Sen., in the 60th year of his age/Died Fri night last in Pleasant Valley in 82d year of her age, Mrs. Brown, widow of late Rudolph Brown; she had 86 grand children and 36 great grand children

649. TLM Nov 2 1826/Died Wed 1st inst in the 49th year of age, Mrs. Maria Newcomer, consort of David Newcomer, of this co, leaving husband and family of children, after long illness/Died recently in Phila, Selleck Osborn, poet and editor of several newspapers

650. TLM Nov 9 1826/Married Sat 21st Oct by Rev Medtart, Hillery B. Talbott to Mrs. Margaret L. Bennett/Married Tues last by same, John D. Fisher to Miss Sarah South/Married 24 Oct by Rev Ruthrauff, Abraham Shanefelt, to Miss Nancy Lechrone

651. TLM Nov 16 1826/Died in this place Wed last, Mrs. Catharine Irvine, wife of Jacob Irvine, in the 70th year of her age

652. TLM Nov 23 1826/Married Thurs evening last, by Rev Lemmon, George M. Potts, Esq. of Frederick to Miss Cornelia, dau of Gen. Samuel Ringgold, of this town/Married in Greencastle, Sun 5th inst, by William Wood, Esq. Bartholomew Thacher to Miss Barbara Hammell, both of this co/Married in Greencastle Thurs last by same, John Streepey to Miss Mary Miller, both of this co/Marriage Extraordinary! On Monday (13th) in Woodstock, Mr. Leonard Lonas, a doughty old gentleman who has weathered out 87 winters, to the buxom Miss Katy Mumau, aged 42 - The snow headed groom dropped a tear over the grave of his former wife but two weeks ago and his dulcinea Miss Katy, buried her father the evening before the wedding day. So wags the world - No accounting for tastes or fashions. Cupid is a sly God - no wonder he is always laughing. - Sentinel

THE TORCHLIGHT AND PUBLIC ADVERTISER (Hagerstown)

653. TLM Dec 14 1826/Married Tues last by Rev Ruthrauff, John Cameron to Miss Ann M'Fall, both of Shepherds-town, Va

654. TLM Dec 21 1826/Married Tues 12th inst by Rev Denius, Jacob Necodemus to Miss Rawana Hess, dau of David Hess, Esq./Married Thurs last by Rev Medtart, James Chambers of Frederick City, to Miss Mary Hahn, of this place /Married same day by same, Samuel Kaffman to Miss Cordelia James/Chambersburg, Dec 19 - Died in this borough, yesterday morning, of the prevailing fever, William S. Buchanan, Esq. attorney at law, a young gentleman who has just entered upon the practice of law/Died in this borough at the res of John Aughinbaugh Wed night last of the prevailing fever, Henry Aughinbaugh, aged 25 yrs/Died lately in Mercersburgh, Mrs. Magaw, aged lady - Frank. Repos.

655. TLM Dec 28 1826/Married Thurs last by Rev Isaac Kellar, Samuel Zellers to Miss Margaret Young, both of this co/Married 4th inst, by Rev Brunner, Mahlon Jennings to Miss Mary Collins/Married by same Thurs last, Elisha B. Miller, of Franklin Co, Pa, to Miss Sarah, dau of David Newcomer, of this co/Died very suddenly, yesterday morning, in the 58th year of her age, Mrs. Catharine Leight, wife of Benjamin Leight, of this town

656. TLM Jan 4 1827/Married 24th ult by Rev F. Ruthrauff, David Dasher, to Mrs. Christiana Glossbrenner, both of this place/Married 26th ult in Balt by same, David Ruthrauff, of Franklin Co, Pa, to Miss Eliza Hake, of the former place/Married 19th ult by Rev Isaac Kellar, George Keefer to Miss Susanna Fogwell, both of this co/Married 26th ult by same, Thomas Brady of Franklin co, Pa, to Miss Sarah Martin of this co/Married Thurs last by Rev James Reid, David T. Wilson to Miss Susan Bean, dau of Barton Bean, all of this co/William Weise offers reward for apprentice boy named Samuel Snider, being guilty of very bad conduct, about 20 yrs of age, 5 ft 4 1/2 inch, light hair, fair complexion

657. TLM Jan 11 1827/Died at his res near Smithsburg, Fri 22d ult, in the 65th year of his age, James M'Kissick, old inhabitant of this co/Died on board the U.S. Schooner Grampus, on her passage from Pensacola to Havana, on the morning of the 30th of Nov, Lieut. Com'dt Joseph Cassin, of the U.S. Navy, and at 4 o'clock in the afternoon of the same day his remains committed to the deep - Norfolk Beacon of Dec.

658. TLM Jan 18 1827/Married Tues last by Rev Bruner, John Summer to Miss Sarah Rowland, all of this co/Died at Green-Castle on Fri last, after a severe indisposition, Solomon Newcomer, in the 17th year of his age, youngest son of Mr. C. Newcomer, Jr. of this town

659. TLM Jan 25 1827/Married Wed evening 17th inst by Rev Brooke, Dr. Thos. Hammond, of Sharpsburg, to Miss Ann Shepherd, dau of late Capt. Abraham Shepherd, of Jefferson co, Va./Married Thurs 18th, by Rev I. Keller, John Tice to Miss Maria, dau of Col. John M'Lain, all of this co/Married 18th inst at Williams-Port by Rev F. Ruthruff, Jacob Picking to Miss Eleanor Williams, both of the same place/Married in Green-Castle, on 11th inst by Wm Wood, Esq. Daniel Hedrick to Miss Margaret Myers, both of this co/From a letter from the Post-Master at Potosi, Missouri, we learn that James Milli-

THE TORCHLIGHT AND PUBLIC ADVERTISER (Hagerstown)

gan, formerly of Hagers-town, died in that place, sometime in Dec last/Died at res of his dau (widow of late James Scott) in Cumberland, Joseph Cresap, Esq. at an advanced age/John Brewer, Esq., Chief Clerk of the House of Delegates of Md., died Sat evening last at Annapolis

660. TLM Feb 1 1827/Married Thures last by Rev Ruthrauff, William Stoops to Miss Amelia Startzman, dau of Peter Startzman, all of this co/Married Thurs 18th ult by Rev Medtart, Thomas Albert, to Miss Hannah Cross/Married Tues morning last by same, John Hansher, to Miss Ann O. Rorriock

661. TLM Feb 8 1827/Married at Williams-port Sun evening last by Rev Rothrauff, John Nitzel, to Miss Eliza Hammond, both of that place/Married Tues 6th inst by Rev James Reid, Solomon Shefy of Adams co, Pa, to Miss Catharine McNeel, dau of John McNeel, of Frederick Co/Died 25 ult at his res in Rockville, Col. Upton Beal, about 58 yrs, upwards of 30 yrs, clerk of Mont co court/Died at Mansfield, Ohio, 21st ult, in the 34th year of her age, Mrs. Catharine Stoudt, wife of William Stoudt, late of Hagers-town/Died Sun last, Jacob Irwin, old inhabitant of this place/Died - Michael House, another of the small remnant of Rev heroes, at his res in this town, Thurs last in the 76th year of his age

662. TLM Feb 15 1827/Died yesterday morning, after a long pulmonary illness, Mrs. Margaret Hanenkampf, widow of late Dr. Hanenkampf, and eldest dau of Peter Humrickhouse, of this place - dau, wife, parent/Married 1st inst, by Rev Clarkson, Jacob Shaffer of Mercersburg, Pa, to Miss Lydia Smith, dau of Fred'k Smith, of Licking creek, near Mercersburg/Married Thurs last by Rev N. B. Little, Philip Wingert, Esq. of this place, to Miss Martha Tomlinson, dau of Benj. Tomlinson, Esq. of Allegany Co/Married Sun last by Rev Denius, David Barkman, to Miss Rebecca Gryton, both of Boonsborough/Married Mon last by same, John Emmerson to Miss Margaret Bridgman, both of Shepherds-town, Va

663. TLM Feb 22 1827/Died 12th inst, after an illness of 18 hrs, Mrs. Elizabeth Gaither in 41st year of her age, wife of Zachariah Gaither, at the Big Spring, in this co/Died 13th inst in 16th year of her age, Miss Catharine Emert, dau of John Emmert, of this co/Married Sun 28 ult by Rev Keedy, James Harper to Mrs. Hovermale, both of this co/Married Sun 4th inst by Rev Helfenstein, of Frederick city, John Knode to Miss Susana Cronise, both of Sharpsburg/Married Thurs 8th inst by Rev Bruner, John Troup, to Miss Sally Teischer

664. TLM Mar 1 1827/Equity case - Jacob Leckrone, Peter Sailor, Jun., Martin Bachtel vs Sarah Shanefelt, Peter Snider & Mary his wife, Henry Shanefelt, Andrew Shanefelt, Daniel Shanefelt, Susanna Shanefelt, David Shanefelt, John Shanefelt, William Shanefelt and Jacob Shanefelt

665. TLM Mar 8 1827/Married at New York, Lewis Silver, merchant of Balt, and formerly of this place, to Miss Leah, dau of Jacob Abrahams, of New York /Married 15th ult by Rev Robert Kennedy, Rev John H. Kennedy, Pastor of the 6th Presby Church, Phila, to Miss Harriet M'Callmot of Crescentsville/Married Thurs 22d ult by Rev Isaac Kellar, Benjamin Brown to Miss Matilda Moudy/Married Tues last by same, Philip Ottenberger, to Miss Lydia Frantz,

88

THE TORCHLIGHT AND PUBLIC ADVERTISER (Hagerstown)

all of this co/Died in Balt Co, 22d ult Edward Reside, native of Scotland, in the 82d year of his age; he had resided in that co 50 yrs/Died 27th ult in Pleasant Valley, Henry Eakle, in the 76th year of his age/Died in this place Tues morning last, at an advanced age, Mrs. Magdalena Stemple, consort of late Christian Stemple

666. TLM Mar 15 1827/Died Fri last in Green-Castle, Pa, Miss Rebecca Coffroth, in the 19th year of her age, leaving father and mother/Married 1st inst by Rev F. Rothrauff, Jacob Rinehart to Miss Elizabeth Westenberger/Married 8th inst by same, Peter Brewer to Miss Sarah Cross, all of this co /James Watson, Clear Spring, offers reward of 6 cents and 3 false spokes for indented apprentice to wagon making business, named John Tracy, about 18 yrs of age, 5 ft 8-10 inch, stout and well built, inclinded to be lazy

667. TLM Mar 22 1827/Married 18u ult by Rev Geo. Geeting, Adam Sumers to Miss Nancy Hines/Married 21st by same, John Beatty to Mrs. Sarah Mix/Married 7 inst by same, Joel Doup to Miss Mary Schlosser/Married same day by same, Alexander Downs to Miss Mary Ann Stiffler, all of this co/Married 6th inst by Rev Rawhousk, John Byers to Miss Fanny Ditwiler, of Pa/Married 8th inst by Rev M. Bruner, Andrew Shank to Miss Esther Hoover/Married 15th inst by same, Lewis Kellar to Mrs. Margaret Lekrone/Married 20 inst by same, Abraham Van Metre to Miss Maria C. Van Metre/Married Tues 13th inst by Rev Isaac Kellar, John Gibbony of this co to Martha Gibson of Bedford Co, Pa/Married Thurs last by same, William Davis to Mrs. Elizabeth Clayton, both of this co/Married Wed last by Rev M.L. Fullerton, Humphrey Fullerton, of Westmoreland co, Pa, to Miss Elenora G. Davidson, of this co/Died Thurs last, Miss Catharine, dau of Stephen Rigler of this borough, aged about 9 yrs - Chambersburg Repository

668. TLM Mar 28 1827/Married Tues 13th inst, by Rev Medtart, Jacob Bowman to Miss Lucy M'Afee/Married Thurs last by same, William Jones to Miss Sarah Ann South/Married Thurs last by Rev Isaac Keller, John Barnett to Miss Amelia Moudy/Married same day by same, John Albert to Miss Nancy Hoover /Married Sun last by Rev F. Ruthrauff, Henry Wallmeyer to Miss Elizabeth Zoll/Died Mon last at his res in Sharpsburg, John Beard, at an advanced age/Died Mon last in this town, Mr. Gaver, at an advanced age/Died at his res near Sharpsburg, 21st inst, Joseph Smith (eldest son of George Smith, Esq. of Sharpsburg) in the 38th year of his age; discourse delivered in Meth Episc Church by Rev John Matthews of Shepherds-town, Va/Died Thurs evening last, after a lingering illness of many months, Mrs. Ann Rawlings, relict of late Solomon Rawlings, of this place, interred in Meth Episc burial ground; she was long a member of the Meth Episc Church

669. TLM Apr 5 1827/Died at res of Alexander Mitchell, near Hagers-town, Thurs last, Mrs. Nancy Stewart, dau of late Col. John Carr of this co, and relict of Rev George Stewart of the Associate Reformed Church, long confined by a chronic disease/Died at Cave-town Sun, Mrs. Susan Boyd, wife of Marmaduke W. Boyd, Esq. and dau of Col. Jonas Hogmire/Equity case - Margaret Ham and George Hedrick vs Peter Ham, John Ham and others. Object of the bill is to obtain decree for sale of estate of Peter Ham, decd, and a division of the proceeds amongst his devisees, after allowing out of the same to Margaret Ham, such as her equivalent to her life estate therein. The bill

THE TORCHLIGHT AND PUBLIC ADVERTISER (Hagerstown)

states that Peter Ham, by his will devisees all his estate to his wife Margaret Hamm for life, except a tan-yard in Sharpsburg, which he gave to his two sons John and Joseph Ham, and ofter the death of his wife the said estate to be sold and proceeds divided among his children, Peter, John, Joseph, Catharine, Sarah and Elizabeth, and his grand daughter Sarah Ham. Defendants Peter Ham, John Ham, Joseph Ham and Sarah Ham now married to Michael Rouner, all reside out of the state of Md/Equity case - Martin Beam vs Jacob Beam and other. The bill is to obtain a decree for sale of tract devised by Jacob Nesly of Lancaster Co, Pa, to his dau Barbara Beam and his son Joseph Nesly. The bill states that Jacob Nesly of Lancaster Co, Pa, decd was many yrs ago seized of a tract of land in Wash Co, Md, which by his will he devised one undivided third part to his dau Barbara and remaining 2/3 part of his son Jacob Nesly. Jacob Beam married said Barbara and purchased from said Jacob Nesly, the younger, his undivided 2/3. Barbara Beam died many yrs ago and left following children and grand children, to wit: John Beam, Martin Beam, the complainant, Samuel Binkley and Catharine (dau of said Barbara) his wife and the following grand children: Jacob B. James, Henry James, Isaac James, Elizabeth James and --- James; all of whom, except the first names, are under age of 21, being the children of her decd dau Elizabeth and David James, husband of said Elizabeth, who is still living. All said defendants are non-residents of Md

670. TLM Apr 5 1827/John Cravens and Ruhamah his wife vs Elizabeth Chapline, Jesse Roach & Mary Ann his wife, James N. Chapline, Isaac S. White & Adam Myers. Object of bill is to obtain payment of two bonds executed by James N. Chapline, one to complainant Ruhamah and the other to Mary Ann Chapline, now Mary Ann Roach. The bill states that the said bonds were given to Ruhamah and Mary Ann for part of the purchase of a tract which the said James N. Chapline as one of the heirs of Jeremiah Chapline, decd, elected to take. Elizabeth Chapline, guardian of said Ruhamah and Mary Ann had applied a bond of the same amount due the said Ruhamah to the use of Mary Ann. Elizabeth Chapline, Jesse Roach and Mary Ann his wife, are non-residents of the state of Md

671. TLM Apr 12 1827/Married 29th ult by Rev Ruthrauff, Daniel Steffy, to Miss Sarah Hartel/Married 4th inst by same, John A. Cavan, Esq. to Miss Barbara A. Saunders, all of this co/Married Tues last by same, John Beck to Miss Elizabeth Kinkle/Married same day by Rev Brunner, Samuel J. Cowney, Merchant, to Miss Ann Maria Conrad of this town/Died 24 Mar of a pulmonary disease at the res of his mother, in Tuscarora Valley, Pa, Dr. James Foster, formerly of this place/Died Mon last in the 50th year of her age, Mrs. Ann F. Boteler, wife of Dr. Henry Boteler, of Shepherdstown - Free Press

672. TLM Apr 19 1827/Died Thurs 5th inst at his res near Conococheague creek, Anthony Hauer, in the 70th year of his age/Died Mon last in the neighbourhood of Williams-Port, Peter Sensell, aged about 75 yrs, oldest tenant on Ringgold's Manor, where he has resided about 45 yrs - husband and parent/Died Fri last in the 75th year of her age, Amelia Dusing, wife of Philip Dusing, of this town/Married Wed last by Rev F. Ruthrauff, Benjamin Oswald, editor of the Lancaster (Ohio) Gazette, to Miss Sarah Ann Brennum, of this co

THE TORCHLIGHT AND PUBLIC ADVERTISER (Hagerstown)

673. TLM Apr 26 1827/Married at Boonsborough, Tues evening 17th inst by Rev William Clingan, Henry S. Shaffner, of this co, to Miss Rachel W. Meredith, of the former place/Married Mon 16th inst by Rev Ryan, Henry A. Kelly, to Miss Margaret M'Gonnigal, both of this place/Married Thurs last by Rev Geo. Geeting, Jacob Grim to Miss Margaret Geltmacher, both of Pleasant Valley /Married lately, by Rev Francis Moore, John M'Kinney to Mrs. Mary Jackson, both of Harpers-ferry. This is the 5th time for the blooming bride (now about 28) and the third time that the silken knot has been tied by the same minister/Died Wed week, of a lingering illness, Mrs. Elizabeth Willis, consort of William Willis, of Frederick, and formerly of this place, in the 43d year of her age/Died Sun morning last, at Cotocton Furnace, Frederick Co, in the 43d year of her age, after a long and painful illness, Mrs. Harriet Brien, wife of John Brien, Esq. and dau of Col. John M'Pherson of Frederick, Md/Died Mon morning last, John Hollins, in the 68th year of his age, native of England, emigrated to Balt in 1783, where he has resided ever since

674. TLM May 3 1827/Married Thurs 26th ult in Green-Castle, by Rev M.L. Fullerton, Peter Bun, of Franklin Co, Pa, to Miss Mary Louns, of this co /Married Tues morning last by Rev Bruner, James Swisler, Jr. to Miss Ann Waugh, both of this place/Bedford Pa Gazette of Apr 26 says that some day last week, Richard Shirley, jr. of Greenfield township, in this town, went out with a pistol to shoot birds. In attempting to put the pistol into his coat pocket it accidentally went off, and wounded him so severely, that he survived only a few days. He was about 23 yrs of age

675. TLM May 10 1827/Married Sun 29 Apr, by Rev Deluel, Dr. James A. Buchanan of this co to Miss Anne Maria Nelson of Balt city/Married 3d inst by Rev John Winter, Martin S. Brown of Winchester, to Miss Elizabeth Smith, dau of S. Smith of Middle Way, Jefferson Co, Va/Married same day by Rev Isaac Keller, Thomas Kellar, Esq. to Miss Eliza Jane Martin, all of this co/Married in Boonsborough, Sun last by Rev William Clingan, Henry Heck, to Miss Drusila Chaney, all of that place/Married in Liverpool, England), Capt Duffey, of the brig Laura, to Miss Hamilton, celebrated sailoress of that vessel/Died Sun last in the 81st year of her age, Mrs. Susan Foutz, of this co/Died Mon last in the 20th year of his age, Lucas Baker of this co/Married in Martinsburg, Va, Tues 8th inst by Rev Jackson, Rev John Thompson Brooke, to Miss Louisa Rebecca Hunter, 3rd dau of Col. David Hunter of that place

676. TLM May 17 1827/Married Thurs morning 3d inst by Rev Waugh, Washington W. Hitt, M.D. of this co, to Miss Mary Reynolds, of Balt City/Married Sun last by Rev Geo. Lemmon, Jacob Kapp to Miss Barbara Keller, both of Shenandoah Co, Va/Died at Martinsburg Sun week, in the 49th year of his age, John Alburtus, late Editor of the Shepherdstown Journal, formerly Editor of the Martinsburg Gazette/Otho Shipley of Balt Co, 23 miles from the city of Balt, on going to the spring about 5 weeks since, found one of his children, 3 yrs old, dead in the spring, in 3-4 inches of water, evidently killed by a 10-year old negro girl of Shipley/Married 10th by Rev Bruner, Jacob Ward to Miss Hester Miller

677. TLM May 24 1827/Married Tues 15th inst by Rev John Ruthrauff, William Wood, Esq. to Miss Mary McGinnies, both of Greencastle, Pa/Married 17th inst by Rev F. Ruthrauff, Jacob Kuhn, to Miss Juliann Schroyer, both of this

THE TORCHLIGHT AND PUBLIC ADVERTISER (Hagerstown)

co/Married 22d inst by same, Freeman Little, to Miss Mary Ann Yeakle, both of this place/Married Wed last by Rev Medtart, Pointon Webb to Mrs. Margaret Young, both of this co/Died at her res in the neighborhood of Clear Spring, Fri morning last, Mrs. Barkman, in the 75th year of her age/Died Sun morning last, in the 72d year of his age, Capt William Lewis of this town. He participated in the battles of Trenton, Princeton, Brandywine, Germantown, Monmouth, and engaged in several skirmishes, and closed his military struggles at the battle of Miami, serviving as Captain under General Wayne, in 1793

678. TLM May 31 1827/Married 16th inst in Phila, Rev J. Beecher of Shepherdstown, VA, to Miss Hannahretta Mitchell, of the former place/Died in George-town, D.C. on Thurs last, John May, (book-seller) formerly of this place/Died in Columbus on 15th inst George Hashee, Esq. Editor of the Ohio State Journal, aged about 40 yrs, member of Ohio legislature - Lancaster Gaz./Died Mon night last in Green-castle, after a lingering illness, Miss Maria M'Clelland, dau of Dr. John M'Clelland, of that place/Michael Peiffer, living at Booth's mill, Wash Co, Md, offers reward for apprentice to the milling business, named Henry Saunders, about 17 yrs of age, 5 ft

679. TLM Jun 7 1827/Married at Mercersburg, Pa, Sat last by Rev A.M. Jewett, Joseph Shannon to Miss Sarah Isabella Sterett, all of that place

680. TLM Jun 21 1827/Died in this place Fri last, Peter Hefflich of Hagerstown, in the 85th year of his age, and on Sat at the res of Matthew Murray, Joshua Murray, Sen. of Frederick Co, in the 62d year of his age/Death of Hon. William Wilson, representative in Congress from Ohio. He was ill before he left the city on his return home, March last; and his illness, a bilious complain gradually increased until it terminated in his death on 29th ult, at Newark, Ohio

681. TLM Jun 28 1827/Died Tues last, after a long and painful illnes, Susan Kroft, wife of Jacob Kroft, in the 69th year of her age

682. TLM Jul 19 1827/John Horn, Hagers-town, offers reward for George Pentz, apprentice to the pump making business, about 18 yrs of age, 5 ft

683. TLM Jul 26 1827/Married 10th inst, William Stoudt, formerly of this place, to Mrs. Mary Sanderson of Richland co, Ohio

684. TLM Aug 2 1827/Married Thurs last by Rev Medtart, Jacob Newcomer to Miss Eliza Kausler, dau of Jacob Kausler, all of this co

685. TLM Aug 9 1827/Married Thurs 19th ult by Rev G. Geeting, John Boyers, to Miss Mary Hines/Married Tues 24th by same, Henry Peckley to Miss Ann Nafe, both of Sharpsburg/Married Thurs last by same, Jacob Barger to Miss Rebecca Jones, all of this co/Married same day by Rev J. Medtart, John Wolgamot, jr. to Miss Mary Ann Firey, dau of Jacob Firey, both of this co/Married Thurs 26th ult by Rev R. Kenedy, John Duffield, Esq of Licking Creek to Miss Mary Ann Shannon, of M'Connellsburg, Pa/Died at P. Hurt's Tavern, 8 miles North of Nashville, 12 Jul, after a short illness, Major Robert Bailey, of Bucksville, Ky, formerly a res of this City, and well

THE TORCHLIGHT AND PUBLIC ADVERTISER (Hagerstown)

known in this District and in Virginia. His character was a chequered as his fortunes, and if both had many shadows, they were not without some redeeming spots of brightness - Nat. Intel.

686. TLM Aug 16 1827/Married Thurs last, Joseph Watson to Miss Catharine Kealhaffer, all of this town/Died in Hagers-town, Fri morning last, in the 74th year of his age, Col. Adam Ott, Rev officer of merit, and formerly sheriff of Wash Co; commissioned as an officer of the Pennsylvania line in Jan 1776; in 1796 electoral candidate for Thomas Jefferson/Died in Funkstown Fri last, George Russ in the 27th year of his age, native of Richmond Va; had no relatives here to lament his loss

687. TLM Aug 23 1827/A laboring man named Joseph Miller, who about cleaning a well in Leitersburg, Tues last, was precipitate by accident to the bottom of distance of 65 ft, on solid rock and had one of his ankles shattered to pieces, but was living yesterday afternoon/Died at his res in Williams-Port Fri last, William Albert, in the 48th year of his age

688. TLM Aug 30 1827/Married Sat 18th inst at Lancaster, Pa, by Rev Dr. Endress, Rev Ludwig Mayer, Professor in the Theological Seminary at Carlisle, to Miss Maria Smith, of Lancaster/Married at Clear Spring, Thurs 16th by Rev Jeremiah Mason, Capt Overton G. Lowe to Miss Mary Ridenour

689. TLM Sep 6 1827/Married Tues 21st ult by Rev M'Crusker, Francis Dugan of Va, to Miss Lucretia M'Cardell, of this co/Married Sun morning last by Rev Kroh, William M. Flautt to Miss Mary Allender, all of this co/Married Mon morning last by Rev Medtart, Jonas Shilling to Miss Margaret Lancaster /Died Tues 4th inst in the 66th year of her age, Mrs. Elizabeth Bragonier, wife of Jacob Bragonier of this co

690. TLM Sep 13 1827/Married Thurs last, George Couter to Miss Keziah Bramble, both of this place/Married Tues last by Rev M. L. Fullerton, David W. Deever to Miss Elizabeth Steuart, both of this co/Married same day by same, James Davis to Miss Mary Ann Murray, dau of Matthew Murray, all of this place/Died in this place, Sun evening last in the 55th year of his age, William Sprigg, Esq. formerly District Judge in Louisiana/Equity case - Daniel S. Bertolet, and Ann his wife vs William Boone, Geo. Boone, William Gearhart and Sarah his wife, William Runyan and Mary his wife, Andrew Taylor and Elizabeth his wife, Benjamin Kline and Harriet his wife, Jonathan Evans and Margaret his wife, Rachel Boone, Franklin Boone, Daniel Boone, Harriet Boone, Margaret Boone, and Elizabeth Boone. Object of bill is to obtain sale of certain real estate. Complainants state that George Boone, late of Berks Co, Pa, died seized of real estate in Wash Co which has descended to complainant Ann, and the defendants as heirs of said George Boone and that it will be to the benefit of all perons concerned to have the real estate sold. Said defendants all reside out of the State of Md. Defendants Franklin, Daniel, Harriet, Margaret and Elizabeth, children of Charles Boone, decd, are under age of 21 yrs

691. TLM Sep 20 1827/Died Mon 10th inst, Mrs Susan Crove, in the 36th year of her age, wife of Philip Grove, Esq. of Sharpsburg

THE TORCHLIGHT AND PUBLIC ADVERTISER (Hagerstown)

692. TLM Sep 27 1827/Married 17th inst by Rev Henry Kroh, Samuel Grove to Miss Ann Stephenson, all of this co/Died Sun last, at an advanced age, Peter Shooper, for many yrs an inhabitant of this place

693. TLM Oct 4 1827/Married Tues 25th ult by Rev J. Medtart, John Johnston to Miss Isabella Day/Married Thurs 27th by same, Wm. Byers to Miss Mary Knodle/Married Sun last by same John Fritz to Miss Catharine Shriver/Married Thurs evening last by Rev G. Geeting, John Smith to Miss Margaret Harman, both of Sharpsburg/Died at his res near Cave-town, Fri 21st ult, Jacob Ridenour, soldier of the Rev/Died 18th ult at his res in Mansfield, Richland Co, Ohio, Josiah Smith. He had recently been on a visit to this place and on his return home was taken sick as Washington, Pa. He left a widow and 4 small children/Died in Tarlton, Pickaway co, Ohio, 17th ult, Mrs. Orpha Binkley, in 22nd year of her age, after a distressing illness of nearly 3 weeks, consort of George S. Binkley, merchant of that place. She left a husband and 2 small children - Lancaster (Ohio) Gazette

694. TLM Oct 11 1827/Married 29th Sep by Rev M. L. Fullerton, Benj. Linebauch to Miss Catharine Banode/By same on 2d inst Benj. Medcalf to Miss Lucretia Bean/By same Wed 3d, Wm. M'Atee to Miss Ann Boyd, dau of Walter Boyd, Esq. of this co/Died 6th inst, Mrs. Elizabeth Angle, consort of Jacob Angle, jr. and dau of David Martin of Franklin Co, Pa, in the 35th year of her age, leaving husband and 6 small children/Died same day Mrs. Yeakle, wife of John Yeakle of this place in the 53rd year of her age/Died at New York, Wed 26 Sep at res of George Suckley, Esq. Rev Freeborn Garretson, of the Meth Epis Church, in the 76(?)th year of his age/Died Sun (30 Sep) after a short illness, Rev Christian Frederick Ludwick Endress, D.D.; he was born Mar 12 1775, came to Lancaster, Oct 6 1815, since which time he has performed the duties of pastor of the German Luth Congregation of this city - Gazette

695. TLM Oct 18 1827/Died 23 Aug 1827, near Pinckneyville, Mississippi, 2 children of Charles S. Clarkson, Esq. Sarah Bella, aged 7 1/2 yrs and Mary Smith, aged 6 yrs and some months/Died Fri evening last in Sharpsburg, Nathan W. Hays, in the 36th year of his age. He left the house of his brother, Dr. Hays on Thurs morning for Green Castle in good health; the following day he returned about noon, and died in a few hours after, with that distressing malady, the Quinsy/Married 25th ult at Western River, Culpepper Co, Va by Rev Jones, William Bussard, of Georgetown, D.C. to Miss Mary Ann, eldest dau of John C. Scott, Esq./Married Sun last by rev Medtart, John Brendel, to Miss Hannah Hahn, both of this place/Married Tues last by rev Keller, at Springfield, res of Edward G. Williams, Esq. Daniel Weisel, Esq. of this place, to Miss Matilda S. dau of late Amos Davis, Esq. of this co

696. TLM Oct 25 1827/Married in Cumberland on Tues evening 16th, by Rev J.J. Jacobs, Doct. Charles V. Swearingen to Miss Sarah Scott, dau of the late Jas. Scott, of that place/Married 21 inst by Rev Geo. Lemmon, Daniel Palmer to Miss Sophia Smith, both of this co/Died Fri morning last, in 31st year of his age, after a short illness, at the res of his brother, Thomas Farmer Van Lear, son of the late Col. William Van Lear, of Williams-Port /Died in Twinsburg, Portage Co, Ohio, on 21st inst, Moses and Aaron Wilcox,

THE TORCHLIGHT AND PUBLIC ADVERTISER (Hagerstown)

aged about 50, twin brothers born in Connecticut on same day, married on same day, wives being sisters; engaged in mercantile business together at Middletown, and failed together; from thence they removed and settled themselves, together in this state, at a place which from they derived the name of Twinsburg; taken sick on the same day, continued sick the same length of time; they died the same day; buried same grave - Cleveland Herald/Dreadful accident - On 24th ult a girl named Maria Griffin, aged 12 years, dau of Dudley Griffin of Centreville, Allegheny Co, while riding on horseback to a neighbor's, the horse by some means took fright and threw the rider from the saddle, her foot hannging in the stirrup leather. She was thus drawn about 80 rods, the horse under full speed. She expired a few minutes after the horse stopped

697. TLM Nov 8 1827/Married Thurs 25th ult by Rev Samuel Helfenstein, John Warner to Miss Ellen Hammon, both of this co/Died at his res near Hancock, in this co, after a short illness, on Mon morning 29th ult, Dr. Lancelot Jacques, aged about 72 years, native of England, emigrated to this country early in life; educated at New Ark school. He served a short time as a surgeon in the American army during the Rev war and three times elected to the Legislature of Md; also filled several other public situations/Died 29th Sep last at res of her son, Samuel Mills, on Elk Ridge, Anne Arundel Co, Md, Mrs. Elizabeth Miller, in the 76th year of her age, relict of the late William Miller of this co/Died in Northport, Col. Thomas Knowlton, aged 69, rev soldier; three times taken prisoner and escaped twice, once while a fellow soldier was shot by his side/Died in Jackson, Mo., Col. Stephen Renney, aged 67; native of Connecticut, served in the army during entire rev war; received wounds, in several battles; presented sword by General Lafayette for his gallantry; served as Captain to Lieut. Colonel.

698. TLM Nov 15 1827/Married Thurs 18 ult by Rev Matthews, Thomas B. Dunn of Antietam in this co, to Miss Matilda B. Beall, dau of late Hezekiah Beall, of Jefferson Co, Va/Married 8 inst by Rev Denius, John Geeting to Miss Rosanna Snyder, both of this co/Married Thurs last at Cave-town, by Rev M.L. Fullerton, Henry Lizer to Miss Mazy Justice

699. TLM Nov 22 1827/Died Thurs evening last, at the res of Col. Daniel Malott, Wash Co, Md., Thomas M'Quinny, soldier of the Rev, in the 89th year of his age; native of Ireland, enlisted at Elkton, in the 5th Md. Regt, served under Maj. Lansdale, Capt. Muse, and Capt. Lynn, of Allegany. Soon after the war he removed to this co. Buried Sat at the Stone Church, near Maj. Baker's store/Died near Cadiz, Harrison Co, Ohio, on the 17th Aug last, Neale Peacock, formerly of Wash Co, Md., many years a soldier of the Md. Line. He fought with the gallant Howard at the Eutaws and the Cowpens; he served also under Gen. Green and other illustrious chiefs

700. TLM Nov 29 1827/Married 1st inst by Rev F. Ruthrauff, Jacob Hoover to Miss Nancy Stouffer, both of this co/Married 22d inst by same, David Hughes, of Georgetown, D.C. to the amiable Miss Margaret Mong, of this co/Married same day by Rev M.L. Fullerton, George France to Miss Sarah Ann Pheasant /Married same day by same, Joseph Miller to Miss Mary Ann Loman/Died 10th inst at his res at Warminster, Va, Hon. St. George Tucker, about 77 yrs of age/Died morning of 16th inst at Green-Castle, Mrs. Eleanor B. McClellan,

THE TORCHLIGHT AND PUBLIC ADVERTISER (Hagerstown)

wife of Dr. John McClellan, of that place, in the 41st year of her age/Died Sat last at Williams-Port, in this co, John S. Towson, son of Jacob T. Towson, Esq.

701. TLM Dec 6 1827/Married 15th ult by Rev M. Bruner, George Miller to Miss Margaret Iler/Married 29th by same, Samuel Welty to Miss Elizabeth Middelkauff/Married same day by same, Samuel Confer to Miss Mary Baker, all of this co/Married Tues last by same, John Myers to Miss Mary Domer/Married same by same, Isaac Myers to Miss Lonas Miller/Married Sun last by Rev James Reid, Caleb Maner to Miss Elizabeth Shererd/Married 22d ult by Rev G. Lemmon, Aaron Heesecker, of this co, to Miss Margaret Rightstine, of Jefferson Co, Va/Married by same on 4th inst, John Doctor to Miss Mahala Leary, both of Shenandoah Co, Va/Equity case - Elizabeth Kuhn and Frederick Fishaugh, vs. Daniel Sheets and Elizabeth his wife, John Bower and Sarah his wife, Moddelena Kuhn, Joshua Smith and Catharine his wife, Judith Bockman, Jacob Kuhn, Abraham Hawken and Anna his wife, Jacob Kauffman and Amelia his wife, and Marmaduke M. Boyd. Object of the bill is to obtain order for sale of real estate of Jacob Kuhn, decd, to pay his debts. The bill states that Jacob Kuhn, late of Wash Co, died intestate, and Elizabeth Kuhn and Frederick Fishaugh obtained letters of administration on his pers estate. Jacob Kuhn left following person his heirs and representatives: John Kuhn, who died since the death of said Jacob, Elizabeth Kuhn, who m Daniel Sheets, Moddalena Kuhn, Judith Kuhn who m Abraham Bockman (who is since dead), Sarah Kuhn who m John Bower, Jacob Kuhn, Christiana Kuhn who died without leaving any legitimate children, Anna Kuhn who m Abraham Hawken, Catharine Kuhn who m Joshua Smith of Virginia and Amelia Kuhn who m Jacob Kauffman of Pa. After the death of said Jacob Kuhn, said John Kuhn, John Bower and Sarah his wife, and Jacob Kauffman and Amelia his wife, sold their rights to real estate to Marmaduke W. Boyd, of Wash Co, Md/Equity case - George Harsh and Elizabeth Shafer vs David Harsh, John Stinebaugh and Mary his wife and Henry Harsh. Object of bill is to obtain sale of real estate in which complainants and defendants are jointly interested. The bill states that Jacob Harsh, Wash Co, decd, died intestate, leaving 182 acres of land. He left 5 children heirs, to wit: the complainants and Henry Harsh and Mary who m John Stinebaugh, and David Harsh. Said Mary and her husband Stinebaugh and David Harsh, left the state. Henry has conveyed his interest to John Stinebaugh /Equity case - Margaret Ham and George Hedrick, vs Peter Ham, John Ham & others. Joseph Ham one of the defendants has died intestate, since the filing of the bill in this cause, leaving David Ham and Margaret his heirs at law, who are infants under age of 21, res in state of Ohio

702. TLM Dec 13 1827/Died Wed night 5th inst in 62 year of her age, Mrs. Catharine Cramer, consort of Jonas Cramer, of this town/Died in Balt on Sun 2d inst, Rev Dr. George Roberts of the Meth Church/Died Thurs last, John M'Kinney of Harpers-Ferry, in the 26th year of his age. He had been married but 8 months, and was the 5th husband of Mrs. Mary Jackson, who is yet under the age of 29

703. TLM Dec 20 1827/Death of Liberty D. Little Tues last at 4 o'clock, aged 18 yrs, 11 months and 14 days, youngest son of David T. Little/Died Sat last at her res near Hagers Town, in the 67th year of her age, Mrs. Margaret Shall, wife of George Shall/Married Thurs 29th ult by Rev Matthews, George

THE TORCHLIGHT AND PUBLIC ADVERTISER (Hagerstown)

Beckenbaugh, Esq. of Frederick Co, to Miss Martha V. dau of James Leggett, Esq. of Sharpsburg, in this co

704. TLM Jan 3 1828/Married Thurs Dec 13 by Rev Geo. Lemmon, John Farrow, to Miss Margaret McCaul/Married Tues Dec 13 by Rev George Geeting, Adam Gouff, to Miss Charlotte Cretzinger, both of Pleasant Valley/Married Thurs last by same, Henry I. Keedy, to Miss Leah Clapper, both of Pleasant Valley /Married same day by Rev Denius, Daniel Keedy, to Miss Sophia Miller, both of Pleasant Valley/Married Tues last by Rev Kurtz, Peter Protzman to Miss Susan Ridenour, both of this co/Married same day by same, William Renner, to Miss Susan Nyswander, both of this co/Married Wed last by Rev Reid, Jacob I. Tritch, to Miss Elizabeth Dundore/Married in this place, last evening by Rev Lemmon, Robert T. Corson, to Miss Christiana, dau of William Brown, Esq. of Winchester, Va/Married Tues last by Rev Kurtz, David Beeler, to Miss Sophia, dau of Gerard Stonebraker/Died at Sharpsburg on morning of 25th ult after a few hours illness, John Clarke, in the 61st year of his age, old inhabitant of Sharpsburg; confined to his bed for more than 12 yrs with a paralysis of the lower extremities; received constant attentions of his wife/Died Fri last at the mill of John Kennedy, Esq. near Hagers Town, Lewis, the (old Antietam) Fisherman, at an advanced age/Isaac Hershey, 2 miles from Funkstown, offers reward for bound boy, Gotleib Lichstine, 18 yrs of age, 5 ft 3 4 inch

705. TLM Jan 10 1828/Married Mon evening last, in Funks-town, by Rev Kurtz, Ira Hill, A.M. to Miss Lydia Wilson/Died Wed 2d inst at Harry's town, George Kneedy/Died Thurs 3d inst in Hagers Town, John Kriner, Brass Founder

706. TLM Jan 17 1828/Married Tues 1st inst by Rev Reid, John Jacob Tritch to Miss Elizabeth Dundore, all of this co/Married Thurs last by Rev Fullerton, David Finefrock, to Miss Mary Ann Finefrock/Married same day by same, Lewis Weeber, to Miss Sibilla Airheart, all of this co/Married 3d inst by Rev R. Post, Roberdeau Annin, to Miss Helen C. McCormick, both of Wash City/Died 26 Dec, Miss Mary C. Schnebly, eldest dau of Henry Schnebly, Esq. in the 16th year of her age/Died in this town, Thurs last at the res of his brother Jacob Powles, Daniel Powles, aged 31 yrs and one day. The decd was res of Balt/Died Tues morning last, Mrs. Elizabeth Schnebly, wife of Henry Schnebly, Esq. of this co

707. TLM Jan 24 1828/Died very suddenly Fri 11th inst at Miller's mill, in this co, Caspar Folk, of Franklin Co, Pa, in the 52d year of his age/Died Sun evening last at the Cottage, near this place, John Neibert, in the 78th year of his age, old inhabitant of this co, leaving numerous offspring and relatives/Died Tues last at the res of Miss Ann Maria Inglis in this place, Miss Jane, dau of late rev Dr. Inglis of Balt

708. TLM Jan 31 1828/Died in Hagers Town on Thurs last, Peter Hose, in the 83rd year of his age/Died Mon last in Hancock after a short illness, John Brady, merchant of the firm of Brady and Wason, in the 40th year of his age/Died yesterday in this place after a long illness of an advanced age, Jacob Tutweiler

THE TORCHLIGHT AND PUBLIC ADVERTISER (Hagerstown)

709. TLM Feb 7 1828/Died at the house of his son-in-law, Major Peter Seibert, on Beaver Creek, on Sat last, Jacob Knode, Sen, at an advanced age

710. TLM Feb 14 1828/Died in this place Fri last, after a short illness, in the 17th year of his age, Samuel Smith, son of Mrs. Elizabeth Smith, of this place

711. TLM Feb 21 1828/Died at his farm in this co, Sun last, John Barnett /Died in this place Mon last, Francis M'Mullen, at an advanced age

712. TLM Feb 28 1828/Married Thurs last, near Hancock by Rev Hutchinson, Daniel Brosius to Miss Eleanora B. Johnston/Married Thurs 14th inst by Rev Kroh, Archibald McAfee to Miss Magdalena Ganter/Married Thurs 21st by same, Frederick Unger to Miss Mary Fishaugh/Married same day, John Bantz to Miss Elizabeth Landis/Married same day by Rev Bruner, Anthony Snyder of Licking creek, Wash Co, to Mrs. Margaret M. Boyd, of Shepherds-town, Va/Died Fri last at his res near Funks-town, John Winders, industrious and respectable farmer, after a protracted and painful illness/From National Intelligencer - Death of Major General Jacob Brown, Commander in Chief of the Army of the U.S., at his res in this city, after a brief illness of 3-4 days

713. TLM Mar 6 1828/Married 10 Jan by Rev Kellar, Jonathan Tice to Miss Rebecca Melone/Married 20 Feb by same, William Denis to Miss Clara P.E. Lenkhorn, both of Va/Married Thurs last by Rev B. Kurtz, Nathaniel Swingley to Miss Eliza, dau of John Shearer, all of this co/Died Tues morning last while on a visit to her friends in Frederick, Miss Maria Ringgold, eldest dau of Gen. Samuel Ringgold, of this co

714. TLM Mar 13 1828/Married Thurs last by Rev Kroh, Daniel Clevidence to Miss Elizabeth Band, both of this co/Died Fri evening last in Hagers Town, Master Daniel Merrick son of J. I. Merrick, Esq. - Herald/Died Fri 20th ult at his res in this co, Edmund M'Coy, in the 52d year of his age/Died at res of his father, near Hancock, in this co, on the 20th inst, in the 20th year of his age, John Moore, son of Alexander Moore/Died Tues 4th inst near Clear Spring, after a short illness, Abraham Troxell, leaving widow and 9 children

715. TLM Mar 20 1828/Married Sun 9th inst by Rev Winter, Jacob Peterman, to Miss Harriet Baxter, all of Williams-Port/Married Thurs last by Rev B. Kurtz, Jacob Fiery to Miss Barbara Hershey, both of this co/Married same day by Rev Bruner, Henry Ainsworth to Miss Mary Julius, all of this place/Married same by Rev Kellar, Philip H. Coakley of the State of New York, to Mrs. Sarah Smith of Williams-Port, in this co/Died in Blair's Valley on Thurs last, James Blair, in the 93rd year of his age, one among the first settlers of this part of Wash Co, and bore a part in the many skirmishes with the Indians/Died Sat last near Hagers Town, Mrs. Sarah Heyser, consort of William Heyser, Jr. and dau of Peter Artz of this town

716. TLM Mar 27 1828/Married Thurs last by Rev Kellar, Daniel Middlekauff to Miss Theresa Newcomer, both of this co/Married same day by Rev Bruner, John Moyer to Miss Mary Tice, both of this co/Married Sun last by Rev Jeremiah Mason, Henry Gorlaugh to Miss Mary Hamison/Died Sun last in this place, Master John Ragan, son of the late Col. John Ragan/Died Mon last,

THE TORCHLIGHT AND PUBLIC ADVERTISER (Hagerstown)

Mrs. Sophia Rudasil, consort of Michael Rudasil of this co, in the 46(?)th year of her age/Died Mon night last, Mrs. Elizabeth Rench, in the 48(?)th year of her age, consort of Daniel Rench, Esq. of this co

717. TLM Apr 3 1828/Died 15th ult after a lingering illness, Henry Newcomer, in the 56th year of his age, worthy farmer of this co/Died Sat evening last in this town, after protracted illness, Mrs. Maria Artz, consort of Peter Artz, in the 54th(?) year of her age/Married Thurs 27th ult by Wm. Wood, Esq. James Ship to Miss Sarah Crawford, both of this co/Married same day by same, John Stile, to Miss Mary Burns, both of this co/Married Tues last by Rev Robert Wilson, Perry Prather, to Miss Charlotte Johnson, both of this co/Married same day by Rev Bruner, Jacob Alter of Cumberland co, Pa, to Miss Eliza Tice of this co/Married same day by Rev Benj. Kurtz, Jonathan Smith to Miss Dorothy Bruner, all of this co/Henry Middlecauff vs John Ott & others. Object of bill is to obtain decree for sale of house and lot in Hagers Town, property of Adam Ott, decd. In year 1819 complainant became endorser for Adam Ott, decd on his promissory note to Hagers Town Bank. Said Ott died intestate without lineal heirs and his heirs at law are John Ott, a brother of the said Adam, Jacob Ott and Michael Ott, sons of his brother Michael, decd, Jacob, George, Polly, Catharine, Margaret, Julian and Sally Ott, children of his brother Jacob, decd, Peter Fisher, Adam Fisher, John Rigert and Catharine his wife, which said Peter, Adam, and Catharine are the nephews and niece of said Adam Ott

718. TLM Apr 10 1828/Married Tues 25 Mar by Rev J. Winter, Upton Dowel, to Miss Ann Smith, both of this co/Married Thurs 3d April by same, Benjamin Crow, to Miss Maria Lefever, both of Williams-port, Md./Married Thurs 27th ult by Rev M.L. Fullerton, Samuel Miller to Miss Elizabeth Sptiznogle, both of this co/Married Thurs last by same, Henry Gordon of Franklin Co, Pa, to Miss Matilda Bowman, of this place/Married Thurs last by Rev B. Kurtz, John W. Cooper to Miss Henrietta Fields/Married same day by same, Samuel H. Little to Miss Ann M. Fields, daus of Wm. Fields, of this town/Married Tues evening last by Rev Isaac Keller, Dr. John Clagett Dorsey to Miss Louisa Ann Hughes, 2nd dau of Samuel Hughes, Esq. of this place/Died 1st inst in 32d year of her age, Mrs. Elizabeth Ruckle, consort of Samuel Ruckle, merchant of Sharpsburgh, after several months of severe and distressing illness/Died at Pittsburgh, 26 March, Mrs. Jane Van Lear Ramsey, wife of Col. John Ramsey, and dau of late Matthew Van Lear, Esq. of Wash Co, Md. in the 45th year of her age - Gazette./Died in this town Sat last after a long and severe indisposition, Lewis Charles Bodman, in the 76th year of his age. He was born in Aura Trimberg, Wurtzburg Co, Germany, an affectionate parent

719. TLM Apr 17 1828/Married Thurs evening last by Rev Helfenstein, Chester Coleman of this place, to Miss Eliza R. Graham of Frederick Co/Married same day by Rev Keller, Andrew M. Farmer to Miss Catharine Ensminger, all of this co/Married same day by Rev Bruner, Samuel Pretzman, to Miss Mary Bender, all of this place/Married same day by Rev Winter, Marmaduke W. Boyd, Esq. to Miss Rebecca, youngest dau of Col. Jonas Hogmire, all of this co/Married Tues morning last by Rev B. Kurtz, Samuel Boyd, to Miss Margaret Bender, all of Hagers Town/Died Sat last near Witmer's mill, Abraham Ditto, old inhabitant of this co

THE TORCHLIGHT AND PUBLIC ADVERTISER (Hagerstown)

720. TLM Apr 24 1828/Married Thurs last by Rev B. Kurtz, David H. Keedy, of Boonsborough to Miss Elizabeth youngest dau of John Hanna, of this co/Died Sun last at her res in this place, Mrs. Catharine Engleman, in the 64th year of her age/Died 17th inst in the 37th year of his age, William B. Cheney, of this co

721. TLM May 1 1828/Married Tues evening 15th ult by Rev Speer, H. J. Rahauser, merchant of Washington, Pa, formerly of this place, to Miss Jane Stewart, of Greensburgh, Pa/Married Thurs last by Rev Bruner, James M'Laughlin to Miss Amelia, dau of David Newcomer, all of this co/Married same day by Rev Robert Wilson, Samuel S. Prather to Miss Jemimee McBee, both of this co/Married this day by Rev Kroh, David Zeller, to Miss Elizabeth Lantz, all of this co

722. TLM May 8 1828/Married Thurs 17th ult by Rev Henry Kroh, Adam Flora to Miss Elizabeth Unger/Married Thurs 24th ult by same, John Keller to Miss Elizabeth Newcomer/Married Thurs week, William Doyle to Miss Margaretta Byer, dau of Capt J. Byer of this co/Married Thurs last by same, Joseph Lighter to Miss Ann Zeigler/Married same day by Rev B. Kurtz, Josiah B. Dever, of Harpers-Ferry, to Miss Amelia Sheneberger of Funks-town/Married Tues 22d ult by Rev Clingan, Joseph Austin to Miss Ann, dau of Gabriel Nourse, Esq., all of this co/Married Thurs 23d ult by Rev Geo. Geeting, Abraham Eacle to Miss Nancy Ann Ott, both of this co/Married Sun 26th ult by same, John Pennell to Miss Elizabeth Baker/Died recently at the res of his son, Jacob Huyett, near Cave-town, Ludowick Huyett, in the 90th year of his age, one of the oldest of Wash Co/Died at the Antietam Iron Works, 20th ult, after a few hours illness, Mrs. Elizabeth Dunn, of Pa, in the 64th year of her age

723. TLM May 15 1828/Melancholy Event! - Daniel Cyester, in a moment of mental derangement, precipitated himself from the bridge at Williams-Port, into the Creek, a distance of about 30 feet, and was drowned, on Sat night last. He was in the 43d year of his age, res in Va, adjacent to Williams-Port several yrs; was in easy circumstances, recently sold out and intended starting for the Western Country on Tues last. He left a wife and 3 small children. Remains committed to the grave with Masonic ceremony/Married Thurs last by Rev B. Kurtz, Peter Wetzel to Miss Ann Moyer, all of this co /Married Sun evening last by same, Leonard Balthis to Miss Amelia Grove, both of Va/Died 1st inst, aged about 65 yrs, Christian Beeler, old citizen of this co/Died Sat morning last, James Williams, son of Edmund Fitzpatrick, of this place, aged 2 yrs, 6 months, 16 days/Annapolis Rep. May 13 - Sun morning last, Jeremiah Townley Chase, Esq. died

724. TLM May 22 1828/Married Tues last by Rev Fullerton, Dr. Elijah Bishop, of this co, to Miss Ann Hoye, of this place/Died Wed 14th inst in this town, Mrs. Sarah Houston

725. TLM May 29 1828/At a frolic at the house of Henry Wells, near the mouth of Middle Island Creek, Tyler co, Va, Jesse Wells, the father of Henry Wells, struck a young man named William Steed, on, or near the neck so severely that he died instantly/Severe thunderstorm in Prince George's County, May 23rd; lightning struck a kitchen on the farm of Mrs. Williams, of Lower Marlboro, and killed 5 of 11 persons who had taken shelter in it: 2

THE TORCHLIGHT AND PUBLIC ADVERTISER (Hagerstown)

2 men, 2 women, and a boy/Died Thurs last at his res in this co, John Cheney/Died same day, Jeremiah Cheney, after a lingering illness

726. TLM Jun 5 1828/Married Thurs 8th ult by Rev Geo. Geeting, John Shackleford, to Miss Mary Ellen James/Married same day by same, John Rohrback, to Miss Rosanna Myers, all of this co/Married same day, by Rev McCauley, John Barks, to Miss Mary Rernsperger of Frederick Co

727. TLM Jun 12 1828/Married Tues last by Rev B. Kurtz, Samuel M'Cauley to Miss Ann Stonebraker, all of this co/Died Wed morning last about 8 o'clock, after a lingering illness, Miss Matilda Reynolds, dau of Major John Reynolds, of this place

728. TLM Jun 19 1828/Married Tues last by Rev Kurtz, James Dilly, to Miss Sarah Benkhart, both of Va/June 17 - Death of John Yeakle Thurs last at half past 11 o'clock in the forenoon, aged 56 yrs, after a long and severe illness/Died Sun 15th inst at 9 o'clock at Tammany Mount, Mrs. Mary Van Lear, relict of the late Matthew Van Lear, in the 69th year of her age, after a protracted indisposition/Died yesterday afternoon, Miss Maria Humrickhouse, dau of Peter Humrickhouse of this place

729. TLM Jun 26 1828/Married in Harbaugh's Valley on 15 inst, by Rev French, M. Michael Waltman to Miss Polly Pittie, after a short courtship of 50 yrs

730. TLM Jul 3 1828/Married in Boonsboro', on 8th ult, by Rev William Clingan, Jas. Brown to Miss Lydia Mowror/Married Thurs evening last by Rev Bruner, William Reese, of Hancock, to Miss Eliza West, of Clear Spring/Married same evening by same, Abraham Dusing to Miss Magdalena Dusing, of this co/Married Tues last by Rev Isaac Kellar, Henry Foutz to Miss Sarah Grosh, both of this co/Died in this place, Mon evening last, after a long illness, Miss Susan Hughes, dau of late Col. Daniel Hughes, of this place

731. TLM Jul 10 1828/Died early Tues morning, Mrs. Margaret Wise, consort of William Wise of this town, in the 37th year of her age

732. TLM Jul 17 1828/Died at Natchez on 17th ult, after an illness of 5 days, Matthew Murray of this place/Died at his res in this town yesterday morning, Isaac Smith

733. TLM Jul 24 1828/Died Thurs evening 17th inst at his res 3 miles north of Hagers Town, Christian Miller, aged 80 yrs, 6 months, 22 days/Died at Balt July 17, John Montgomery, Esq. late major of the city/Died Sat last at his res near Cave-town, Walter Boyd, Esq. an old inhabitant of this co, for many yrs a practical Surveyor of this section of co

734. TLM Jul 31 1828/Died 19th inst at his res in Somerset, Perry Co, Ohio, Jacob Binckley, Sen., formerly a citizen of Hagers Town. After eating his dinner on the 18th, he was visited by an apolectick stroke, of which he died the following day about 2 o'clock, aged about 61 yrs/Died at her res, 3 miles from Hagers Town, Tues last, Mrs. Dorothy Ridenour, consort of John Ridenour, in the 68th year of her age

THE TORCHLIGHT AND PUBLIC ADVERTISER (Hagerstown)

735. TLM Aug 7 1828/Married Thurs evening last, by Rev Winters, Wm. W. Beecher, to Miss Maria Guthrie, both of Clear-Spring/Married same day by Rev Bruner, David Chrest, to Miss Elizabeth Stoops, all of this town/Married same day by Rev James Reid, Samuel Henderson, to Miss Mary Allison, all of this town /Married Tues last by Rev Benj. Kurtz, William Beams, to Miss Ann Morrison, both of Frederick Co/Married Tues last John Stemple, merchant, of this place, to Miss Jane Smith, of Huntingdon co, Pa/Died Mon evening 28th inst, at his res near the Green Spring, Old Furnace, in this co, Daniel Mc-Coy, after a long illness, leaving widow and 6 children/Died Thurs last at his res in this co, at an advanced aged, Christian Middlekauff

736. TLM Aug 14 1828/Died at his res near Sharpsburg, Mon morning last, Archibald Ritchey, Esq. after a long illness

737. TLM Aug 21 1828/Married Thurs 14th inst by Rev James Reily, Henry Smith, of Waynesburg, Pa, to Miss Jane Staley, of Cave-town, in this co/Married same day by Rev B. Kurtz, John Barnhiser, to Miss Susanna Brown, both of Frederick Co/Married Sun last by same, Abner Williams to Miss Mary Sheeter, both of this co/Married 7th inst by Rev M. Bruner, Henry Beser(?) to Miss Ann Brown, both of Va

738. TLM Aug 28 1828/Married at York, Pa, Tues 19th inst, by Rev James R. Reily, Capt. John Wolgamot, of this co, to Mrs. Eve Worley, of Franklin Co, Pa/Died at her res below Funkstown, Mon last, Mrs. --- South, consort of Gera South/Died Tues morning last, in this place, Henry Kellar, son of Philip Kellar, aged 22 yrs/Died Mon last at his res in Franklin co, Pa, Nicholas Martin, son of David Martin of the same co

739. TLM Sep 4 1828/Married Mon 25th ult by Rev B. Kurtz, John Kauffman to Miss Elizabeth Nyswander/Married Thurs last by Rev M. L. Fullerton, Robert C. Arbuckle to Miss Letha Ann Harn, both of this co/Died Mon 25th ult at New Haven, Connecticut, J. Ashmun, Esq. late Colonial Agent of the "American Colonization Society," at Liberia/Died 23d inst in Staunton, Va, Rev Enoch George, one of the Bishops of the Meth Episc Church, aged about 60 yrs

740. TLM Sep 11 1828/Died Thurs night, 4th inst, at an advanced age, Christopher Griffith, long a res of this place/Died Tues last in this place, Jacob Bowman, old inhabitant of this co/Died Sat week, at his res in this co, after a few days illness, David Martin, son of the Rev Nicholas Martin, of Franklin co, Pa/Died Mon night, 25th ult, Jas. B. Ray, governor of Indiana, recently re-elected

741. TLM Sep 18 1828/Married Thus last by Rev B. Kurtz, John George, Jr. to Miss Elizabeth Schlenker, all of this co/Married same day by same, Jacob Haynes, of Harpers-Ferry, Va, to Mrs. Sarah Marmaduke, of Shepherdstown, Va /Married Thurs 11th inst by Rev Bryson, David Newcomer, of this co, to Mrs. Bethsheba Johnson, of Balt

742. TLM Sep 25 1828/Died Mon evening last, after a protracted illness, Miss Elizabeth Gaither, dau of Henry Gaither, late of this co; remains interred in Episc Church Yard

THE TORCHLIGHT AND PUBLIC ADVERTISER (Hagerstown)

743. TLM Oct 2 1828/Married Sun last by Rev Emmert, William Knodle to Miss Rachael Kauffman, dau of Christian Kauffman, all of this co/Married Tues last, Henry Middlekauff, to Mrs. Mary Kilpatrick, all of this place/Died Fri monring last at her res in this place, Miss Margaret Maffet, aged about 56 yrs

744. TLM Oct 9 1828/Died of billious fever at Jefferson Barracks, Mo, 22 Aug, 1st Lieut. James Grier of the 5th Infantry. Since his graduation at the Academy in 1821 his services and employments on extra duties have been highly honorable/Died Sat night last, Mrs. Huyett, consort of Daniel Huyett, near Cave-town, in this co, apparently in good health 24 hrs previously, leaving husband and children/Died Sun last, Mrs. Stouffer, wife of Christian Stouffer, near Funks-town/Died at the res of Judge John Buchanan, yesterday morning, Matilda, youngest dau of John I. Stull, Esq. of George Town, D.C. /Married in Mercersburg, Thurs 2d inst by Rev T. B. Clarkson, Jas. Williamson, M.D. to the amiable Miss Catharine, dau of Daniel Shaffer, Esq. all of that place/Married in the vicinity of Xenia, Ohio, on 2d inst by Rev Towler, Henry Kealhofer, Jr. formerly of this place, to Miss Anna P. Beall

745. TLM Oct 16 1828/Died Sat evening 4th ult, between hours of 9 and 10 o'clock, Mrs. Mary Huyett of this co, in the 41st year of her age. She had been in a delicate situation for the last 12 months. On the morning of her decease she complained of giddiness, which was succeeded by fainting. Nothing serious, however, was apprehended; and arrangements having been made to accompany her brother to town, she expressed her assent not to postpone it. On her arrival in town she continued to have slight symptoms of fainting and medical assistance was immediately applied to. And yet no serious apprehensions were entertained by her medical attendant. On her arrival at home, early in the evening, she was bled according to his directions, and every appearance seemed favourable to a recovery. But it was delusive./Died at about 5 o'clock on Sabbath afternoon, Cornelia Rebecca, youngest dau of Rev James Reid, of this place, aged 16 months; her death was occasioned by a very slight scratch of a nail, so as barely to shew blood, on Wed last. Sat morning a violent fever and symptoms of tetanus appeared

746. TLM Oct 23 1828/Married Tues evening 14th inst, by Rev Robert Kennedy, Doctor James Johnson Beatty to Miss Sarah Ann Muir, both of Clear Spring /Died Wed 8th inst, Mrs. Hannah Hamilton, wife of John C. Hamilton, and dau of late Charles M'Cauley, of this co

747. TLM Oct 30 1828/Married Thurs last by Rev B. Kurtz, Henry Newcomer to Miss Mary Ann, youngest dau of Major Peter Seibert, of this co/Died Sun evening last, near this place, after a lingering illness, Mrs. Selenary W. Ragan, consort of Jonathan Hager Ragan, leaving husband and a little dau

748. TLM Nov 6 1828/Died Tues evening last, at an advanced age, Gotleib Mittag, old inhabitant of this place/Married Thurs last by Rev B. Kurtz, Robert Vinsonheller, of Shepherds-town/Married same day by same, John Yontz, to Miss Prudence Entler, all of Shepherds-town, Va/Married same day by same, Samuel Anderson, to Miss Sarah Yontz, all of Shepherds-town, Va

THE TORCHLIGHT AND PUBLIC ADVERTISER (Hagerstown)

749. TLM Nov 13 1828/Married at Williams-Port on Thurs 6th inst by Rev Winter, William Steel to Miss Sally Prechfield, all of this co/Married Sun evening last by Rev James Reid, Dr. J.W. Roper of Harpers Ferry, Va, to Miss Ann Cecilia Thomson, of this place

750. TLM Nov 20 1828/Married in Bucks Co, Pa, Jacob Lukens, aged 81, to Miss Rachael Childs, aged 25. She is a niece to her husband, an aunt to her mother and sister to her grandmother/Married Tues last by Rev B. Kurtz, David Sprecher to Miss Mary Bear, both of this co/Died at a very advanced age, Wed last, George Kellar, one of the oldest citizens of this co/Died Sat last in Boonsborough, Mrs. Mary Hamilton, dau of Wm. Hess, of Hagers Town /Died Sat last, Mrs. Elenora Allison, wife of Andrew Allison of this place /Melancholy accident - On Thursday last, after the receipt of the full returns in this electoral district, a number of the Jackson party repaired to the two pieces of cannon opposite sides of our town for the purpose of rejoicing at their triumph. The pieces were fired nearly at the same moment and both bursted. No injury was sustained at the bursting of that on the West of the town. On the East the case was different - George Bowers lost his life; his head was severed from his body and carried nearly 100 yards into an adjoining field./John B. Lynch of this co, died on Friday last. He had received a serious injury in the foot a few days previous by its being caught in a threshing machine. This injury was followed by amputation which however, did not avail to the saving of his life.

751. TLM Nov 27 1828/Married Thurs last by Rev B. Kurtz, Thos. Lowry to Miss Elizabeth Haffley, all of this place/Married same day by Rev Geo. Geeting, Henry Piper to Miss Elizabeth, dau of Jacob H. Keedy, of this co /Married same day by same, Joseph Rohrer to Miss Elizabeth Thomas, both of Pleasant Valley/Married in Williams-Port Tues evening 25th inst by Rev J. Winter, George Albert, of Hagers Town, to Miss Mary Ann Herr, of the former place/Married Tues evening, 12th inst by Right Bishop Onderdonk, Rev Jehu Curtis Clay, Rector of the Episc Church of Norristown and Perkiomen, and formerly of this place, to Miss Simmons Edey, dau of late Richard Edey, Esq. formerly of the Island of Barbadoes/Married in city of Balt Fri, 14th inst, by Rev Wyatt, Jonas Green, Esq. Editor of the Annapolis Gazette, to Miss Mary Atkinson, of the former place/Died 22d inst, Mrs. Sarah M'Williams, consort of Capt. Robert P. M'Williams, in the 22d year of her age, leaving 2 infants, the youngest only 8 days old, and husband; remains interred in Luth burying ground in Sharpsburg; funeral discourse delivered by Rev John Matthews of Shepherdstown/Died Sun 16th inst in city of Balt, after a long illness, and in the 29th year of his age, Luke Tiernan, Jr., 2nd son of Luke Tiernan, esq. of that city

752. TLM Dec 4 1828/Married Sun last by Rev Geo. Geeting, Jacob Kost, to Miss Catharine Snavely, both of this co/Married same day by same, James Smith, to Miss Sophia Long, both of Pleasant Valley/Married Thurs evening last by Rev M.L. Fullerton, William Yeakle, to Miss Harriet M. Hoye, of this place/Equity case - David Cheney, vs David Nighswander and others. Object of bill is to obtain decree for sale of real estate of Jacob Nighswander, decd, for payment of debts. The bill states that said Jacob Nighswander died largely indebted to complainant and sundry others. Heirs of said Jacob Nighswander, the following res out of the state, namely: David Nighswander,

THE TORCHLIGHT AND PUBLIC ADVERTISER (Hagerstown)

Emanuel Nighswander, George Welhouser and Elizabeth his wife, Daniel Nighswander, John Barnhart, David Barnhart, Peter Barnhart and Matthew Barnhart /Equity case - Daniel A. Bertolet and Ann his wife, vs. William Boone, George Boone and others, heirs at law of George Boone, decd. Petition has been filed by Andrew Sayler and Elizabeth his wife, Benjamin Kline and Harriet his wife, Jonathan Evans and Margaret his wife, William Runior and Mary his wife, and Jeremiah Boone and Rachael his wife, setting forth that by the last will of said George Boone, duly executed according to the laws of Pennsylvania, but insufficient to pass any interest in real estate lying in Md, certain part os the testator property were devised to several of his children, and the residue sold, but this was insufficient to pay said legacies and proceeds of said prop in Wash Co may be applied to the payment of said legacies/Notice to James Ramsay, John Van Lear Ramsay, Mary Jane Ramsay, Eliza Ramsay, Sally Ramsay, Nancy Ramsay, Sophia Allis Ramsay, Susan Emma Ramsay and Frances Ramsay, of Pa, which said James, etc... are devisees of Mary Van Lear, decd, late a defendant to the bill of complainant of Otho H. Williams and others, in Wash Co Court

753. TLM Dec 11 1828/Married Thurs 27 Nov by Rev B. Kurtz, David Ridenour to Miss Susan Ebrecht, all of this co/Married Thurs last by same, Charles G. Lane, to Miss Maria F. Kirkpatrick, both of this place/Married same day by Rev Geo. Geeting, Thomas Blake, to Miss Anna Morrison, both of this co/Married Sun last at Green-Castle, Pa, by the Rev Ruthrauff, Jacob Smith to Miss Susanna Keefer, both of this co/Reward for apprentice to tailoring business, named Daniel Moats, about 20 yrs of age, offered by John P. Hammer

754. TLM Dec 18 1828/Married Thurs last by Rev Rahauser, Henry Freaner to Miss Sarah Chambers, both of this place/Married 2d inst by Rev Williamson, Dr. A. T. Dean, formerly of Chambersburg, to Miss Adeline C. Junkin, dau of Richard McCrain, of Dauphin co/Died Sat morning last in this place, David Bish, in the 33rd year of his age, leaving wife and two young children/Died Tues evening last about 11 o'clock, William Hess, Sen, after an illness of 8 days; he has braved the tempests of 76 winters and for upwards of 40 yrs been citizen of this place

755. TLM Dec 25 1828/Married Thurs last by Rev B. Kurtz, John Swope, to Miss Mary Ann Petry, all of this co/Married same day by Rev Isaac Kellar, John Sensel, to Miss Catharine R. Schnebly, both of this co/Married Tues last by Rev B. Kurtz, Samuel H. Alter to Miss Catharine Westeberger, both of this co/Married Thurs 25th ult, Martin Wheelan from the Falls of St. Anthony, Mississippi, to Miss Elizabeth Price, of Unity, Montgomery Co, Md. The vicissitudes of a soldier's fortune detained him from the arms of his dearest 16 yrs, when he performed a journey of 1600 miles on foot to consummate his early vows - Rockville Amer./Died suddenly, Mon morning 8th inst, at his res in Loudon, Pa, Thomas Williamson/Died Fri morning last in this town, John Henry Miller, in the 72d year of his age/Died Sat last in this town, in the 76th year of her age, Mrs. Christiana House, relict of Michael House/Died Thurs 11th inst at an advanced age, Samuel Downey, of Franklin Co, Pa/Died in this Borough Friday last, in the 75th year of her age, Mrs. Mary M'Clintic, widow of Daniel M'Clintic - Chambersburg Repository.

THE TORCHLIGHT AND PUBLIC ADVERTISER (Hagerstown)

756. TLM Jan 1 1829/Died Fri morning last, after an illness of 15 days, Samuel Updegraff, silver smith, of this place, in the 33d year of his age, leaving orphan, wife and parents

757. TLM Jan 8 1829/Married Sun 7th inst by Rev Geo. Geeting, George Hines, to Miss Sally Yerty, both of Pleasant Valley/Married Thurs 11th ult by same, Jacob Piper, to Miss Nancy Kitzmiller, both of this co/Married Thurs 18th ult by same, Jacob Clopper, to Miss Susan Deitrick, both of this co/Married Thurs week last, by same, Thomas Ainsworth, to Miss Charlotte Mullen/Died Thurs evening last, in this town, Abraham King, aged about 60 yrs; remains interred in Meth burial ground

758. TLM Jan 15 1829/Died in this place Sun last, at an advanced age, Mrs. --- Bowman, widow of the late Jacob Bowman/Died Tues morning last, at the Bell Tavern, Owen McMahon, aged about 30 yrs. He came here last Sep from The Cath Seminary at Charleston, S.C. He is from the county of Langford, Ireland

759. TLM Jan 29 1829/Married 22 Dec by Rev Campbell, John F. G. Mittag, Attorney at Law, to Miss Ann M'Kenna, only dau of Hon. William M'Kenna, all of Lancasterville, S.C./Married Sun week last by Rev Geo. Geeting, John Middlekauff, to Miss Elizabeth Neykirk(?), both of this co/Married on the same by Rev Denius, David Geeting to Miss Eliza Toby, both of this co/Died 15th inst at his res in Georgetown, in the 65th(?) year of his age, Lieut. Col. Isaac Roberdeau of the Topographical Engineers and Chief of the Topographical Bureau in the Department of War, over which he has presided from its erection/Died at his res near Park Head Forge, 13th inst, Isaac Bachtel, Jr. in the 36th year of his age/Died Tues last at her res in this town, Miss Polly Olewein/Died Wed morning at an advanced age, Mrs. Shupe, widow of late Jacob Shupe, decd of this place

760. TLM Feb 5 1829/Died Wed 28th ult, Francis Robison of Franklin Co, Pa, in the 85th year of his age, after an illness of 6 days

761. TLM Feb 12 1829/Married Thurs 5th inst by Rev John Winter, Augustus Lescher, to Miss Catharine Spigler, all of this co/Married same day by same, Samuel Cyester to Miss Eve, eldest dau of Col. Jacob Wolf, all of Williamsport/Married 4 Jan by Rev Jacob F. Definbaugh, Elias Spong, to Miss Catharine Weaver, all of this co/Married 29 Dec by same, Elias S. Grove, to Miss Mary Ann, dau of Joseph Smith, both of Sharpsburg/Died 7 inst at his res near William-Port, in the 39th year of his age, Major Edward Greene Williams, third and last surviving son of late Gen. Otho Holland Williams of the Rev army; remains accompanied to the tomb of his venerated father. He left wife and an only child/Death of Benjamin Varnum Crowninshield, of Salem Mass., born Jan 26 1808; died Jan 26 1829, graduated at Harvard Univ in 1827

762. TLM Feb 19 1829/Married Thurs evening last by Rev John Winter, Jonathan G. Cooper to Miss Elizabeth Bowers, all of Williams-port/Married Sun last by Rev Benjamin Kurtz, John Westenberger to Miss Susan Reynard, all of this co/Further on death of Major Edward Greene Williams; he was born in March 1789, 3rd and only surviving son of late Gen. Otho Holland Williams, grad of Princetown College. He served as a Captain of horse, during a

THE TORCHLIGHT AND PUBLIC ADVERTISER (Hagerstown)

period of the late war, twice returned a delegate from this county to the Legislature; retired from public service shortly after commencement/Died in Sharpsburg 6th inst, Henry Young, old Rev soldier, in the 97th year of his age; he served as a teacher in the German and English languages. He has been an inhabitant of Sharpsburg for upwards of 30 yrs. He was a U.S. pensioner for several yrs; res in the family of William Rohrback for last 5 yrs; interred in German Luth burying ground; discourse delivered by Rev Defenbaugh of this place

763. TLM Feb 26 1829/Married Tues evening last by Rev Isaac Keller, Dr. Samuel H. Rench to Miss Susan Swearingen, dau of John V. Swearingen, Esq. of this co/Died Mon last in this town, aged about 60 yrs, Henry Chrest, native of Germany, for several yrs an inhabitant of this town

764. TLM Mar 12 1829/Married Thurs last by Rev J.C. Bucher, Valentine Cow, to Miss Mary Smith, all of this co/Died 7th inst at his res in this co, in the 50th year of his age, Thomas Rowe

765. TLM Mar 19 1829/Married 3rd inst by Rev Martin Bruner, John Young of Montgomery Co, Md. to Miss Mary C. Shafer of this co/Married Wed last by Rev Benj. Kurtz, Isaac R. Douglass Esq. Attorney at law, of Charlestown, Va to Miss Margaret G. Stephenson, of Leetown, Va/Married Thurs last, by same, Job M'Namee, to Miss Margaret Bragunier, all of this place/Married same day by Rev Martin Bruner, David Hammond, of this co, to Miss Ann Newcomer, dau of Christian Newcomer, Jr. Sheriff of Wash Co/Married 25 ult by Rev Deckenbaugh, John Wisong, of Shepherdstown, Va, to Miss Helen Marietta Hebb of this co/Died Fri last after a short illness, at the house of William Wise, in this place, Miss Mary D. Crawford, dau of late John Crawford, in the 17th year of her age - Herald/Died Tues last at an advanced age, John Crumbaugh, old inhabitant of this place/Died in Harrisburgh Mon 9 inst, after a short illness, John De Pui, Clerk of the Senate of Pa and res of that town - Chronicle.

766. TLM Mar 26 1829/Married in Liberty township, Adams co, Pa, by Rev J. C. Bucher, of Cave-town, Wash Co, Md., John Boyd to Miss Catharine Catron, both of Adams co, Pa/Married Tues last by Rev B. Kurtz, John Blake to Miss Catharine Hammel, both of this place

767. TLM Apr 2 1829/Married Thurs last by Rev Kellar, Alexander Stephens, to Miss Mary Cahill, both of this co/Married same day by same, David Hauthorn, to Miss Mary Chaney, all of this co/Married Tues last by Rev Samuel K. Hushour, Charles A. Fletcher, to Miss Elizabeth Ziegler, dau of Frederick Ziegler, all of this co/Married Fri last in Williams-port, by Rev J. Winter, Henry Gosher, to Miss Elizabeth A. Kinsley, both of Va/Died night of Sat 21 Mar, at his res in Martinsburg, Va, Col. David Hunter, in the 68th year of his age/Died Thurs last at the res of Miss Inglis, in this town, after an illness of 3 weeks, in the 77th year of his age, Derick Peterson, Esq. formerly of Phila/Died suddenly Sat last, Conrad Blentlinger, in the 77th year of his age, old inhabitant of this town/Died Thurs last, Jacob Dechert (?), Esq. Post Master, of Chambersburg

THE TORCHLIGHT AND PUBLIC ADVERTISER (Hagerstown)

768. TLM Apr 9 1829/Married Thurs evening last by Rev Winter, John Cyester, to Miss Elizabeth Weisel, all of Williams-Port/Married Thurs last by Rev Benj. Kurtz, Henry Beakly, to Miss Elizabeth Ceavier/Died Thurs last at her res near Baker's Cross Roads, in this co, Mrs. Elizabeth Gary, aged 91 yrs, 6 months, 25 days, leaving 7 children, 36 grandchildren, 78 great grand children, and 2 g.g. grand children/Henry Hyster, about 16 yrs of age, ran away from the poor house (Balt), apprentice to the Segar business, about 4 ft 8-9 inch/Equity case - George Bean, vs Sophia Ann Kapp, Frederick Kapp & others, heirs at law of Michael Kapp, decd/Equity case - Henry Pfautz, Peter Kautz and Catharine his wife vs. Nancy Pfautz (widow), Nancy Pfautz, Michael Pfautz, Saml. Pfautz, Jos. Pfautz, Elizabeth Pfautz, John Pfautz and Jacob Pfautz. The bill is to obtain sale of real estate of which Henry Pfautz, Sen. died seized, for the benefit of his children and heirs. Henry Pfautz Sen. died intestate some time in 1826, leaving estate to his children, Nancy Pfautz, Michael Pfautz, Samuel Pfautz, Joseph Pfautz, Elizabeth Pfuatz, John Pfautz, Jacob Pfautz and complaints Henry Pfautz, Jr. and Catharine the wife of Peter Kautz, and also leaving Nancy Pfautz his widow. The bill also represents the whole of the defendants, except Nancy Pfautz is non compos mentis, are infants (under age of 21) and non-residents of the state of Md/Robert Downey and Mary Downey, vs William Braddon and Mary his wife and others. Object of the bill is to obtain sale of real estate of which Samuel Downey, died seized, for benefit of his heirs. Samuel Downey died intestate in 1828, leaving real estate to Robert Downey and Mary Downey and William Braddon and Mary his wife, Ann Downey, Samuel Downey, John Downey, Rebecca Lyon, Ruth wife of Robt. Burns, Susan Downey, Ruth Downey, John Downey, Edmond Downey, Basil D. Downey, Maria Downey, Harriet Downey, John Downey and William Downey. The bill represents the following defendants of full age and non-residents of state of Md: William Braddon and Mary his wife, Ann Downey, Samuel Downey, Rebecca Lyon, Robert Burns and Ruth his wife, and following namned infants under age of 21, also non-residents: John Downey, Susan Downey, Ruth Downey, John Downey and Edmond Downey

769. TLM Apr 16 1829/Married Thurs last by Rev B. Kurtz, Philip Stockslager, to Miss Sarah Schmutz/Married same day by same, Charles Edelen, to Miss Elizabeth Ridenour/Married Thurs evening last at Montpelier, by Rev Drane, Dr. John O. Wharton, to Miss Elizabeth A. T. 2nd dau of late John Thompson Mason, Esq/Married Tues evening last, by Rev Brunner, David P. West to Miss Attilia Heffleich, of this place/Equity case - Henry Nyman, John Eakle, vs Jacob Brandner, Samuel Brandner and others. Object of the bill is to obtain decree for sale of real esate of George Brandner, decd who died seized of considerable real estate in Wash Co which descended to his heirs at law, namely, Samuel Brandner and Michael Brandner of full age, and Levi, Jonas, Samuel, Susanna Brandner, children of Jacob Brandner, all of whom res out of state of Md. Also Andrew Brandner and Eliza Brandner infants and who m Christian Poffenberger, and are res of state of Md. George Brandner the younger, since the death of his father, sold and conveyed all his right to Jacob Snyder. Said Jacob Snyder hath since died, leaving following children, George Snyder and Jacob Snyder of full age and Elizabeth, David, Sarah, Joseph, Mary, Susanna, Solomon, Nancy and Ruanna Snyder, infants. The widow is in possession of dower right

THE TORCHLIGHT AND PUBLIC ADVERTISER (Hagerstown)

770. TLM Apr 23 1829/Married Sun 5th inst in city of Frederick, Md, by Rev D. F. Shcaffer, Joseph A. Roof, of this place, to Miss Christiana Criglow, of the former place/Married by Rev M. Bruner, Wesley Manning to Miss Mary Sager/Married by same, George Glaize to Miss Lucinda Ann Rogers, of Va/Married Thurs evening last, by Rev Drane, Dr. Charles Macgill, of Martinsburg, Va, to Miss Mary, eldest dau of Richard Ragan, Esq. of this place/Died in Balt Tues 14th, of a lingering illness, Henry Locher, Jr. in the 53d year of his age, for many years an inhabitant of this co. He left a large family /Died at his res in this co, Fri last, after a long and painful illness, in the 61st year of his age, Robert Hughes, Esq. He had filled several important offices.

771. TLM Apr 30 1829/Married Thurs 16th inst by Rev John Winter, Elie Prather to Miss Catharine Hanes, all of this co/Married Thurs 23d by same, Isaac Baer to Miss Ann Donoho, both of this co/Married Tues last by Rev M.L. Fullerton, David C. Newcomer to Miss Eleanora Catharine, youngest dau of Thomas Grieves, of this place

772. TLM May 7 1829/Married Sun 12th ult by Rev S. K. Denius, John Coblentz, to Miss Sarah Remsberg, both of Frederick Co/Married 16th ult by same, Jonathan Thomas, to Miss Rosanna Mumma, both of this co/Married Thurs evening last by Rev Rahauser, William Boyd, to Miss Eliza Shugers, both of this place/Died in this town, yesterday morning, after a few days illness, Capt. Thomas Post, formerly Sheriff of this co, aged 55 yrs and 7 months, leaving wife and 6 children

773. TLM May 14 1829/Married 28 Apr by Rev R. Wilson, Basil Prather to Miss Temperance Mason, dau of Rev J. Mason, of this co/Married Thurs last by Rev B. Kurtz, Jacob Nepper to Miss Mary Francis, both of Clear Spring/Married same day by Rev M'Naughton, George W. Sellers, to Miss Rebecca Geyer, all of Mercersburg, Pa/Died yesterday in Williams-Port, after a lingering pulmonary affliction, Mrs. Jane Friend, widow of the late Gabriel Friend/William Pool has been committed to the jail of this co, charged with the murder of a mulatto man named Joseph Smith, prop of George Shiess, of this co, on the 10th inst. Acording to the inquest - "by two blows inflicted on his head with a piece of timber in the still house of said Geo. Shiess, in the moment of excitement and anger, produced by irritative language from the deceased."

774. TLM May 21 1829/Married in Balt Tues 12th, by Rev Duncan, Parker Blood, of this place, to Miss Clarine, eldest dau of Captain Lodowick Leeds of that city/Married Thurs last by Rev B. Kurtz, George Carson to Miss Matilda, dau of George Hershey, all of this co/Married same evening by same, Richard Welsh to Miss Margaret Gower, both of Funks-town/Married 12th inst by Rev Elliott, Francis Wyeth, editor of the "Harrisburg Argus," to Miss Susan H. Maxwell, dau of William Maxwell, of Franklin co, Pa/Died in this place this morning, after a few weeks' illness, William Fitzhugh, Jr., Esq. in the 43d year of his age. He was the late Jackson elector for this district.

775. TLM May 28 1829/Married 13th inst by Rev Geo. Geeting, Joseph Clayton, to Miss Louisa Showman, both of this co/Married Thurs last by same, Jacob Miller, to Miss Elizabeth, eldest dau of Jacob Schnebly, all of Pleasant

THE TORCHLIGHT AND PUBLIC ADVERTISER (Hagerstown)

Valley/Married Sun last, by same, John Huffer, to Miss Leah, eldest dau of John Blecher, all of Pleasant Valley/Married in Balt, Tues week last, by Rev Joseph Frye, Samuel Keener, to ...na dau of Mrs. Maria McCl... of that city /Died at Meadville, at the house of his son, Jesse Magaw, on 1st inst. Dr. William Magaw, formerly of Franklin co, Pa, aged about 89 yrs, patriot of the Rev; served as Surgeon in the Pennsylvania Line, during the whole of the war

776. TLM Jun 4 1829/Married in Carlisle Tues week by Rev ... Duffield, Rev John W. M'Cullough, to ... Mary Louisa Duncan/Married Tues last by Rev Martin Bruner, Samuel L. Gysinger, to Miss Elizabeth Julius/Married Thurs last by same, Andrew Rench to Miss Jane Price, all of this co/Died 1 Apr, near Middletown, Frederick Co, Catharine Bucher, formerly of Hagers Town, in the 93d year of her age/Died 23d inst in Brunswick Co, Va, Dr. Richard Field, Senior Editor of the Petersburg Intelligencer, in the 62d year of his age /Died at the house of Mrs. Kendal in this place, Joseph Taylor, Esq. ... Washington City, in the 56th year of his ... He arrived her about 2 weeks ago, with his Lady on his way to the Bedford Springs for the benefit of his health, but his journey was arrested in consequence of his illness, which ended in his death after several days of severe suffering

777. TLM Jun 11 1829/Married in Greencastle, Pa, Wed evening, 3d inst by Rev Buchanan, James Ramsey, of Phila, to Miss Jane C. Young, dau of late Rev Young, of that place/Married Tues last by Rev Smith, Henry A. Leonard, of Hancock, to Miss Mary Ann Duckett, of this place/Died in this place, Sun morning last, after a lingering illness, Mrs. Margaret Howthorn, consort of William Howthorn/From Hamilton (Ohio) Telegraph of May 29 - died last evening at his res adjacent to this place, after a tedious illness, John Cleves Symmes/From Opalousas Gazette of May 6 - Death of James Dixon, son of English emigrant, born in St. Mary's co, Md, 7 Jan 1797, studied medicine under Dr. Dorsey of Hagers Town; attened lectures in Phila and commenced practice in 1818 in this place; married 1824 dau of Judge King of this place; died 30 May 1829/Charlestown Repository of May 20 - Died Sat 9th inst, Mrs. Jane Robinson, wife of Archibald Robinson, near Shepherdstown, member of Presby Church

778. TLM Jun 18 1829/Married Chambersburg Thurs last by Rev Moeller, Hugh C. Raney, to Miss Neomy Duble, both of this place/Died in this place Tues night last, after a protracted illness, Thomas B. Hall, Esq. in the 43d year of his age, leaving numerous family of children. He was once Lottery Commissioner of the State/Equity case - Elizabeth Chaney vs Jeremiah Chaney and others. Object of the bill is to obtain decree for sale of real estate of John Chaney, decd for payment of his debts. He died indebted to complainant. The administration of his personal estate has been committed to Fanny Cheney, his widow. Of the heirs of John Chaney, the following res out of the state, namely, Naomy Johnson, Levi Foy and Mary his wife, John Swearingen and Amelia his wife, William Daily, John Corney and Naomy his wife, Patrick McClary and Hannah his wife, John Isenberger and Deborah his wife, Sarah Lane, Richard Chaney and Rebecca his wife, Elizabeth Lane, John Lane, David Lane and Julian Lane

THE TORCHLIGHT AND PUBLIC ADVERTISER (Hagerstown)

779. TLM Jun 25 1829/Died in this town Fri last, Mrs. Julianna Ott, relict of late Col. Adam Ott, in the 69th year of her age/Died same day at res of his mother in this town, Conrad Blendlinger, aged about 40 yrs/Died suddenly, Sat morning, at his res near Funks-town, Christian Stover, old inhabitant of this co/Died Tues morning last, after a protracted pulmonary indisposition, Miss Nancy Douglass, eldest dau of Robert Douglass, Esq. of this place

780. TLM Jul 2 1829/Married Thurs week last, by Rev Geo. Duffield, Rev Daniel Zacharias, of York, Pa, to Miss Jane, dau of Joseph Hays, Esq. of Carlisle, Pa/Married Sun last by Rev Bruner, Frederick Grosh, to Mrs. Elizabeth Zimmer, all of Funks-town/Married Mon last, by same, James Gillan, to Miss Eliza Jane Hanson/Married Sun 28th ult by Rev Jno. Winter, Robert P. McWilliams to Miss Ann Hebb, all of this co/Died in Shepherds-town, Va, Jun 21, 1829, about 3 o'clock, P.M. Dr. Benjamin F. Hickman, aged about 32 yrs. Of his early life we know little. After receiving a liberal education, he commenced the study of medicine with Dr. Cramer, of Charlestown, Va. After graduating he entered the matrimonial state and became a res of Sharpsburg, Md; he was member of Meth Episc Church. Shortly before his death, he was removed to Shepherds-town/Death of Thomas Harris, Esq. in Annapolis

781. TLM Jul 16 1829/Died at her grandaughter's Sun night last, in the 97th year of her age, Elizabeth Ann Orndoff, widow of Major Christian Orndoff, formerly of this co. Is is supposed that not less than 500 of her children's children, are now living. Two of her children, one 60, the other 70 yrs of age, witnessed her interment. Up to the 6th generation followed her to the tomb

782. TLM Jul 30 1829/Married Thurs last by Rev Bruner, Samuel Coblentz, to Miss Elizabeth Poffenberger, all of Middletown Valley/Married Tues last, Isaac Morgan, to Miss Elizabeth Gerhard/Died Sat last, after a short illness, Mrs. Margaret Barks, long a res of Pleasant Valley/Died same day, Miss Margaret Carns, of ths same place/Died at Marseilles, France, very suddenly, on the 29th of May last, Rev Michael De Bourgo Egan, President of Mount St. Mary's Seminary, near Emmittsburg. He sailed from this co in Oct last for the benefit of his health - Adams Sentinel.

783. TLM Aug 6 1829/Married Thurs last by Rev M.L. Fullerton, Peter Wright, to Miss Susan Staubs, both of this town/Died Wed last, after a short illness, Mrs. Mary Grimes, wife of Joshua Grimes, Esq. of Boonsborough/Died Fri night last, George Hammer, in the 67th year of his age, of this town/Died Sun morning last at the Globe Tavern in this place, John P. Pierce, a peaceable and unoffending man.

784. TLM Aug 13 1829/Died Fri last at his res in Pleasant Valley, after a short illness, Samuel Rohrer, in the 45th year of his age/Died in this place, Sun last, after a severe and protracted illness, Mrs. Mary Inglis, late of the city of Balt, in the 85th year of her age/Died at Havana 2d June last, Charles T. Monahan, native of Hagers Town, in the 23d year of his age, victim to prevailing yellow fever/Married Sun last by Rev J. Winter, Joseph Bowers to Miss Catharine Hines, both of Sharpsburg/Married Tues last by same, Jacob Sprecher top Miss Margaret Miller, both of this co

THE TORCHLIGHT AND PUBLIC ADVERTISER (Hagerstown)

785. TLM Aug 20 1829/Married Sun last by Rev John Winter, Martin Yontz, to Miss Catharine Deal, all of Va/Died Thurs night last, at her res near Smithsburg in this co, Mrs. Eve Oswald, in the 54th year of her age/Died Sat night last, in this town, Christian Brining/Died Mon 3d inst, Benjamin Franklin Hickman, only son of Charles Rowe, of this co, in the 5th year of his age

786. TLM Aug 27 1829/Married Thurs last by Rev B. Kurtz, Samuel Falder to Mrs. Margaret Kuhn, both of this co

787. TLM Sep 3 1829/Married in Williams-Port on 32d ult by Rev J. Winter, Gideon Landeger to Miss Rachael Grabell, both of Va/Died suddenly of a bilious cholic, Mon 24th ult, in Sharpsburg, Md., John Myres, Sen., leaving wife and 4 children/Died Thurs evening last, in this place, Thomas McCormick, in the 37th year of his age, leaving wife and several small children /Died Tues last, at her res in Funks-town, Mrs. Sarah Witmer, wife of late Daniel Witmer, of Lancaster Co, Pa/Died Sun last, in Balt, James Beale Davidge, M.D., professor of surgery in the Md. univeristy/Bedford Gazette - Died at the house of Humphry Dillon in this borough, Tues night last, Joseph Patterson, of Balt, generally known as "Patterson the Gambler." His disease was violent and his dissolution rapid. He is said, by those who knew him, to have had some good traits of character; but certainly his life was a war with every thing sacred in society

788. TLM Sep 10 1829/Married 6th inst by Rev J. Winter, James Clayton to Miss Sarah Boyd, all of Sharpsburg/Married Tues last by Rev Keller, Henry Bowers, to Miss Mary Shrouds, both of Va/Married Tues last by Rev Bruner, Joseph Lynn, to Miss Catharine Suver, all of Loudon, Va

789. TLM Sep 17 1829/Married Thurs last by Rev Isaac Keller, Henry Himes to Miss Amy Downes, both of this co/Married same day by Rev Buchanan, Solomon Calkglesser to Miss Elizabeth Kline, both of Hagers Town/Married Thurs 27th ult by same, Gabriel Jefferson Keen, to Miss Rebecca McKee, both of this co/Married Sun last by Rev Ruthrauff, Francis Renner, to Miss Katharine Staubs, both of this place/Married same day by Rev Bruner, Christian Winter, of this place, to Miss Catharine Cramer of Funks-town/Married Tues 9th inst by Rev Dr. Matthews, William T. Compton, to Miss Isabella K. Boyd, dau of late Samuel Boyd, Esq. all of Martinsburg

790. TLM Sep 24 1829/Married Thurs last by Rev Dr. Matthews, Joseph Ground to Miss Barbara Reel, both of Sharpsburg/Married Sun last by Rev Drane, William Philson to Miss Susan Clowser, all of this co/Married Tues last by the same, George H. Beck to Miss Mary Ann Householder, both of this co/Died in this place on Thurs last, Mrs. Kinkle, at an advanced age/Died at his res in this town, last night, after a short illness, in the 24th year of his age, John Brendle, 2nd son of George Brendle

791. TLM Oct 1 1829/Married at Green-Castle, Pa, Thurs 17th inst by Rev Matthew L. Fullerton, W. B. Copeland, merchant of Steubenville, Ohio, to Miss Jane, only dau of late Mr. A. Watt, decd of the former place/Married Tues last by Rev B. Kurtz, John M. Schlect, merchant, of Washington City, to Miss Elizabeth C. Ridenour, of this co

THE TORCHLIGHT AND PUBLIC ADVERTISER (Hagerstown)

792. TLM Oct 8 1829/Married Thurs last, Otway McCormick to Miss Sarah Ann Alexander, all of Brucetown, Va/Married Sun last, George Cauliflower Eakle to Miss Susan Dundore, all of Funks-town/Married Thurs last, at Carlisle, Pa, John Peterman to Miss Catharine Ohlwein, dau of Charles Ohlwein, all of Hagers-town/Married Tues last by Rev Kurtz, Dr. William H. Grimes of Clearspring, to Miss Susan Harbine, of this co

793. TLM Oct 15 1829/Married Thurs evening last, by Rev Drane, George Ross Beall, Esq. to Miss Ellen Schnebly, eldest dau of Daniel Schnebly, Esq. all of this place/Married same evening, by Rev Fullerton, Benjamin F. Yoe, Esq. to Miss Narcissa Post, dau of late Capt. T. Post, all of this place

794. TLM Oct 22 1829/Married Thurs last by Rev B. Kurtz, Samuel Giddinger to Miss Sarah Gantz, all of this co/Married same day by same, William Weis to Miss Margaret Schwartzwelder, all of this town/Married Tues by Rev M. Bruner, Josiah Kershner, to Miss Catherine Stine, all of this co/Died at Frederick-town, at the house of his son-in-law, Wm. Schley, Esq. on Sun last, in the 60th year of his age, General Samuel Ringgold, of this co. The decd had frequently represented this Congressional district in the Congress of the U.S. and Washington co in the House of Delegates and in the Senatorial Electoral College of the State; interred in the family burial ground, at Fountain Rock/Died at his res in Prince George's Co, Md., in the 75th year of his age, Col. William Dent Beall, distinguished officer of the Rev Army; his last public service being in the Legislature of the State/Died Wed morning 14th of Oct at his res near Cave-town, Wash Co, Md., after a short illness, John Shank, in the 46th year of his age, leaving widow and 9 children

795. TLM Nov 5 1829/Married Tues last in Chambersburg, by the Rev Rahauser, John A. Keaty, to Miss Susanna Wolgamot, both of this co/Married Wed last in the same place, by same, John Teischer, to Miss Mary Wolgamot, both of this co/Died Tues morning last, after a short illness, Mrs. Christiana Newman, in the 72d year of her age, for many yrs an inhabitant of this co/Died Sun last at the res of Daniel Zeller, Louisa Anna, 2d dau of Rev N. B. Little, who had been here on a visit from Cumberland, aged 11 months and 23 days

796. TLM Nov 12 1829/Married Tues last by Rev Kurtz, Jacob Mouser, to Miss Margaret Markwald, both of Va/Married Thurs last by Rev Geo. Geeting, Elias Mumma, to Miss Susan, eldest dau of Daniel Miller, all of this co/Married Tues evening last, by Rev M. L. Fullerton, James Johnson, M. D. to Miss Jane, 2d dau of Joseph Gabby, Esq. of this co

797. TLM Nov 19 1829/Married in Carlisle, Pa, Thurs, Oct 29, by Rev George Duffield, Rev Lewis H. Baucher, of Boonsborough, to Miss Clarissa M. Brooks, of the former place/Married Thurs last by Rev B. Kurtz, Andrew Irwin to Miss Ann Ferrin, both of Funks-town/Married Tues evening, Nov 3, at Cabelldale, Ky, by Rev Samuel Steele, Rev John C. Young, Pastor of the 2d Presbyterian Church, Lexington, to Miss Frances A., eldest dau of the late J. Cabell Breckenridge, Esq.

798. TLM Nov 26 1829/Married 3d inst at Mansfield, Ohio, by Rev H. O. Sheldon, Thomas T. Donaldson, merchant of Zanesville, to Miss Elizabeth Ann Walker, of Mansfield, both formerly of this place/Married Sun last in Lei-

THE TORCHLIGHT AND PUBLIC ADVERTISER (Hagerstown)

tersburg, by Rev J. C. Bucher, David Haverstick, to Miss Margaret Harrison, all of this co/Married Tues last by Rev W. Jones, Dr. James H. Clagett, of Mont Co, to Miss Elizabeth A. Garrett, eldest dau of Edward Garrett, esq. of this co/Married same day by same, Dr. John D. Garrett, of Frederick co, to Miss Matilda Garrett, 2d dau of Edward Garrett, Esq/Died in this place, Tues night last, after a long illness, John Creager, in the 47th year of his age /William Pool found guilty of manslaughter in the killing of a black man, property of Geo. Shiess, Esq, Wash Co. He was sentenced to 3 years in penitentiary, 3 months to be confined to the solitary cells

799. TLM Dec 3 1829/Married Tues last by Rev Crok of Balt circuit, Cornelius Staley, of Frederick Co, to Miss Ruhannah Snavely, dau of Adam Snavely, of this co/Married lately by Rev Wilson, Archibald I. Findlay, Esq. of Chambersburg, Pa, to Miss Sophia Van Lear, of Cincinnati, Ohio, dau of late Matthew Van Lear, Esq. of this co/Equity case - Ann Weaver vs David Weaver. The bill states that said David m said Ann several yrs ago, since which time she has borne him 2 children, both infants of tender yrs; that he has abandoned them and gone off to the western country, where he now resides; that Wm. Albert the father of said Ann, lately died, bequeathing to Ann an equal portion of his estate. The bill is to compel David to give up any claim to her portion in order that she support herself and children/Equity case - Jacob Bentze, John Monninger and others, vs David Neikirk, Mary Short, Elizabeth Night and Susanna Barr. Object of bill is to obtain decree for sale of real estate of Jacob Bentze, late of Wash Co. The bill states that Jacob Bentze died intestate around 1827, seized in fee simple of real estate in Wash Co, leaving Jacob Bentze a son and daus Eve who m John Monninger, Elizabeth who m --- Night, Mary who m David Short, Susanna who m Peter Barr, and Catharine who m John Neikirk, his children and heirs. Catharine Neikirk died in 1820 leaving issue Elizabeth, George, John, Jacob, Daniel, Johanis, Henry, Michael, Joseph, Samuel and David Neikirk her children. Mary Short and Susanna Barr reside out of the state of Md/Jacob Snively adm of George Schnebly, decd, vs Michael Beard, Peter Beard, Jacob Beard, George Beard, Philip Beard, David Beard, John Beard, Samuel Beard, David Troxell, Elizabeth Troxell, Peter Troxell, Margaret Troxell, Daniel Beard, Andrew Beard, Jacob Hull, John Hull and Catharine Hull, heirs and representatives of Philip Beard, decd. Object of the bill is to obtain decree for sale of real estate of Philip Beard, decd for payment of his debts. The bill states that said decd was indebted to Eve Schnebly, to secure the payment of which he executed to her his single bill. That said Eve assigned and transferred said single bill to George Schnebly for a valuable consideration. That after the death of said Philip an action was brought on said bill and judgment recovered agnst Michael Beard, administrator of said decd, in Wash Co Court of the use of said George Schnebly. After recovery of said judgment, George died intestate. Letters of admintration on his personal estate were granted to complainant by the Orphans' Court of said co. A certain portion of the heirs of Philip Beard are non-residents of Md, to wit, Peter, Jacob, George, John, and David Beard and Peter Troxell & Margaret his wife, and Jacob Hull and John Hull.

800. TLM Dec 10 1829/Married Tues last by Rev George Geeting, John Brown, to Miss Hannah Brown, both of this co/Died at his res two miles west of Hagers-town, Fri night last, of a pulmonary affection, David Oster, in the

THE TORCHLIGHT AND PUBLIC ADVERTISER (Hagerstown)

31st year of his age/Died Mon last in this town, Adam Glossbrenner, aged about 47/Died Mon last in this place, Mrs. Sally Harry, relict of George M. Harry, and dau of Mrs. Ann Chesley, of Hagers Town/Died in City of Phila, Tues last, Rev William Ashmead, formerly pastor of the Presby church in Lancaster, Pa/Died Wed last at his res in Frederick, after an illness of a few days, Col. John M'Pherson, in the 69th year of his age

801. TLM Dec 17 1829/Married near Pulaski, Tennessee on 17th ult, Turner F. Jack, formerly of Hagers Town, to Miss Caroline Lydia Perry, dau of James Perry, Esq.

802. TLM Dec 24 1829/Married in Frederick Sat evening 28 ult, by Rev D. F. Schaeffer, George Figely, of this place, to Miss Eleanor Yowler, of that city/Married 13th inst by Rev J. C. Bucher, James Hurley to Miss Maria, dau of Jacob Thomas, all of this co/Married 17th inst by same, Geo. Bowers to Miss Nancy Shank, dau of John Shank, decd, all of this co/Married Tues evening 15th inst, Dr. Francis M. Burckhart to Miss Catharine Ann Rosenberger, dau of Anthony Rosenberger, all of Berkeley Co, Va/Married Thurs evening last by Rev M. Bruner, William Tanley to Miss Amelia Dennison/Married Tues last by Rev B. Kurtz, David Witmer, to Miss Mary, 2d dau of John Horine, Esq. all of this co

803. TLM Dec 31 1829/Married in Frederick Co, Wed last, by Rev Smaltz, David Flory(?), of Wash Co, to Miss Mary Ann Lambert, of Frederick Co/Married Thurs last, by Rev Bucher, Ludwick Tritle, to Miss Catharine Martin, both of this co/Married same day by Rev B. Kurtz, Joseph Cratzinger, to Miss Rebecca M'Crea, all of this co/Married Thurs last, by Rev Denius, John Hoskins to Miss Catherine Rohrbach, all of this co/Died in this place, Mon last, at the res of Martin Rickenbaugh, Thomas Kean (hatter) in the 58th year of his age/Died same day, Mrs. Margaret Miller, in the 64th year of her age, widow of the late John Miller, decd, of this place/Died yesterday morning, Mrs. Sarah Thornburg, in the 37th year of her age, wife of George Thornburg, of this place

804. TLM Jan 7 1830/Married Thurs last by Rev B. Kurtz, Charles M'Cauley to Miss Elizabeth Ruch, all of this co/Married same day by Rev M. Bruner, Benjamin Watkins to Miss Margaret Haverstick, all of this co/Married Sun evening 20th ult by Rev Robert Wilson, William Harvey to Miss Eliza Rice, both of Williams-Port/Married at Martinsburg, Va, Thurs evening, 24th ult, by Rev Young, John Clise to Miss Sophia Locke, both of William-port

805. TLM Jan 14 1830/Married Tues evening last by Rev Jewett, Capt. Henry I. Shafer, of Funks-town, Md. to Miss Maria, youngest dau of William M'Kinstry, Esq. of Mercersburg, Pa/Married in Balt Tues morning, 5th inst, by Rev Henshaw, John R. Jones, Merchant, to Miss Rebecca Goll, formerly of Hagers Town/Married Tues 29th ult by Rev Dr. J. S. Reese, Rev Frederick Stier, formerly of this place, to Mrs. Eleanor Spencer, of Talbot Co, E. Shore of Md./Married 17th ult by Rev Bucher, Lewis Tritle of Frederick co, to Miss Catharine Martin, dau of Stephen Martin of this co/Married Tues last by Rev B. Kurtz, John McCoy to Miss Nancy Connelly, all of this co

THE TORCHLIGHT AND PUBLIC ADVERTISER (Hagerstown)

806. TLM Jan 21 1830/Married Thurs last by Rev Drane, Daniel Ridenour, to Miss Sarah Bean, all of this co/Married at Martinsburg, Va, Tues evening last, by Rev Monroe, John T. Evans, Esq. of Ky, to Miss Susan, dau of Capt. James Maxwell, of the former place/Died at her res in Sharpsburg, Mon evening 21 Dec, in the 79th year of her age, Mrs. Catharine Miller, consort of the late David Miller/Died Sun evening last, Mrs. Elizabeth Dusing, wife of John Dusing, of this co, in the 48th year of her age/Died at the res of Wm. Brazier, in Hagers Town, Sun last, at an advanced age, Mrs. Julian Heller(?) /Died at the res of James F. Williams in this town, yesterday morn- ing, in the 25th year of his age, John Cross/A man by the name of Elijah Elliott, res in Va, near Williams-Port, put an end to his existence on Wed week, in a fit of melancholy by suspension. He was a married man of about 25 yrs of age

807. TLM Feb 4 1830/Married Sun evening last by Rev M. Bruner, John Weis to Miss Adeline G. Lancaster, both of Shepherds-town, Va/Married Tues evening 26 ult, in City of Balt, by Rev Peyton, Henry Dundore, formerly of this place, to Miss Eliza West, of that city/Died Sat last, at the res of Mr. Wilms, on Long Meadows, 4 miles from Hagers Town, at an advanced age, Richard Wise/Died same day, Mrs. Ridenour, consort of Jacob Ridenour, of Harrystown/Died Sun morning last in this place, Mrs. Coliflower, consort of George Coliflower, merchant, leaving husband and 9 children

808. TLM Feb 11 1830/From Franklin Repository – Died of a lingering illness, at his res in Atrim township, 1st inst, Nathan M'Dowell, Esq. in the 72d year of his age. In the 19th year of his age, Mr. M'Dowell was called to the army of his country, then struggling for its independence, in which he served under Gen. Harmar, marched to the western frontier, to protect it from Indian outrage. In July 1788 he was honored with the command of a small force of 25 men. This small party ascended the Muskingum and encamped in the wilderness at the distance of 80 miles from the main army. In the night they were attacked by the Tawawa and Chippawa Indians, but in consequence of a gallant defence the assailants were repulsed with considerable loss. By this engagement the victors were reduced by killed and wounded and missing to 10 in number/Died Sat morning last, Mrs. Rebecca Tilghman, consort of Thomas Tilghman of this co/Died Thurs last at her res in this place, Mrs. Susan Hahn, at an advanced age/David Little offers reward for apprentice to the tailoring business, named Charles Selser, between 19 and 20 yr of age

809. TLM Feb 18 1830/Married Thurs 4th inst at Elizabeth-town, Lancaster Co, Pa, by Rev Frederick Ruthrauff, Joseph Strite, of this co, to Miss Elizabeth Strite, of the former place/Married Mon evening 8th inst by Rev Riddle, Rev Benjamin Kurtz, Pastor of the Luth Church in this town, to Miss Catharine Baker, dau of Henry W. Baker, Merchant, of Winchester, Va/Married Thurs last by Rev M. Bruner, John Weaver, to Miss Phebe Waters, all of this co/Married same day by same, Conrad Billmyer, of Jefferson co, to Miss Mary Martin of Berkeley co, Va/Married same day by Rev J. Diffenbacher, Capt. John Cushwa, of this co, to Miss Elizabeth Brewer, dau of Jacob Brewer, Esq. of Mercersburg, Pa/Married same day by Rev Rahauser, Mr. Alexander M'Cammon, to Miss Susannah M..tag, both of this place/Married 28th ult by Rev Funk, David Zuck, to Miss Elizabeth Negly, dau of Jacob Negly, Esq. all of Frank-

THE TORCHLIGHT AND PUBLIC ADVERTISER (Hagerstown)

lin co, Pa/Married Mon last by Rev Buchanan, Jacob C. Snyder, Esq. to Mrs. Sally Beard, both of this co/Married Thurs by Rev John Bryson, John C. Montgomery, Esq. of Danville, to Miss Debra Kerr, youngest dau of Jacob Kerr, of Turbut township, Northumberland co, Pa. The day after the marriage Mr. and Mrs. Montgomery started in a sleigh from her father's res and had proceeded but a short distance when the horses took fright and upset the sleigh, by which she was thrown against a fence and killed!/Died in Chambersburg, Wed morning last, in the 95th year of her age, Mrs. Rachel Aston, relict of Capt. Owen Aston - Repository/Died Thurs night last, at his res about 4 miles from Hagers Town, after an illness of only 4 days, Charles M'Cauley, aged about 28 yrs/Died at his res in Balt Co, 5th inst, Col. Peter Little, late a Representative in the Congress of the U.S., from the district in which he resided/Died in Nashville, Tenn, 23d July last, of a bilious fever, William Keen, Jr., native of Balt. Promoted by an enterprising spirit to interest himself in the mercantile line, he tore himself from the bosom of his family and friends, to avail himself of an opening in the South and West. The death of Mr. Keen was hastened in a considerable degree by a severe wound received in the side during the battle of North Point, near Balt. Frequent but unsuccessful attempts were made to extract the ball. In this engagement he justly received the praise of his commander, Capt. Montgomery. He fell on the battle ground, a wounded bleeding victim for his country - a prisoner of war only 18 yrs of age

810. TLM Feb 25 1830/Died last week, D. Steward Potter, youngest son of Daniel Potter of this co, in the 2d year of his age

811. TLM Mar 4 1830/Married Tues 23d ult by Rev Bruner, Rev Solomon K. Denius of Boonsborough, to Miss Mary Ann Shafer, dau of George Shafer, Esq of the same place/Married Thurs last by same, Henry Rohrer to Miss Susan Allebaugh, both of this co/Married same day by Rev B. Kurtz, Henry Dusing to Miss Mary Ann Rutter, both of Frederick co/Married same day by same, Maurice Baker to Miss Elizabeth Fayman, both of Va/Married evening of 22 Feb at house of Louis Fletcher, of Boonsborough, by Rev S. K. Denius, Samuel Snider, of this place, to Miss Ann Maria, of Balt City, dau of late Zephaniah Chaney, of Balt co

812. TLM Mar 11 1830/Married Tues evening 2d inst by Rev H. Haverstick, Samuel Charles, Editor of the "Civilian," to Miss Margaret Wineour, dau of Henry Wineour, all of Cumberland/Married Thurs last by Rev B. Kurtz, John Drill, of Frederick co, to Miss Elizabeth Protzman, of this place/Married same day by same, Jonas Petry to Miss Emeline Weaver, all of this co/Married Tues last, in Martinsburg, Va, by Rev Medtart, Jacob Reitzell, of this place, to Miss Rebecca Hughes, of the former place/Died in Balt Sat 27th ult, Mrs. Eleanor Clagett, in the 76th year of her age, relict of the late Alexander Clagett, Esq. formerly of this place/Died at Antietam Iron Works Sat 20th ult, Thomas Blake, in the 39th(?) year of his age, leaving widow and children

813. TLM Mar 18 1830/Portion missing/...remains interred in St. Paul's Church Yard/Died Fri morning last in the 82d year of his age, Rev Christian Newcomer, for many yrs Bishop of the German Meth Society; crossed the Allegheny mountains 20 times, attended the first Camp Meeting, which was held in

THE TORCHLIGHT AND PUBLIC ADVERTISER (Hagerstown)

the lower part of this state. Nine days before his death he left home for the purpose of serving his Lord and Master, when his horse took firght, threw him and broke several of his ribs; he lingred and expired shouting praises to the the God of his salvation; reamins attended to the family burial ground, near Beaver Creek, 5 miles from Hagers Town/Died Sat last, Mrs. Catharine Billmyer, in the 48th year of her age, cosnort of John Billmyer, of this town/Died Sat morning last, in the 22nd year of his age, John Swope of this co, after a lingering pulmonary indisposition/Died Mon afternoon, Malvina McClennah, aged 1 year and 10 days, dau of James Swisler, Jr/Died lately at Raleigh, N.C. at the res of Gavin Hogg, Esq. the Rt. Rev John Stark Ravenscroft, D.D. Bishop fo the Prot. Episcopal Church, in N. Carolina, in the 58th year of his age

814. TLM Mar 25 1830/Married Thurs last by Rev M. Bruner, Daniel Shanefelt to Miss Sarah Funk, all of this co/Married same day, by same, David Spielman, of this place, to Miss Catharine Sayler, all of this co/Married same day, by same, William Halley, to Miss Sarah Haverstick, all of this co/Married same day by Rev Robert Wilson, Reuben Rogers, to Miss Mary Ann Kring, of Harrisonburg, Va/Married same day by Rev John Winter, George I. Brewer, to Miss Elizabeth dau of Lancelot Jacques, Esq all of this co/Married Sun last by same, William Kreigh, to Miss Margaret McClary, all of this co/Married Tues last by same, William Boyer to Miss Regina Stickley, both of Va /Married Thurs week by Rev Geo. Geeting, Joseph Hout, of Jefferson Co, Va, to Miss Mary, dau of Henry Rohrback, of this co

815. TLM Apr 1 1830/Married 11th ult by Rev Brown, John Middlekauff, of this co, to Miss Catharine Cushwa, of Berkeley co, Va/Married Thurs last by Rev Bruner, Jacob Marken, to Miss Rebecca Garman, both of Frederick Co/Married 18th ult by Rev B. Kurtz, Jacob Beard to Miss Lea Beard, both of this co/Married Thurs last by same, Jacob Bowser, of Sandusky, Ohio, to Miss Ann, dau of David Startzman, of this co/Married Tues last by same, Henry T. M. Briscoe, to Miss Elizabeth Entler, both of Shepherdstown, Va/Died in this place Fri last, Mrs. Showaker, consort of Martin Showaker/Died Sun night last in the 60th year of his age, John Schleigh, Sen., Inn-keeper, of this place

816. TLM Apr 8 1830/Married Tues evening last by Rev M. L. Fullerton, Peter Suter, to Mrs. Catharine Martin, both of this place/Married Sun evening last, by Rev Bruner, David Swope, to Miss Maria Renner, all of this co

817. TLM Apr 15 1830/Married Thurs last by Rev B. Kurtz, David Ridenour to Miss Margaret 2d dau of Jacob Kausler, all of this place/Married same day by same, John Winders, to Miss Rebecca Slenker, both of this co/Married Fri last by same, George Kitchen to Miss Maria Gant, both of Va/Married Sun last by Rev M. Bruner, John Reed to Miss Amelia Robinson, all of this co

818. TLM Apr 22 1830/Married in city of Balt Tues 6th inst by Rev Joshua Wells, Archibald Cameron of Shepherds-town, Va, to Miss Ann, dau of Paul Ruckle, merchant in that city/Died Sat 10th inst at his res in this co, after an illness of about 6 weeks, in the 54th year of his age, Christian Hershey, farmer of this co/Died Sat evening, Harriet, dau of John Brien, Esq. of Catoctin Furnace, about 13-14 yrs of age - Reservoir

THE TORCHLIGHT AND PUBLIC ADVERTISER (Hagerstown)

819. TLM Apr 29 1830/Married 15th inst by Rev B. Kurtz, William Startzman to Miss Sophia Miller, all of this co/Married Wed last by same, Asa Hervey Hoge to Miss Rebecca McPherson Lupton, both of Winchester, Va/Died Tues 20th inst at the res of her grand-mother (Mrs. Deborah Scott) in Cumberland, Mary Catharine Swearingen, aged 4 yrs, 6 months/Died Tues evening last, in this place, Miss Sophia Ann Kapp, in the 21st year of her age/Equity case - Elizabeth Chaney vs Jeremiah Chaney and others. Object of bill is to obtain decree for sale of real estate of John Chaney, decd, who lately died indebted to complainant and others. Administration of his estate has been committed to Fanny Chaney his widow. Of the heirs of John Chaney, the following res out of the state of Md, namely, Naomy Johnson, Levy Foy and Mary his wife, John Swearingen and Amelia his wife, William Daily, John Corney and Naomy his wife, Patrick McClary and Hannah his wife, John Isenberger and Deborah his wife, Sarah Lane, Richard Chaney and Rebecca his wife, Elizabeth Lane, John Lane, David Lane and Julian Lane

820. TLM May 6 1830/Married Tues last by Rev Bruner, George Zentmyer, to Miss Nancy Boyer, of Frederick co/Died at Green Castle, Thurs last, after a protracted illness, Frederick Weitzell, in the 27th year of his age, eldest son of John Weitzell, formerly of this town/Chambersburg Repository (newspaper) - Died at his res near this Borough, Sat afternoon last, of the consumption, in the 66th year of his age, Hugh Brotherton

821. TLM May 13 1830/Died of a pulmonary disease, Mrs. Knavel, wife of George Knavel, in the 44th year of her age, leaving husband, 3 children and an aged mother/Died at res of Wm. Price, Esq. in this town, yesterday morning, after a lingering illness, Miss Sophia Duckett, youngest dau of late Dr. Richard Duckett, of Prince Georges co, Md/Married Thurs last by Rev B. Kurtz, Samuel Furrey to Miss Susan Siderstick, all of this co/Married Sun last by same, Lewis L. Lee of New York, to Miss Catharine Winders, of this co/Married Sun 9th inst by Rev Winter, Joseph Garish to Miss Catharine Albert, all of Williams-Port

822. TLM May 20 1830/Married in New York 5th inst, Rev Matthew L. Fullerton of Hagers Town, to Miss Ann Duryee, dau of late Isaac Heyer, of New York /Married Thurs last by Rev Jones, of Charlestown, Va, Jacob H. Grove, merchant of Sharpsburg, to Miss Mary Hite, dau of Col. Hite, of Jefferson co, Va/Died in this town, at the res of her son Joseph Boyd, Thurs last, Mrs. Eleanor Boyd, aged 93 years/Died Fri last, Miss Elizabeth Oldwine in the 36th year of her age, dau of Charles Oldwine, of this town/Died Sat last at Mont Alto Iron Works, in Franklin co, Pa, James C. Hughes, in the 31st year of his age, son of Samuel Hughes, Esq./Died Mon evening last, after a lingering illness, Miss Susan Dusinger, in the 52d year of her age, 2d dau of Philip Dusinger, of this place/Died Wed 28th ult, at her res in this co, in the 51st year of her age, Mrs. Sarah Winders, widow of the late John Winders/Died in George-town, D. C. Thurs evening last, in the 59th year of his age, Daniel Bussard, Esq. a member of the Board of Aldermen. - Columbian Gazette/Samuel Gilbert, 4 miles from Hagers Town, offers reward for Philip Henley, 15 yrs of age, about 5 ft 6 inch, slender made, fair hair, quick and free spoken and very inquisitive, indented apprentice

THE TORCHLIGHT AND PUBLIC ADVERTISER (Hagerstown)

823. TLM May 27 1830/Married Tues last, by Rev Funk, Samuel Eyerly of Wash Co, to Miss Mary Ann Sleider, of Cumberland Co, Pa/Married Thurs last by Rev B. Kurtz, John Horine, Esq. to Mrs. Frances Cheney, all of this co/Married same day by Rev Drane, Elias Welck to Miss Elizabeth Johnson, both of this co/Married same day by same, Gera South to Mrs. Sarah Watts, all of this co/Marriage on 22d ult at Marietta, by Silas Cook, Esq., Charles Samuel Swartwout Barron, of Belmont Co, to Miss Mary Wilhelmine Fustin Caroline Louise Fredericke Zeigler, of Marietta

824. TLM Jun 3 1830/Jacob Easterday gives notice that his wife Feronia Easterday has left his bed and board; he is determined not to pay anything of her contracting

825. TLM Jun 10 1830/Married Thurs last by Rev B. Kurtz, William Bodmann to Miss Susan A. dau of John Kealhofer, all of this place/Married same day by Rev Bruner, John Bigham to Miss Mary Ann Kershner, both of this co/Married at Balt Sun 30th ult, by Rev D. McCilton, Henry H. Zimmerman, of this place, to Miss Mary Ann, eldest dau of Basil Legg, of Queen Ann co/Married Thurs 13th May by Rev Geo. Geeting, Jacob Domer to Miss Rachel Dennison, both of this co/Married Thurs 20th ult by same, Archibald Lamarr to Miss Susan Brown, both of Pleasant Valley/Married Thurs 27th ult by same, John Myers to Miss Mary Myers, both of this co/Died 26th ult, James N. Chapline, residing near Sharpsburg, aged 33 yrs. Although during a good part of Mr. Chapline's life some irregularities of conduct were occasionally observable, yet according to his own acknowledgements, hte early instructions of a most pious mother, frequently checked him in his hours of levity and mirth

826. TLM Jun 17 1830/Married Tues 1st inst, by Rev George Geeting, John Benner to Miss Harriet Koons/Married same day by same, George Snavely to Miss Eliza Baker/Married Thurs last by same, James Tannehill to Miss Elizabeth Hoffman/Married same day by same, John Bender to Miss Barbara Slice /Married Sun last by Rev Winters, Jacob Johnston to Miss Eliza Snavely, all of this co/Married Thurs last by Rev Buchanan, Abraham Trago, of Harpers-Ferry, Va., to Miss Juliann Hawken of this place/Married Thurs last by Rev Bacher, Elie Crampton, Esq. to Miss Maria, dau of David Rohrer, Esq. of Pleasant Valley, Md/Died Sun last, Mrs. Ault, consort of Jacob Ault, of this place

827. TLM Jun 24 1830/Married at Waynesburg, Sun last by Rev Buchanan, Jacob McCleary, of Cave-town, to Miss Margaret Padin, of Funks-town/Married Tues evening last, by Rev B. Kurtz, Philip Kreigh, to Miss Leah Hammer, of this place/Married same evening, by Rev Bruner, Thomas Murray, of Balt City, to Miss Mary Beard, of this place/Died Tues last, after a short illness, Capt. Robert P. McWilliams, of Sharpsburg

828. TLM Jul 1 1830/Married Thurs 3rd ult, by Rev Hoshour, Daniel Flora, of Smithsburg, in this co, to Miss Catharine McLanahan, of Waynesburg, Pa/Married Thurs 10th ult by same, John Craddock to Miss Margaret A. Mong, of this co/Married 19th ult, in the city of Balt, by Rev Wilmer, Jonathan M. Robinson of this co, to Miss Sarah Ann Holland, of that City/Married Thurs evening last, by Rev B. Kurtz, Daniel Stewart Hammacher to Miss Susan Bender, dau of George Bender, all of this town/Married same evening, in Sharpsburg,

THE TORCHLIGHT AND PUBLIC ADVERTISER (Hagerstown)

by Rev Drane, Rebe John Alexander Adams, Rector of St. Pauls Church, Sharpsburg, to Mrs. Mary Anna Ritchie/Married at Lexington, Ky, Thurs evening Jun 17, by Rev Dr. Fishback, Jonathan D. Hager to Miss Sarah Springle, both of that place

829. TLM Aug 5 1830/Married Sun last by Rev M. Bruner, Adam Kellar to Miss Ann Maria Beckenbaugh, both of Middletown, Frederick Co, Md/Married Tues last by Rev John Light, Perry Prather, Esq. to Miss Elizabeth, dau of the late Ab'm Troxell, both of this co/Died at his res about 3 miles from Williams-Port Thurs evening last, after an illness of 4 days, John Ash, in the 57th year of his age

830. TLM Aug 12 1830/Married at Greencastle, Thurs last by Rev Buchanan, Levi B. Moles, of Clear Spring, Md, to Miss Esther Martin of the former place/Married at Lexington, Ky, by Rev Chapman, James O. Harrison, Attorney at Law, to Miss Margaretta Ross/Died Mon 2d inst, about 3 miles from Williams-Port, in the 30th year of his age, Frederick Moudy, after an illness of 9 hours, which defied medical relief, leaving wife and several children - Repub. Banner

831. TLM Aug 19 1830/Died in Pleasant Valley, Jul 29th, Perry (Perny?) Barney Conner, aged 12 yrs, 9 months/Died at the same place 9th inst, Lydia Conner, aged 18 yrs, 4 months and 4 days. Both were children of Hugh and Sarah Conner

832. TLM Aug 26 1830/Married Thurs last by Rev George Geeting, Samuel Kitzmiller to Miss Mary Palmer, both of this co/Died in Boonsboro', Sun 22nd inst, after much and painful suffering, Mrs. Susanna Funk, in the 78th year of her age; funeral discourse by Rev Kurtz

833. TLM Sep 2 1830/Married at Rockland in this co, Tues evening, by Rev Drane, William Holliday, Esq. of Queen Anne's co, to Miss Ann E.,. 3d dau of Col. F. Tilghman/Died at Bellefontain, in Logan co, Ohio, Thurs 5th inst, after an illness of a few hours, of billious cholic, Jacob Sides, formerly of this town

834. TLM Sep 9 1830/Married at Cincinnati, evening of 17th Aug by Rev Finlay, George A. Bender, of Hagers Town, to Jemima, youngest dau of Col. Charles Hales/Married Thurs last by Rev Kurtz, Daniel Baugher of Frederick co, to Miss Elizabeth Swope, of this co/Married Thurs 26th ult by same, Emanuel Herr, to Miss Catharine Petry, all of this co/Died 21st ult after a protracted illness, in the 64th year of his age, Robert Cheney, sen. Esq., farmer of our co/Died at the res of Col. H. Runnels, in Monticello (Miss.) Fri 6 Aug, Thomas D. Lecompt, aged about 39 yrs, native of the Eastern part of Md, and has resided in this place for a considerable length of time - Advocate.

835. TLM Sep 16 1830/A Negro man, property of Hilleary Talbott, of Shepherds-town, Va, put an end to his existence, Wed week, at the Tavern of Mr. Morrison, near Boonsborough, by hanging himself with his wagon line. It is said this man nuroed Cox when an infant, and had been melancholy ever since Cox's execution/Married Tues 20th ult by Rev Reck, Thomas H. Crampton, to

THE TORCHLIGHT AND PUBLIC ADVERTISER (Hagerstown)

Miss Ann M. Keller, both of Pleasant Valley/Died in Bedford Co, Pa, on 30 July last, Mrs. Mary Kershner, widow of the late George Kershner, of this co, in the 85th year of his age. She was a native of Wash Co.

836. TLM Sep 23 1830/Married Fri last at Greencastle, by Rev Rothroff, Jacob Ault to Miss Naomi De Butts, both of this place/Died Sat last, at Mount Tammany, near Williams-Port, Mary Jane Ramsay, dau of Col. J. Ramsay, of Pittsburgh, Pa, in the 21st year of her age/From the Shepherdstown Pioneer, of Sep 15 - Died Tues last at the res if William Taylor, in this co, after a short but severe illness, Daniel B. Newcomer, in the 23d year of his age, member of Meth Episc Church; ramains conveyd to his father's res near Hagers Town

837. TLM Sep 30 1830/Married Thurs last, near Sharpsburg, by Rev John Alexander Adams, Samuel Moats, to Miss Sally Domer, both of this co/Married Thurs last by Rev Bruner, Daniel Ankeny, to Miss Elizabeth Miller/Married same day by same, George Miller, to Miss Gertrude Kenny, all of this co/Died Wed evening last, Dorothy Blentlinger, in the 71st year of her age, of this place/Died at his res on night of the 19th inst, after a short but long threatened illness, Samuel Avey, in the 30th year of his age, farmer of this co. Mr. Avey has been for upwards of a year much afflicted with a cough, which subjected him to a pain in the breast at time, and invariably, a shortness of breath under the least exertion. He left a wife and 2 children. The day before his death he solicited his brother and sister to pray for him .../William C. Thomson died Wed morning 22d inst at Morristown,Ohio, after an illness of 6 days, in the 29th year of his age. He had been on a tour of 5-6 weeks, with a friend, thro' the western states, and was taken ill, on his return, at Zanesville; but, anxious to reach home, urged forward as far as Morristown, where the malignity of his disease at once terminated his homeward journey. But little more than five yrs ago, he came among us, a stranger.

838. TLM Oct 7 1830/Married Thurs 23d ult, by Rev B. Kurtz, John Robison to Miss Hannah Thomas, both of this co/Married Thurs last by same, John Jacob Bodinger, to Mrs. Margaret Boward, both of this place/Married same day, by same, William H. Kitzmiller to Miss Catharine M. Crayton/Died Thurs evening last, after an illness of several weeks, Mrs. Elizabeth, consort of William Boullt (Bouilt) of Williams-Port

839. TLM Oct 14 1830/Married Sun 3d inst by Rev Wm. R. Rhinehart, Frederick A. Grim, to Miss Elizabeth Geltmacher, both of this co/Married Thurs last, by Rev Drane, Nathaniel Kershner, to Miss Maria Deal/Married same day by Rev Winter, Aaron Piper, to Miss Margaret G. Martin, both of Sharpsburg/Married Thurs evening 16 ult, by Rev J. Buchanan, George Besore of Waynesboro', to Miss Eliza, dau of Jacob Snively, of Antrim township/Married 9th ult by Rev David Stoner, of Waynesboro', to Miss Ethelinda elder dau of Jacob Besore, formerly of Greencastle/Died 4th inst in this place, Mrs. Ann Maria Biershing, in the 69th year of her age, formerly of Frederick/Died Fri last, Samuel Spickler, in the 33d year of his age, native of this co. He was thrown from his horse on the race ground, near this town, the horse in full speed; and the injury he received in his head from a concussion of the brain, occasioned his death in 4-5 hours afterwards - Herald/Died suddenly

THE TORCHLIGHT AND PUBLIC ADVERTISER (Hagerstown)

in consequence of a fall, on 10th inst, at Mt. St. Mary's College, Emmittsburg, Fitzhugh Dorsey, of Hagers Town, aged 17 yrs and 8 months. He was a native of Hagers Town (long article with testimonials from the school)

840. TLM Oct 21 1830/Married Thurs 7th inst by Rev Duffield, Rev John M. Krebs, to Miss Sarah Holmes, dau of Andrew Holmes, Esq. of Carlisle/Married Thurs last, by Rev M. Bruner, John Miller of this co, to Miss Ann Dillahunt of Franklin Co, Pa/Married Sun last by same, John Haller, to Miss Catherine Roads, both of this co/Married Tues last by same, Henry Miller, of Frederick co, to Miss Mary Leckrone of this co/Died at Annapolis, Fri last, Colonel William Done, Delegate elect to the Legislature of Md., for Somerset Co

841. TLM Oct 28 1830/Maried Tues last by Rev L. H. Johns, William Lewis of Cumberland, to Miss Eliza Brosius, dau of Jacob Brosius, of Wash Co/Married Thurs last by Rev Martin Bruner, Jacob Buzzard, to Miss Margaret Keplinger /Married same day by same, Martin Rohrer, to Miss Mary Funk, all of this co/Married Mon evening last, by same, Henry Price, to Miss Juliet Ann Ong, both of Va/Married in Frederick, Thurs last, by Rev Shafer, Daniel Hollar to Miss Ann Maria Gelwicks, both of that place

842. TLM Nov 4 1830/Married Thurs 21st ult by Rev Monroe, Samuel Ruckle, of Sharpsburg, to Mrs. Mary Butler of Jefferson Co, Va/Died Mon 25th ult in Pleasant Valley, John Calamin, soldier of the Rev, in the 84th year of his age/Died Tues 26th ult in Pleasant Valley, Mrs. Susan Thomas, consort of George Thomas

843. TLM Nov 11 1830/Married Thurs last by Rev F. Rahauser, Otho H. W. S. Miller to Miss Mary Ann Firey, both of this co/Died in this town Fri night last, after a lingering illness, Hezekiah Miller, in the 36th year of his age/Died Sun evening at the res of his brother, about 2 miles west of this town, Jacob Oster, in the 27th year of his age, after a lingering illness

844. TLM Nov 18 1830/Married at Sharpsburg, on the 14th inst by Rev John A. Adams, Benjamin Leckman, to Miss Mary Ann Lowry/Died in this place Thurs last, after a painful illness, Mrs. Judith Ann Quantrill, consort of Capt Thomas Quantrill, in the 45th year of her age/Lancaster, Ohio, Nov 9 - died in Clearcreek township, in this co, Sat last, Col. George Nigh, at an advanced age. He was a native of Wash Co, and emigrated to Fairfield co, at an early period of its existence - Gazette./Gettysbsurg, Pa, Nov 9 - Died 4th inst at Shepherds town, Va, after an illness of two weeks, of the billious inflammatory fever, Rev David Jacobs, late teacher of the Languages in the Gettysburg Gymnasium, aged 24 yrs, 11 months, 12 days. He was a native of Franklin co, Pa, and graduate of Jefferson College. He acquired his Theological knowledge, in part, in this Seminary, and took charge of the Classical department in 1827. Being in a delicate state of health, he determined to take a tour southward, for his benefit. Accordingly, he left his place for Charlestown, S C, about the middle of Sept. last, but upon his return, in consequence of the dampness of the weather, he was taken ill at Woodstock, Va, but continued his journey to the above mentioned place

845. TLM Nov 25 1830/Married Thurs last, by Rev School, Samuel Strite, of this co, to Miss Martha Snively of Franklin co, Pa/Married same day by Rev

THE TORCHLIGHT AND PUBLIC ADVERTISER (Hagerstown)

Martin Bruner, Henry Landis, to Miss Lavinia, dau of Jacob Middlekauff, all of this co/Married same day by same, David Ridenour, merchant, to Miss Catharine Harbine, both of Clear-Spring/From the Carlisle Volunteer - Married 21st ult, George Thornburg, to Miss Sophia Oldwein, both of Hagers Town - in Manchester by Dr. Wm. Cooley, John Clark to Miss Clara Green - in New York, Wm. Weaver, Esq. of Lynchburg, Va to Mrs. Eliza Woodman/Died in this place on Fri last, Charles Ohlwine, aged 75 yrs, 3 months, 22 days, of his place, in which he lived for upwards of 50 yrs, among the few remaining Rev Heroes. He attached himself to the company of Captain Pike, of the 4th Regt of Light Dragoons. Engaged at the battles of Monmouth and Bunkers Hill. After the war he resumed his occupation, a stone mason. Being reduced in circumstances, he succeeded another Rev patriot, as crier of the Orphans' Court of his native co, where he was continued by the different courts until his decease - Herald.

846. TLM Dec 2 1830/Married in Charlestown, Tues evening 23d ult, Rev Jacob Medtart, pastor of the Luth church, Martinsburg and Shepherdstown, formerly of this place, to Miss Ann Likens, of the former place/Married at Shippensburg, Pa, on same day, by Rev Wilson, Peter Artz, senior, of this place, to Mrs. Catharine Clippinger, of the former place/Married Thurs last by Rev Jeremiah Mason, Benjamin Prather, to Miss Catharine Miller, both of this co/Married Sun last, in Greencastle, pa, by Rev F. Sholl, Jacob M. Mekimmey to Miss Elizabeth Criner, both of this place/Married in Hinsdale, Henry Tyrrol to Miss Calistha Nigh, after a courtship of 30 minutes

847. TLM Dec 23 1830/Married Thurs last, by Rev B. Kurtz, William Stewart, of this co, to Miss Elizabeth Watts, of ths place/Married Thurs evening last by Rev Winter, Isaac Lefever, of Williams-Port, to Miss Ann Martin, of this co/Married Tues last, by Rev M. Bruner, Abraham Krieger, to Miss Sarah Zentmyer, both of Frederick co/Married Thurs week last, by Rev Winter, Cephas Bartleson, to Miss Margaret, dau of Michael Kreps, all of Williams-Port/Died in this town, Wed week last, Mrs. Sabina Bowman, relict of the late Baltzer Bowman, in the 70th year of her age

848. TLM Dec 30 1830/Married Thurs last, by Rev J. Reck, John Price of Franklin co,Pa, to Miss Catharine Barr, only dau of Jacob Barr, of Wash Co, Md/Married same day by Rev Bucher, Elias Shutt, to Miss Mary Keedy, both of this co/Married Sun last, by Rev M. Bruner, Peter Ambrouse, to Miss Susannah Wilt, both of this place/Married Tues evening 21st inst by Rev Ryan, John Fahey, to Miss Margaret Morgan, both of this place

849. TLL Mar 23 1824/Married Tues last by Rev J. R. Reily, Henry Funk to Miss Susana Miller, all of this co/Married Thurs last by same, Erwine Miller, of Franklin co, Pa, to Miss Jane Williams, of this co

REPUBLICAN BANNER (Williams-Port)

850. RBL vol. 1, No. 1, Jan 2 1830/Married Sun evening 20th ult by Rev Robert Wilson, William Harvey to Miss Eliza Rice, both of this place/Married at Martinsburg, Va, Thurs evening 24th ult by Rev Young, John Clise, to Miss Sophia Locke, both of Williamsport/Died at Balt, Sun morning, 27th ult, in

REPUBLICAN BANNER (Williams-Port)

the 59th year of his age, after a very short and severe illness, Nicholas G. Ridgely, Esq. of the firm of McDonald & Ridgely, of Balt

THE HAGERSTOWN MAIL

851. HMM Vol. 1, No. 21, Nov 21 1828/Died Sun 9 inst in 45th year of his age, Samuel Cox of Harpers-Ferry/Died Fri last, Dr. George A. Hayden, of Harpers- Ferry/Died Sat last in 26th year of her age, Mrs. Margaret Bowers, wife of John Bowers of Harpers-Ferry/Died at Charleston, 2d inst, Major Gen. Thomas Pinckney, in the 79th year of his age

THE FARMERS' REGISTER AND MARYLAND HERALD

852. FRL Jun 17 1828/Died Thurs last, John Yeakle, Chairmaker, in the 56th year of his age, of this town

853. FRL Sep 15 1829/Married in Cumberland Wed evening last by Rev N. B. Little, John Egshaw of that place to Mrs. Mary Stange, formerly of Hagerstown

854. FRL Sep 29 1829/Died Wed last in the 46th year of his age, Rev Jonathan Helfenstein, for many yrs the Pastor of the German Reformed Church at Frederick

855. FRL Dec 29 1829/Chancery Case - William Price, Sophia B. Hays and others vs Henry Neighkirk and Nancy his wife, Samuel M. Hill and others. To revise original bill filed by William Williams Chapline agnst James Chapline, Christian Orndorff and Jacob Hess on 23 Oct 1790 and to renew bill of revivor and supplement filed by Joseph Chapline in 1809 as administrator and grantee of said William Williams Chapline agnst above defendants and Jacob Mumma, Frederick Rohrer, David Furey, John Buchanan and Robert Smith. Robert Smith died about 1818. David Furey died many yrs ago. Daniel Keedy is deceased. James Chapline died several yrs ago intestate and insolvent; his children and heirs: Alitha who m William Wallace, Romena who m John Miser, Joseph Chapline, Heros Chapline, Atlas Chapline and Cyrus Chapline - all of whom reside out of the state of Md.

856. FRL Jan 5 1830/Married at Falling, Va, John H. Pleasants, Esq., editor of Richmond Whig, to Mary L. P., dau of Henry Massee, Esq. of ths former place

INDEX

The index number refers to the number of the paragraph in this book, not to the page number. Titles (military rank, Dr., Mr., etc.) have been included in the index only in cases where the given name was not available.

ABERNATHY Elizabeth 61; William 61
ABRAHAM Leah 665
ABRAHAMS Jacob 665
ADAMS Elijah 10; Henry 604; John 512; John A. 844; John Alexander 837; Louisa 10; Rebe John Alexander 828; Rebecca 604
ADDISON Henry 413; Rev 413
AINSWORTH Henry 715; Thomas 757
AIRHEART Sibilla 706
ALBERT Ann 799; Catharine 325, 622, 821; George 751; John 325, 590, 668; Margaret 279; Thomas 660; William 687, 799
ALBRIGHT Miss 99
ALBURTUS John 676
ALDER Marcus 549
ALEXANDER Sarah Ann 792; Valentine 241
ALLBRIGHT Daniel 21
ALLEBAUGH Susan 811
ALLEN Elizabeth 221; Paul 80, 639; Rebecca 364; Rev B. 415
ALLENDER Harriet 262; Mary 689; William W. 299, 446
ALLISON Andrew 750; Catharine 310; Elenora 750; Mary 735
ALMAND Mary 621
ALTER David 355; George 590; Jacob 717; Samuel H. 755; Sophia 567
AMBROUSE Peter 848
ANDERSON Martha 630; Samuel 533, 748
ANGLE Elizabeth 694; Henry 304; Jacob 694
ANKENEY George 291, 440; Henry 398; John 291, 440; Sophia 398
ANKENY Daniel 837; George 572; Henry 625; Susan 625
ANNIN Roberdeau 706
ANTHONY Charles 375
ANTRIS Rev 449
ARBUCKLE Robert C. 739
ARDINGER Peter 478
ARMSTRONG Robert 150; Sarah 561
ARNOLD Anthony 69; Johnzee 114; Mary 69, 98; Nancy 114; Squire 185
ARTHUR Henry 72; Susanah 72
ARTZ Maria 598, 717; Peter 598, 715, 717, 846

ASH John 829
ASHBURY Ann 501; John 236, 501; Joseph 617
ASHMEAD William 800
ASHMUN J. 739
ASTON Owen 809; Rachel 809
ATHEY Dennis M. 38; Margaret 177
ATKINSON Mary 751
AUBERT Catharine 557
AUGHINBAUGH Henry 654; John 654
AULT Jacob 826, 836; Mrs. 826
AUSTIN Joseph 722; Rev 42
AVEY Samuel 837
AVY Michael 248

B... Isaac 282
BABB Harriot 295
BACHER Rev 826
BACHTEL Isaac 367, 759; Martin 664; Mr. 273
BAER George 619; Isaac 771
BAHN Major J. 550
BAILEY Robert 685
BAKER Abraham 563; Alexander 604; Barbara 563; Catharine 208, 563, 604, 809; Daniel 563; Eliza 826; Elizabeth 563, 604, 722; Henry W. 208, 809; Isaac 251, 274; Jacob 634; John 231, 274, 563, 604; Justina 563; Levi 172; Lucas 675; Major 699; Mary 701; Maurice 604, 811; Nathan C. 587; Nicholas 604; Richard 604; Rozanna 515; Samuel 610, 618
BALCH Rev 64
BALL Alfred 373; Henry W. 211; Notly M. 610
BALTHIS Leonard 723
BANCORD Elizabeth 593
BAND Elizabeth 714
BANODE Catharine 694
BANTZ John 712
BARE Isaac 458; Jacob 336; Martin 281
BARGDOLL Easter 298; John 298; Peter 298; Samuel 298
BARGER Jacob 685
BARKER Ann 50; William 50
BARKLEY Christian 75

INDEX

BARKMAN David 662; Frederick 462; Henry 462; Jacob 462; Mrs. 677; Peter 462
BARKS John 726; Margaret 782
BARKUS Betsy 110; John 110
BARNES Ezra 281; Rev 629
BARNETT Elizabeth 494; John 519, 668, 711
BARNHART David 752; John 752; Matthew 752; Peter 752
BARNHISER Christiana 488; John 737; Matthias 488
BARNS Rev 155
BARR Catharine 848; David 285, 427; Frances 341; George 427; Jacob 341, 346, 848; John 572; Peter 799; Samuel 346; Susanna 799
BARRON Charles Samuel Swartwout 823
BARTGIS Matthias 35
BARTLESON Cephas 847
BARTLETT Mary 495
BASCOM Rev 153
BASHORE David 547
BASNET Winey 142
BASNETT Mary 128, 142; Nancy 128, 142; Nehemiah 128, 142; Samuel 128, 142; Sarah 128, 142; Winna 128
BAUCHER Lewis H. 797
BAUGHER Daniel 834
BAUMGARTNER John 646
BAUMWARD Peter 199
BAXTER Harriet 715
BAXTON Pamelia 610
BAYLY Samuel 394, 555; William 394
BEACHLY John 545
BEAKLY Henry 768
BEAL Upton 661
BEALER Susan 457
BEALL Alexander 132; Alpheus 132; Anna P. 132, 744; Aza 75, 132, 157; Benjamin M. 41, 132; Charles F. 132; Christiana 216; Daniel 41, 132; Dennis 138; Eleanor 132; Elie R. 132; Elizabeth 75, 132, 218; Elizabeth B. 41, 132; Ellen 136; George 132; George Ross 793; Gustavus 3, 41, 132; Hamilton 132; Hazel 166; Hezekiah 698; Isaac 41, 132; Isaac M. 132; Isaac W. 41; Jesse T. 41, 132; John 132, 216; John B. 132; John J. 132; Joseph T. 41, 132; Josiah 132; Juliet 132; Lewis H. 132; Matilda B. 698; Matilda S. 550; Mrs. 78; Priscilla 61, 132; Rezin 218; Richard 41, 132; Samuel 4, 41, 132; Samuel B. 41, 132; Thomas 4, 41, 61, 132; Virlinda 132, 157; William 78; William Dent 794; William T. 41, 132
BEAM Barbara 669; Jacob 669; John 669; Martin 669
BEAMS William 735
BEAN Barton 369, 656; Benjamin 431; Charles 614; Elizabeth 317, 461; George 575, 596, 614, 768; Lucretia 694; Mary 575; Sarah 806; Susan 656
BEAR Mary 750
BEARD Andrew 799; Daniel 799; David 315, 460, 799; George 799; Jacob 799, 815; John 668, 799; John G. 618; Joseph 608; Lea 815; Mary 827; Mary M. 535; Michael 562, 799; Peter 799; Philip 799; Sally 809; Samuel 799; Zachariah 235
BEATTY Beal 132; Brook 132; Dr. R. H. 64, 617; Eleanor 132; Elie 48, 591; James Johnson 746; John 667; John C. 132; Lewis 132; Margaret 648; Nancy 132; Otho 132; Thomas 132
BECK Andrew 603; George H. 790; John 671; Susanna 603
BECKENBAUGH Ann Maria 829; George 703
BECKLEY John 545; Sarah 406
BECKLY Jac. 604
BEDINGER Henry 129
BEECHER Rev J. 678; Samuel 289; Sarah 308; William W. 735
BEELER Christian 723; David 704; Jacob 304
BELGG Naomi 194
BELL Andrew 350; Daniel 405; Elizabeth 320; Jacob 350; Margaret 350; Mary 552; Peter 320; Samuel 437
BELT Carleton 199; Thomas 385
BENDER George 634, 818; George A. 834; John 826; Margaret 634, 719; Mary 719; Samuel 642; Susan 828; William 545
BENKHART Sarah 728

127

INDEX

BENNER John 826; Peter 619
BENNETT Margaret 650; Margaret L.
  650; Sylvenus 12
BENSON Perry 126
BENTZ Catharine 506; Samuel 627
BENTZE Catharine 799; Elizabeth 799;
  Eve 799; Jacob 799; Mary 799;
  Susanna 799
BERGMAN Susanna 547
BERKLEY James 177
BERNHISER Mary 430
BERRY Jeremiah 149; Juliet Matilda
  617; William 351
BERTOLET Ann 690, 752; Daniel A. 752;
  Daniel S. 690
BESER Henry 737
BESHORE Daniel 563; Mary 563
BESORE Ethelinda 839; George 839;
  Jacob 839
BETZ Christian 301; Frederick 346;
  Mary 346
BEVANS Samuel 68; Sarah 68
BEVEINS Thomas 114
BIDDINGER Henry 142
BIERSHING Ann Maria 839
BIGHAM John 825
BILLMIRE Catharine 645
BILLMYER Catharine 813; Conrad 809;
  John 813
BINCKLEY George 603; Jacob 734
BINKLEY Catharine 669; Ferdinand 603;
  George S. 693; Jacob 603; Louisa
  603; Orpha 693; Samuel 669; Thomas
  603; William 603
BINKLY George 447; Jacob 447
BISH David 754
BISHOP Elijah 724; Elizabeth 360
BLACK George W. 574; James 9, 150;
  Polly 9
BLACKFORD Col. 584; Otho 584
BLACKWELL D. 642; David 83; Harriet
  83, 642
BLAIR Ann 74; Col. T. 74; James 715;
  Thomas 41, 132
BLAKE John 766; Thomas 753, 812
BLECHER John 775; Leah 775
BLENDLINGER Conrad 779; Catharine
  311; Conrad 767; Dorothy 837;
  Sarah 458
BLOCHER Ann 98; George 98; Jacob 212
BLOOD Parker 774

BLUE Garrett 164
BLYTHE Rev Dr. 283
BOCKMAN Abraham 701; Judith 701
BODINGER John Jacob 838
BODMAN Lewis Charles 718
BODMANN Ferdinand 606; William 825
BOERSTLER Daniel 601
BOGS Isabella 113
BOMGARDNER William 621
BOMWART Elizabeth 59; Peter 59
BOND George 690; Mary Ann 620; Sarah
  605
BOON William 752
BOONE Daniel 690; Elizabeth 690;
  Franklin 690; George 690, 752;
  Harriet 690; Jeremiah 752;
  Margaret 690; Rachael 752; Rachel
  690; William 690
BOOSE Catharine 48, 593; John 48, 69,
  593, 624
BOOTH Bartholomew 339, 476; John 316,
  476; Susan 316
BOREN William 620
BOSTATER Jacob 516
BOTELER Amelia 440; Ann F. 671;
  Edward 455; Henry 671; Hezekiah
  440, 517
BOUILT Elizabeth 838; William 838
BOULLT Elizabeth 838; William 838
BOVEY Margaret 338; Mary 253
BOVY Adam 240
BOWAN Rev 155
BOWARD Leonard 155; Margaret 838;
  Michael 507, 643; Nancy 507
BOWART Ann 377; Michael 377
BOWEN Elizabeth 417; James 593; Jane
  N. 560
BOWER George 239; John 385, 701;
  Sarah 701
BOWERS David 281; Elizabeth 242, 762;
  George 750, 802; Henry 788; Jacob
  275; John 851; Joseph 784; Margaret 851; Moses 304; William 518
BOWIE Washington 69
BOWLES John 314; Mary 314
BOWMAN Baltzar 494, 847; Catharine
  552; Elizabeth 275; George 240,
  405, 446; Jacob 668, 740, 758;
  Mary 256, 342, 479; Matilda 718;
  Mrs. 758; Sabina 847; Susan 563

INDEX

BOWSER Christiana 265; Elizabeth 450; Henry 264; Jacob 815; Polly 254; Sarah 570
BOYD Ann 590, 694; Eleanor 822; Eliza 329; Isabella K. 789; John 766; Joseph 329, 822; Margaret M. 712; Marmaduke M. 701; Marmaduke W. 271, 669, 719; Olivia 374; Samuel 719, 789; Sarah 788; Susan 669; Walter 374, 590, 694, 733; William 772
BOYER David 524; Elizabeth Ann 145; Maria L. 269; Nancy 820; Susan 508; William 814
BOYERS John 685
BRADDON Mary 768; William 768
BRADLEY John 452
BRADSHAW George 609
BRADY & WASON 708
BRADY John 708; Thomas 656
BRAGDEN John 540
BRAGONIER Daniel 279, 341; Elizabeth 283, 306, 689; Jacob 689; John 288; Martha 341
BRAGUNIER Margaret 765
BRAMBLE Keziah 690
BRANDNER Andrew 769; Eliza 769; George 246, 769; Jacob 769; Jonas 769; Levi 769; Michael 769; Samuel 769; Susanna 769
BRANNAN Sarah A. Luiza 454
BRANON Sarah Ann Louisa 309
BRANT John 66, 98; Juliana 66; Margaret 98; Thomas C. 367
BRASHEAR Van S. 638
BRATTON Elizabeth 533
BRAZIER William 806
BRECKENRIDGE Frances 797; J. Cabell 797
BRENDEL Catharine 564; George 257, 564; John 695
BRENDLE George 790; John 790
BRENNUM Sarah Ann 104, 672
BRENT Thomas C. 520
BRENTLINGER Frederick 613
BREWA Margaret 241
BREWER Adam 260; Daniel 234; David 242, 565; Elizabeth 277, 809; George I. 814; Henry 367; Jacob 809; Jacob A. 283; John 258, 659; Peter 666; Rosanna 235; Susanna 367

BRIDGMAN Margaret 662; William 381
BRIEN Harriet 673, 818; John 673, 818; Robert Coleman 604
BRINING Christian 785
BRISCOE Henry T. M. 815
BRISON Elvina 598
BROADMARKLE John 136
BROCIUS Eliza 230; Jacob 227, 230
BROMLEY Elizabeth 230
BROOKE Harriet E. 629; Rev 659; Richard 629; Thompson John 675
BROOKHART David 241
BROOKS Clarissa M. 797
BROSIUS Daniel 712; Eliza 841; Jacob 339, 841
BROSSIUS Jacob 476
BROTHERTON Hugh 820
BROWN Ann 737; Benjamin 531, 665; Catharine 630; Charles 542; Christiana 704; Elizabeth 617; George 126, 576; Hannah 800; Jacob 166, 712; James 730; Joel 288, 438; John 473, 552, 800; Martin S. 675; Mrs. 648; Rev 815; Rev J. 575; Rosanna 556; Rudolph 648; Susan 825; Susanna 737; William 704; William D. 637; William M. 314
BRUA Emanuel 275; Jacob 306; Martha 524; Peter 302; Sarah 302
BRUCBAKER Barbara 533
BRUCE Andrew 158; Elizabeth 147; Francis 140; George 158; Upton 147, 197
BRUEBAKER Barbara 533
BRUER Peter 448; Sally 448
BRUMBAUGH Catharine 258; David 311, 458; Elizabeth 243; Jacob 258; Smith Daniel 544
BRUNER Dorothy 717; Martin 765, 776, 841, 845; Rev 658, 663, 674, 676, 712, 715, 716, 717, 719, 721, 730, 735, 780, 782, 788, 789, 811, 815, 816, 820, 825, 827, 837; Rev M. 667, 701, 737, 770, 794, 802, 804, 807, 809, 814, 817, 829, 840, 847, 848
BRUNNER George 262; Margaret 309, 454; Rev 103, 655, 671, 769
BRUTIE Mr. 426
BRYAN Ann 422; John F. 615; Maria 5; Rev 606

INDEX

BRYSON John 809
BUCEY Jemima 120; Paul 120
BUCHANAN Ann Catharine 376; J. M. 87;
  James 529; James A. 675; John 92,
  376, 744, 855; John M. 577;
  Louisiana P. W. 87; Maria Sophia
  92; Mary S. 386; Rev 303, 432,
  577, 579, 588, 631, 634, 789, 809,
  826, 827, 830; Rev J. 839; Thomas
  386; William S. 654
BUCHER Catharine 776; Rev 803, 805,
  848; Rev J. C. 764, 766, 798, 802
BUCKINGHAM Rev 285, 436; Rev P. G.
  308
BUCKLEY Robert 595
BUCKWALTER Benjamin 553; Gearhart
  492; Gerhart 491; Jacob 385; John
  492; Mrs. 491
BUCY Margaret 121
BUN Peter 674
BURCKHART Francis M. 802
BURCKHARTT C. 533; Eleonora 533
BURD John A. 100
BURGAN Rebecca 241
BURGESS Alfred 150; Elizabeth 142
BURKHART Sarah 243, 407
BURNETT Sarah 566
BURNS --- 115; Andrew 116; Catharine
  615; Mary 717; Robert 768; Ruth
  768
BURRELL Elizabeth 518
BUSSARD Daniel 822; Peter 313;
  William 695
BUSSELL Noah 80
BUTLER Anna Catharine 43; John George
  43; Jonathan 33; Mary 842; Rev 119
BUZZARD Jacob 841; John 603
BYER Capt J. 722; Margaretta 722
BYERS Eliza 573; John 573, 667; Nancy
  545; William 693

CAHILL Mary 767
CALAMIN John 842
CALBERT Matilda 632
CALDER Elizabeth 382, 383
CALHOUN Eleanor 19; Samuel 19
CALKGLESSER Solomon 789
CAMERON Archibald 818; John 285, 519,
  653; Maria 519; Susan 582; Susanna
  582
CAMPBELL Barclay 92; James 92; McKean
  92; Randolph 19; Rev 759; William
  19

CARLA Catharine 305
CARLISLE Alexander 20; Robert 138
CARLTON James P. 32; Mary 32
CARNS Margaret 782
CARPENTER Margaret 415; Stephen 551
CARR Amelia 322; Cathrine 547; Col.
  568; Edward 547; Ellenora 568;
  James 547; John 322, 547, 669;
  Mary 547; Nancy 547
CARROLL Charles 383; William 572
CARSON George 774; James O. 266
CARTER Harriet 20; Joseph 122;
  Lucinda 100; Nancy 122; Noah 251
CARVER Daniel 399, 530
CASSEL Jacob 348
CASSIN Joseph 657
CASTLE Amelia 399, 530
CATLETT George 9
CATRON Catharine 766
CAUFMAN Daniel 325
CAVAN John A. 671
CEAVIER Elizabeth 768
CELLAR Barbara 365; George 365; John
  297; Margaret 297
CHAMBERLIN John 129; Rebecca 129
CHAMBERS James 654; Jesse 225; Sarah
  754
CHANDLER Jehu 328
CHANEY Ann Maria 811; Drusila 675;
  Elizabeth 778, 819; Fanny 778;
  Fanny 819; Jeremiah 778, 819; John
  778, 819; Mary 767; Rebecca 778,
  819; Richard 778, 819; Zephaniah
  811
CHAPLINE Alitha 855; Atlas 855; Cyrus
  855; Elizabeth 670; Heros 855;
  James 520, 855; James N. 670, 825;
  Jeremiah 422, 634, 670; Joseph
  436, 462, 481, 855; Mary Ann
  Abigail 481; Romena 855; Susan N.
  422; Susanna 634; William Williams
  855
CHAPMAN Henry 596; Rev 830; Samuel
  596; William 150
CHARLES Elizabeth 358; Samuel 209,
  812
CHASE Jeremiah Townley 723
CHENEY David 752; Frances 823;
  Jeremiah 725; John 725; Mary 565;
  Robert 834; William B. 720
CHENOWETH George L. 553; James B. 362
CHESLEY Ann 800

INDEX

CHEW Benjamin 629
CHILDS Rachael 750
CHREST David 735; Henry 763; Jacob 436
CHRISTIAN Francis Payton 489
CHRITONAN George 242
CISSLER John 209
CLAGETT Alexander 286, 812; Alfred 606; Eleanor 599, 812; Elie 397; Hezekiah 599; James H. 798; Jane 397; Joseph 606; Richard 572; Robert 620; Susan Wilson 606; Thomas J. 581; Zachariah 565
CLAGGETT Martha E. 413
CLAM Mary 607
CLAPHAM Samuel 642
CLAPPER John 411; Leah 704
CLARK Catharine 50; John 845; Jonathan 50; Samuel 558
CLARKE George 470; James W. 351; John 704; John X. 16, 546; Mary Ann 392; Rev 618
CLARKSON Charles S. 695; Mary Smith 695; Rev 662; Rev T. B. 744; Sarah Bella 695
CLARY Ellenor 140; Mary 64
CLAY Charles H. 276, 421; Jehu Curtis 751; Margaret 623; Rev 408; Rev J. 405; Rev J. C. 240, 253, 255, 267, 269, 272, 275, 279, 296, 413, 415, 418, 443, 623; Slator 276, 288, 421; William Annan 623
CLAYTON Elizabeth 667; James 788; Joseph 775
CLEARY Cordelia 49; Daniel 187
CLEMMER Jacob 116
CLEVIDENCE Daniel 714
CLIFTON Mary Ann 42
CLIMER Edward 484; Maria 484
CLINGAN Rev 722; William 673, 675, 730
CLINGEN Rev 642; William 593
CLINGIN Rev 606
CLIPPINGER Catharine 846; John 610
CLISE Elizabeth 169; George 169; Harriet 1; Jane 180; John 1, 22, 180, 804, 850; Rosanna 175
CLOPPER Jacob 757
CLOSE Jonathan 211
CLOWSER Susan 790
CNODLE Ann 601
COAKLEY Philip H. 715

COBAUGH Dietrich 567
COBERT Rebecca 253
COBLENTZ John 772; Samuel 782
COCHRAN Mary 107; Ninian 107
COCKEY Joshua 135
CODDINGTON William 111
COFFROTH Rebecca 666
COLEMAN Chester 719
COLER George 473
COLFLESH John 188
COLHOUN Eleanor 549; John 448; Samuel 549
COLIFLOWER George 807; Mrs. 807
COLLINGS John 67
COLLINS Elijah 504; Mary 193, 655; Pratt 201; Reuben 100; Sarah 560
COMBS Anna 190; Coleman 248, 410; Elisha 190; Elizabeth 329; John 224; Mary 248, 410; Sophia 224
COMPTON William E. 562; William T. 789
CONFER George 275; Samuel 701
CONN Peter 241
CONNE Perny Barney 831
CONNELLY James C. 91; Nancy 805; Rachel 91
CONNER Hugh 831; Lydia 831; Perry Barney 831; Sarah 831; William 170
CONOWAY Eliza 296
CONRAD Ann Maria 103, 671; Christian 373
CONRADT Christian G. 388
CONROY Mrs. 34
CONVERSE Rev 186
COOK Catharine 478; David 326; Nancy 413; Silas 823; Susanna 288
COOKE Colin 634; David 254, 534; Mary 254
COOLEY William 845
COON Frederick 366; Julian 614
COOPER Amelia 631; John W. 718; Jonathan G. 762; Nancy 128, 142; Thomas 128, 142
COPELAND W. B. 791
CORBUS Ann 165
CORDIMAN Jacob 466
CORNEY John 778, 819; Naomy 778, 819
CORSE Nancy 258; William 374
CORSON Robert T. 704
COSKERY Harriet 529
COSS Eliza 541
COUTER Elias 625; George 690

INDEX

COW Valentine 764
COWAN Eliza V. L. 638
COWENS Hugh 182
COWNEY Samuel J. 671
COX Henrietta 596; Samuel 851
COXE --- 206
CRADDOCK John 828
CRAIG Samuel 562
CRAMER Catharine 702, 789; Dr. 780; Jonas 702
CRAMPTON Abraham 306; Ann Mary Maria 591; Elias 306, 453, 596; Elie 826; Elisha 306; Elizabeth 306, 453; John 306, 648; Joseph 306; Josiah 306; Nancy 581; Ruth 306; Sarah Anne 306; Thomas 306, 591; Thomas H. 835
CRATZINGER Joseph 803
CRAVEN John 545
CRAVENS John 670; Ruhamah 670
CRAWFORD Ann Eve 328; John 204, 328, 366, 765; Mary D. 765; Sarah 717
CRAYTON Catharine M. 838
CREAGER John 798
CREGER Rebecca 622
CRESAP Abigail 31; Ellen 20; James C. 145; James D. 31; James M. 4; John 70; Joseph 70, 93, 145, 659; Nancy 66; Phoebe 70; Robert 119, 120, 122; Ruth 119; Thomas 20, 66
CRETZINGER Charlotte 704
CRIGLOW Christiana 770
CRINER Calistha 846
CRISSMAN Michael 304, 454
CRISTMAN Mary 520
CRISWELL Elizabeth 592
CROK Rev 799
CROMWELL Eliza 177; Ellen 434; Joseph 385, 399, 514; Lavania 149; Margaret 385, 514; Mary 542; Nathan 542; Richard 297; Thomas 149, 177
CRONICH David 245
CRONISE Ann Maria 434; George 604; Mary 206; Susana 663
CROSS Hannah 660; John 806; Sarah 515, 666
CROW Benjamin 718; Eliza 538; Jacob 243
CROWNINSHIELD Benjamin Varnum 761
CRUMBAUGH John 765; William 329
CULP William 161

CULVER Henry 84
CUMMING Robert 54, 602
CUMMINGS Lucia 50
CUMMINS John 50
CUNNINGHAM Samuel 350, 642; William 453
CURTIS Josiah 406
CUSHWA Catharine 815; David 494; Elizabeth 494, 565; John 809
CUSTER Emanuel 197
CUTHRIE Stephen 215
CYESTER Daniel 723; John 768; Samuel 761

DAHSER David 656
DAILY William 778, 819
DALE Richard 62
DANGERFIELD Edmund T. 158; Elizabeth 158; Henry 158; John 158; Mary 158
DANIEL John 296
DASH Alcinda Jane 381
DASHIEL George 397
DAUBLE Henry 304
DAUSH Mary 488
DAVID Christiana 367; Elie 367; Jacob 319
DAVIDGE James Beale 787
DAVIDSON Benoni 176; Elenora G. 667; Patrick 550; William 146
DAVIS Amos 596, 695; Ann 281; Edward 281; Elias 342; Elizabeth 135, 342; Elizabeth L. 272, 418; Francis 441; Harriet 309, 454; Harriot 304; Henry 645; Holly 528; Hulda A. 170; James 690; Jesse 342; Jesse F. 240; John 272, 418, 558; Matilda S. 695; Nancy 560; Narcissa 325; Rev 617; Richard 242; Solomon 76, 170, 648; Sophia 242, 596; Susanna 556; Thomas 384; Vincent 556; William 311, 458, 667
DAVY John 401
DAWSON Benjamin 160; William R. 110
DAY Isabella 693
DAYTON George 484; Joseph 484
De BUTTS Naomi 836
De PUI John 361, 495, 765
DEAL Catharine 785; Maria 839
DEAN Dr. A. T. 754; Francis 98; George 399; Mary 641; Ruth 91; William 91
DEARBORN Henry 186

INDEX

DEAVER John 601
DECHERT Jacob 347, 767; Mary 614; Peter S. 347, 614
DECKENBAUGH Rev 765
DEEMER Catharine 377
DEEMS Eliza 155; Elizabeth 211; Frederick 155, 211
DEEVER David W. 690
DEFENBAUGH Rev 762
DEFINBAUGH Jacob F. 761
DEITRICK Elizabeth 366; John 366; Samuel 560; Susan 757
DELAHUNT William 337, 369
DELONG Mr. 37
DELUEL Rev 675
DENEAS Rev 562
DENEEN George 135
DENIES Rev 582
DENINE George 170
DENIS William 713
DENIUS Rev 327, 336, 606, 654, 662, 698, 704, 759, 803; Rev S. K. 342, 772, 811; Solomon K. 811
DENNIES Rev 506, 512, 569
DENNIS Rev 457
DENNISON Amelia 802; Rachel 825
DENNY David 19, 495; Rev 471, 598; Rev D. 332
DEVENNY David C. 536
DEVER Josiah B. 722
DEVICMAN George 123
DEVORE Cornelius 110; Mary 110
DICK Eliza 475
DICKERHOOF John 155
DICKEY Isabella W. 566
DICKSON William 343
DIEFFENBACHER Martin 630
DIFFENBACHER Rev J. 809
DIFFENBAUGH Barbara 102
DILLAHUNT Ann 840
DILLEHUNT William 500
DILLION Humphrey 193
DILLMAN Amelia 480; Henry 289, 480; Mary 289
DILLON Humphry 787; John 568, 641
DILLY James 728
DITTO Abraham 719; Mary 336
DITWILER Fanny 667
DIXON James 777
DOCTOR John 701
DOMER Jacob 825; John 639, Mary 701; Sally 837

DONALDSON Mary 346, 485; Mary Ann 397; Thomas T. 798
DONALSON Eliza 572
DONE William 230, 840
DONNELLY Daniel 464
DONOHO Ann 771
DONOVAN John 596
DOOBLE Catharine 514
DOOMER Margaret 417
DORBY John 631
DORSEY Dr. 777; Fitzhugh 839; Francis 538; Frederick 592, 604; Freeland 592; John Clagett 718; Rev 546; Roderick 223
DOUBLE Andrew 453
DOUGLASS Isaac R. 765; Nancy 779; Robert 248, 410, 779
DOUP Joel 667
DOWDEN Thomas 128, 142
DOWEL Upton 718
DOWNES Amy 789; Charles G. 275; William 578
DOWNEY Ann 768; Basil D. 768; Edmond 768; Harriet 768; John 768; Margaret 309; Maria 768; Mary 768; Robert 768; Ruth 768; Samuel 755, 768; Samuel J. 103; Susan 768; William 768
DOWNING Timothy 265
DOWNS Alexander 667; Eliza 242; Elizabeth 577; Henrietta 577; William 577
DOYLE H. George 283; Mary 280; William 722
DRAKE George H. 38
DRANE Eliza 168; James 148; Rev 769, 770, 790, 793, 806, 823, 828, 833, 839
DRILL John 812
DRURY Ignatius 585
DU VAL Singleton 599
DUBLE Neomy 778
DUCKETT Mary Ann 777; Richard 821; Sophia 42, 581, 821
DUFFEY Captain 675
DUFFIELD George 591, 594, 780, 797; John 685; Rev 776, 840; Samuel 634; William 417
DUGAN Francis 689; John S. 31
DUN Mrs. Russel 452
DUNCAN Mary Louisa 776; Rev 774; Stephen 146; William 456

INDEX

DUNDORE Chritiana 264; Elizabeth 704, 706; Henry 807; Susan 792
DUNN Charlotte 16, 71; Elizabeth 722; Richard 16, 71; Samuel 208; Thomas B. 206, 208, 698
DURYEE Ann 822
DUSING Abraham 730; Amelia 672; Elizabeth 806; Henry 811; John 806; Magdalena 730; Philip 672
DUSINGER Philip 822; Susan 822
DUSSINGER Samuel 392
DUVAL Benjamin 129; Edward W. 129; Era 129; Gabriel 129; Griffen 129; Isaac 129; Jefferson 129; Juliet 129; Martha A. 129; Singleton 599; William 129
DUVALL Benjamin 142; Edward W. 142; Ezra 142; Gabriel 142; Griffin 142; Isaac 142; Jefferson 142; Juliet 142; Matthew 142; William 142

EACLE Abraham 722
EAKER Elizabeth 250; Thomas 250
EAKLE Catharine 563; Elizabeth 639; George 511; George Cauliflower 792; Henry 665; John 769; Joseph 455
EASTER Emanuel 45; Henry 77, 110; Maria 77, 110
EASTERDAY Feronia 824; Jacob 824; Mary 434
EASTON Elizabeth 517
EBERHART John 478
EBERT Elizabeth 295; John 295, 441; Mrs. 441
EBLEHOCK Maria 385
EBRECHT Susan 753
ECKHART John 556; Margaret 556
ECKLES Anna 132; Samuel 132
EDELEN Charles 769
EDEY Richard 751; Simmons 751
EDWARDS Editha 642; Owen 16; Thomas 642
EFFENGER Mary 642
EGAN Michael De Bourgo 782
EGSHAW John 194, 853
EGY Michael 522
EICHELBERGER Frederick 495
EICLEBERGER John 313
EISENHART George 578; Jacob 578

ELLIOT Elie Williams 288, 438; Elijah 205; George M. 266; Rev 452; Robert 288
ELLIOTT David 638; Elijah 806; Eliza L. 337; George M. 337; Martha 617; Rachael 91; Rev 527, 774; Rev D. 549, 550; Robert 438; Sophia 91
EMERT Catharine 663
EMMERSON John 662; Thomas 234
EMMERT Benjamin 220; John 663; Joseph 522; Mary 260; Rev 743
EMORICH Susanna 311
EMORY Frances 328; John 322, 328, 475; Robert 328
EMRICH Susan 458
EMSWILER Jacob 630
ENDERS James 329
ENDRESS Christian Frederick Ludwick 694; Rev Dr. 688
ENGLE Martin 96
ENGLEMAN Catharine 720
ENGLISH James 132; Lucy 132
ENSMINGER Catharine 719; Martin 296; Sarah 275
ENT Capt 396
ENTLER Elizabeth 815; Prudence 748
ERNSBERGER Esther 406
ESPY James 32
EUSTACHIEUS Catharine 593
EVANS John T. 806; Jonathan 690, 752; Joseph 209; Margaret 690, 752; Maria 276, 421; Sarah 634; Thomas B. 576; Washington 151; William W. 634
EVERLY Hannah 50; Joseph 50
EVERSTINE Anne 85; Joseph 64, 170; Lewis 85
EVY Christiana 235
EYERLY Samuel 823

FAHEY John 848
FAIL Elizabeth 449; Jacob 449
FALDER Samuel 786
FARMER Andrew M. 719
FARROW John 704; Nathan 397
FARST Jacob 392
FARVER Christian 564
FAUGHWELL George 481
FAULKWELL Elizabeth 262; Mary 356; Sarah 248
FAUST Henry 356
FAYMAN Elizabeth 811

INDEX

FECHTIG C. C. 300; Christian 30, 376; Frederick 258; George 354; Jacob 30, 152, 569; John 308; Lewis R. 1, 306, 506; R. 376
FECKLER Peter 501
FEIGLEY Nancy 564; Sarah Ann 552; William 542
FELKER Catharine 300, 447
FERGUSON Augustus 484; Charles 484; John W. 484; Joseph 484; William 484
FERRIN Ann 797
FETTER Daniel 9
FIELD Richard 776
FIELDS Ann M. 718; Henrietta 718; William 579, 718
FIERY Elizbeth 258; Henry 293, 391; Jacob 715; Joseph 391, 446, 486; Lewis 391; Mary E. 446; Nancy 349, 486; Susan 304
FIGELY George 802
FIGHT George 398
FINDLAY Archibald I. 799
FINDLEY William 278
FINEFROCK David 706; Mary Ann 706
FINFROCK John 648
FINLAY Rev 834
FINLEY Ebenezer 371; Mary 371
FINNELL Alexander 420; Rev R. 420
FIREY Jacob 581, 685; Joseph 535; Mary Ann 685, 843
FISHAUGH Frederick 701; Henry 309; Mary 712
FISHBACK Rev Dr. 828
FISHER Adam 717; Eliza 627; Elizabeth 109; Euriah 25; Jacob 406; John 296; John D. 650; Jonathan 305; Lucinda 142; Michael 142; Peter 717
FISHERMAN Lewis 704
FITZHUGH Eliza M. 481; Samuel T. 481; William 182, 774
FITZPATRICK Edmund 723; James Williams 723
FLAGG Joida E. A. 629; Joseph 629
FLAUTT William M. 689
FLEMING James 256; Jane 618; Mr. 574
FLEMMING Elizabeth 314
FLETCHER Charles A. 767; Lewis 562; Louis 811
FLICKINGER Leah 143

FLORA Adam 722; Daniel 828; Margaret 309
FLORY Christopher 547; David 803
FOCKLER Peter 369
FOGLER John 640
FOGWELL Susanna 656
FOLK Caspar 707; John 158
FOLY John 120
FOOTE Rev 61; William H. 363
FORD Thomas 235
FORE Catharine 416
FOREMAN George 426
FORMAN Jacob 586
FORSHEY Abel 91; Edward 91; John 91; Margaret 91
FOSTER James 671
FOUGHT Rev 166
FOUKE Ann 615; Henry 62, 615; Mary Ann 62
FOULKE Elizabeth B. 568
FOUTZ Henry 730; Susan 675
FOX Philip 300, 447
FOY Levi 778; Levy 819; Mary 778, 819
FRANCE George 700; Jonathan 91; William F. 228
FRANCIS Mary 773
FRANTZ Lydia 665
FRAZER Owen B. 569
FREANER Henry 754; John 240
FREEMAN Thomas 204
FRENCH Anna 90; Annah 90; Daniel 90; David 90; Elizabeth 404; John B. 2; Joseph 90; Juliana 2; Mary 90; Phebius 90; Rev 729; Robert 90; Samuel 90
FRETHY Edward 16
FREY John 215; Mathias 183
FRICK Charles 617
FRIEND Agness 536; Gabriel 773; Jane 773; John 91; Josiah 91; Kennedy T. 645; Lavinia 91; Oliva 91; Rachel 518; Rebecca 481; Robert T. 268, 536; Sophia 91
FRIESE Jacob 295
FRITZ Jacob 478; John 693
FROST John 148
FRY Harriet 642; Stephen 573
FRYE Joseph 617, 775
FULLERTON Humphry 667; Matthew L. 791, 822; Rev 179, 706, 724, 793; Rev M. L. 667, 674, 690, 694, 698,

135

INDEX

700, 718, 739, 752, 771, 783, 796, 816
FUNK Elizabeth 315; Henry 373, 394, 849; Jacob 524; Joseph 259; Mary 841; Nancy 238; Rev 809, 823; Sarah 814; Susanna 259, 832; Terace 241
FUREY David
FURREY Samuel 821
FURRY Elizabeth 279
GABBY Jane 796; Joseph 796; William 488
GABRIEL Josiah 300, 447
GAITHER Beal 598; Catharine K. 92; Eliza 379; Elizabeth 663, 742; Henry 742; Henry H. 92, 396; Mr. Z. 379; Stuart 267; Zachariah 663
GALLOWAY John 629; Mary 619; Sarah 629
GAMBLE Elizabeth 275
GANT Maria 817
GANTER Magdalena 712
GANTZ Sarah 794
GARAGHTY Michael 504
GARETT Edward 798
GARISH Joseph 821
GARLINGER Jacob 399
GARMAN Rebecca 815
GARRETSON Freeborn 694
GARRETT Edward 798; Elizabeth A. 798; John D. 798; Matilda 798
GARY Elizabeth 768
GAUMER --- 166
GAVER Mr. 668
GEARHART Sarah 690; William 690
GEBHART Rebecca 309
GEETING David 759; George 623, 639, 640, 647, 648, 667, 673, 704, 722, 726, 751, 752, 753, 757, 759, 775, 796, 800, 814, 826, 832; John 698; Rev 392; Rev G. 685, 693; Rev G. L. 607
GEHER Daniel 389
GEHR Samuel 607
GEIGER Eleanora 419, 497; Eliza 293; Henrietta 637; Jacob 293
GELTMACHER Elizabeth 839; Margaret 673
GELWICKS Ann Maria 841; Daniel 628
GEORGE Enoch 739; John 741; Wilson L. 401, 608
GEPHART John 179
GEPHARTT Peter 60
GERE John A. 206
GERHARD Elizabeth 782
GERHART Daniel 238; Rebecca 454; Rev H. 10
GEYER Rebecca 773
GIBBONEY John 305
GIBBONS John L. 568
GIBBONY Ann 625; John 625, 667
GIBSON Martha 667
GIDDINGER Samuel 794
GILBERT David 291; Jacob 237, 319; Samuel 822; Sarah 237
GILES Mark 619
GILL Barbara 403; John 403
GILLAN James 780
GILLIAM Ricahrd 621
GILLIS Samuel H. 171
GILMOR Ann 286; William 286
GILMORE William 598
GLAIZE George 770; Susanna 453
GLASS John 641; Joseph 475
GLAZE Catharine 607; David 279; Elizabeth 426
GLETNER Joseph 641; Mary 240
GLOSS Rosanna 406
GLOSSBRENNER Adam 800; Christiana 656
GOLL Rebecca 805
GOOD Jacob 310
GOODMAN Rebecca 525
GORDON Henry 718; Susanna 531
GORLAUGH Henry 716
GOSHER Henry 767
GOUFF Adam 704
GOULDING Andrew 382
GOWER George 620; Henry 295; Margaret 774
GRABELL Rachael 787
GRAEFF Catharine 574
GRAHAM Eliza R. 719; Louisa L. 520; Tom 588
GRAHAME Thomas 97
GRAY Ann 321; John 607; Samuel 321
GREENAWALT Jacob 392
GREEN Clara 845; Edward 266; Jonas 751; Joseph 242
GREENE William 136
GRICE Jacob 647
GRIER James 744
GRIEVES Eleanora Catharine 771; Eliza Isabella 322; Ellen 179; Mary S.

136

INDEX

577; Phebe 331; Thomas 179, 331, 577, 771
GRIFFIN Dudley 696; Maria 696
GRIFFITH Christopher 740
GRIM Agnes 620; Alexander 306; Benjamin 582; Frederick A. 839; Jacob 673; John 620, 639; Sophia 593
GRIMES Joshua 783; Mary 783; William H. 792
GRIMM Abraham 471
GROSH Elizabeth 262; Frederick 375, 377, 505, 780; George W. 599; Henry 288, 599; Mary 375, 377; Polly 505; Sarah 730; Sophia 570
GROSS Isaac 12
GROUND Joseph 790; Sarah 542
GROVE Amelia 723; Ann 597; Elias S. 761; Elizabeth 459; Hannah 638; Jacob H. 822; Lavinia 606; Peter 459, 597; Philip 606, 691; Samuel 692; Susan 691
GROVES David 89; Sarah 89
GRUBB Mary 128, 142; Thomas 638
GRUBER Christiana 554; John 289, 380, 438, 554; Matilda 380; Theresa 289, 438
GRYTON Rebecca 662
GUARD Jeremiah 91; Oliva 91
GUSLER John 106
GUTHRIE Maria 735
GUYTON Sarah 606
GWINN Walter 147
GYSINGER Samuel L. 776

HAEFLINCH Amelia S. 530
HAFFLEY Elizabeth 751
HAGER Anna 540; Christian 289; Elizabeth 289; Jonathan 485, 540; Jonathan D. 828; Ruth 164
HAHN Hannah 695; Mary 286, 654; Susan 808
HAINES J. F. 642; John 401
HAINS Mary 384
HAKE Eliza 656
HALBERT Archibald 277
HALES Charles 834; Jemima 834
HALL Ann 345; Harriet 236, John 236, 303, 329; Mary 329; Thomas B. 345, 778
HALLER John 840
HALLEY William 814

HAM Catharine 669; David 701; Elizabeth 669; John 669, 701; Joseph 669, 701; Margaret 669, 701; Peter 669, 701; Sarah 669
HAMAKER Elizabeth 490
HAMILTON Ann 290; Hannah 746; Jane 253; John 290; John C. 746; John S. 582; Mary 750; Miss 675; Sarah 620
HAMISON Mary 716
HAMM Elizabeth 549; Mary T. 418; Peter 418
HAMMACHER Daniel Stewart 828
HAMMAKER Elizabeth 356
HAMMAN Elizabeth 452; Philip 452
HAMMEL Catharine 766
HAMMELL Barbara 652
HAMMER George 783; John P. 753; Leah 827; Peter 564
HAMMON Ellen 697
HAMMOND David 765; Eliza 661; Thomas 659
HAMOND John 61
HANAGAN James 626
HANENKAMPF Dr. 662; Margaret 662
HANES Catharine 771; Mary 400, 608
HANNA Elizabeth 720; George 364; Isaac 238; John 720; Robert 645
HANSEL Fanny 72; George 72
HANSHER John 660
HANSON Eliza Jane 780; James H. 566; Rev 306, 568, 582; Samuel 420
HARBAUGH John 563; Juliana 478; Leonard 468; Samuel G. 506
HARBINE Catharine 845; Susan 792
HARDEY George L. 642
HARDIN Elizabeth 9; John 9
HARDY Eliza 157; Margaret 172; William 172
HARLET Mr. 432
HARMAN Margaret 693
HARMER Rev W. R. 269
HARN Letha Ann 739
HARNESS Jemima 138; William 138, 158
HARPER James 663; Kenton 19, 549
HARRIS Alcinda 306; James 246; Samuel 306; Thomas 780
HARRISON Catharine 592; James O. 830; Margaret 798; Samuel 404
HARRY David 614; Elizabeth 310; George M. 800; Jacob 310; John 281, 346, 425, 485, 509, 546;

INDEX

Martha Susan 425; Mary Ann 346, 485; Sally 800; Samuel 546; Susanna 281
HARSH David 701; George 701; Henry 701; Jacob 701
HART Elizabeth 257; Jacob 257
HARTEL Jacob 531; John 275; Sarah 671
HARTLE Hannah 394
HARTMAN Andrew 366; Catharine 366, 415; Christian 366; Henry 366; Jacob 366; John 415
HARVEY Caleb 162; William 804, 850
HARVIN William 557
HARWOOD Benjamin 60
HASHEE George 678
HASLETINE Mortimore 151
HASLETT Margaret 407; Rev S. 116
HATHORN Prudence 560; William 594
HATSENMILLER John 275
HATTER David 605
HAUER Anthony 672
HAUS Rev 99
HAUSE William 574
HAUTHORN David 767
HAVERSTICK David 798; Margaret 804; Rev 209, 216; Rev H. 201, 211, 221, 214, 812; Sarah 814
HAWKEN Abraham 701; Ann 572; Anna 701; Christian 282, 315, 490; David 490; George 490; Jacob 310, 490; Juliana 490; Juliann 826; Margaret 624; Nancy 490; Rosanna 279; Samuel 279, 490; William 490
HAWKINS Thomas 269
HAYDEN George A. 851
HAYNES Jacob 741
HAYS Dr. 695; Dr. J. J. 296; Elizabeth 579; Jane 780; John 122, 563; John J. 365, 443, 462; Joseph 780; Joseph C. 606; Melvina 122; Michael 140; Nathan W. 695; Sophia B. 855
HAYSLET Samuel 215
HAYSLETT Frances 215
HEARTLY William 222
HEASTAND Abby 620; John 620
HEATHERINGTON Andrew 251; John 251
HEATHRINGTON Andrew 274; John 274
HEBB Ann 780; Helen Marietta 765
HECK Charles 174; Henry 675
HEDRICK Daniel 659; George 669, 701
HEESECKER Aaron 701
HEFFLEICH Attilia 769
HEFFLINCH Peter 680
HEFFLYBOWER Catharine 352; Margaret 352
HEFFNER Andrew 461; David 317
HEFLEICH John 433; Magdalena 433
HEFLICH Amelia S. 399
HEISKELL Sidney I. 580
HEISKILL Mary 545
HELD John 232
HELFENSTEIN Charles 637; Jonathan 621, 854; Rev 483, 663, 719; Samuel 697
HELFENSTINE Rev 436
HELLER Julian 806
HELM Meredith 598; William 52
HELMOUTH Rev Dr. 431
HELSER Susanna 282
HEMPHILL James 467
HENDERSON Samuel 735
HENDRIXON John 215; Samuel 28
HENLEY Philip 822
HENRY Francis 561; George 10; Miss --- 10
HENSHAW Rev 397, 805
HERBERT John 317, 461
HERBST Rev 237
HERLEY Rev 413
HERLY William M. 520
HERMAN John 525
HERR Abraham 520; Catharine 287, 436; Daniel 237; Emanuel 834; John 287, 436; John P. 237; Mary Ann 751; Nancy 520; Rudolph 20
HERRING Elizabeth 249
HERRON Alexander G. 572
HERSH David 358, 493; George 243, 407; Henry 381
HERSHBERGER John 536
HERSHEY Andrew 478,491; Barbara 491; 715; Christian 818; David 340; George 774; Isaac 704; Magdalena 340; Matilda 774
HERVEY James 300
HESS David 597, 654; Elizabeth 572; Jacob 855; Matilda 150; Rawana 654; William 750, 754
HESSER Samuel 1. 642
HESTER Gabriel 522
HEWETT Jacob 415
HEYER Isaac 822; Rev 12, 21, 22, 27, 61, 66, 303
HEYSER Sarah 715; William 488, 715
HEZLETT Eliza 327

INDEX

HICKMAN Benjamin F. 780; Benjamin Franklin 785
HIEGEL Michael 516
HIESTER Catharine 484; Daniel J. 484; Gabriel 545; Isaac 484; John 484; Rebecca 484; William 484
HILDEBRAND Isaac 107; Mary 107
HILDEBRANDT Isaac 338
HILL David 248; Elizabeth 572; Ira 705; John 141; Levenia 141; Rev Dr. 580, 626; Samuel M. 855
HILLEARY Joseph P. 173; Margaret 152; Matilda Ann 30; William 18, 30, 152
HILLERY Matilda 569
HILLIARD Christopher 361; Margaret 594
HIMES Henry 789
HINCH Rev 272, 419
HINDS Michael 598
HINES Catharine 784; George 757; Mary 685; Nancy 667
HINT Elizabeth 279
HINTY Elizabeth 423
HITCHCOCK Charles B. 336
HITE Col. 822; Mary 822
HITT Daniel 52, 598; Rev T. 491; Samuel M. 491, 598; Washington W. 676
HOALTZMAN John 155
HOBBS John 129; Sarah 129
HOBLITZELL Adrian 2; Caroline 2; Dennis B. 219; George 128, 142, 227; Hannah 2; Jacob 150; John 2; Lowenso 227; Rebecca 2; William 2, 63, 71, 128, 142
HOFFER Mary 400; Michael 305
HOFFMAN Catharine 33, 287, 581; Christian 350; Christina 487; David 116, 121; Elizabeth 256, 826; George 33; Jacob 254, 306, 350, 487; John 287, 346, 508; John J. 95, 142; Lydia 417; Margaret 34; Maria 116; Mary 246; Thomas W. 610; Valentine 34
HOFFMASTER George 639
HOGAN Sarah 392
HOGE Asa Hervey 819
HOGG Gavin 813; Jemima 268; John 268, 504, 562, 643; Sarah Ann 562; William 504

HOGMIRE Jonas 271, 395, 669, 719; Rebecca 719; Susan 271
HOLKER John 459
HOLLAND Sarah Ann 828
HOLLAR Daniel 841
HOLLIDAY Mary E. 557; William 833
HOLLINS John 673
HOLMES Andrew 840; Hugh 565; Sarah 840
HOLSEY Emanuel 244
HOLTZMAN Elie 149; Frances 146; John 146
HONE Bridget 110; Bridjit 77; Charles 77, 110
HOOK John S. 120; Mrs. 120
HOOPER Abraham 253; Kitturah 569; Sophia 42
HOOVER Esther 667; Henry 91; Jacob 700; John 572; Nancy 91, 668
HOPEWELL Athallah Rebecca 155
HORB Elizabeth 72; Joseph 72
HORINE Barbara 574; John 574, 802, 823; Mary 802
HORN John 682
HORSENEST Mary 608
HOSE Catharine 250, 296; Elizabeth 250, 275; Jacob 327; Margaret 250; Peter 708
HOSHOUR Rev 828
HOSKINS John 803
HOUER Catharine 238
HOUKE George 592
HOUSE Christiana 755; Michael 661, 755
HOUSEHOLDER Elizabeth 604; Mary Ann 790
HOUSER Catharine 473; Isaac 523; Jacob 473; Rachel 309
HOUSLEY Daniel 618
HOUSTON Sarah 724
HOUT Joseph 814
HOVERMALE mrs. 663
HOWARD John E. 471; John Eager 126; Mary 334; William 520
HOWELL Mary 186
HOWER Rosanna 279
HOWTHORN Margaret 777; William 777
HOYE Ann 724; Harriet M. 752; Jane 626; Nancy 48, 591; Paul 48, 591
HRECKLE Joseph 256
HUBBARD David 600
HUBER Elizabeth 279; John 555

139

INDEX

HUFFER Jacob 417; John 775; Samuel 557
HUFFMAN Jacob 75
HUGHES Amelia S. 388; Ann 590; Daniel 467, 590, 594, 616, 730; David 700; Edward 629; Eliza 432; Elizabeth 185; George 126, 185; James 327; James C. 822; John H. 412; Louisa Ann 718; Mr. 608; Rebecca 812; Rebecca L. 594; Robert 169, 770; Samuel 202, 542, 718, 822; Susan 730
HULL Catharine 799; Jacob 799; John 799
HUMRICKHOUS Albert 528
HUMRICKHOUSE Charles 436; Eliza 333; Maria 728; Peter 333, 662, 728; Susan 251
HUNT Job 376, 519
HUNTER David 675, 767; James 62; Louisa Rebecca 675; Mrs. 68
HURDLE Richard 515
HURLEY James 802
HURT P. 685
HUSHOUR Samuel K. 767; Andrew 182, 184; Druse 182; James 247; William 489
HUTCHINSON Rev 712
HUYETT Daniel 744; Jacob 269,722; Ludowick 722; Mary 745; Mrs. 744
HYER Rev 3, 18
HYLAND Ann 544; Elisha 544; John 373; Rachel 281
HYSTER Henry 768

ILER Margaret 701
INGLIS Ann Maria 707; James 613; Jane 707; Mary 784; Miss 767; Rev Dr. 707; William C. 629
INGRAM Elizabeth 269, 415; Joseph 269, 415
INKS Elizabeth 50; George 50
INSKEEP Abraham 176; Ann 129; James 164, 176; Samuel 129
IRELAND Nancy 110; William 110
IRVINE Catharine 651; Jacob 651
IRWIN Andrew 797; Jacob 661
ISAHART Rosa 42
ISEMINGER Barbara 351
ISENBERGER Deborah 778, 819; John 778, 819

ISLER Elizabeth 63, 73; George 63; Jacob 63, 73

JACK Ann 244; Turner F. 801
JACKSON Ann 9; Mary 133, 673, 702; Rev 675; Ruth 306; Susan 588; Thomas 306
JACOB Rev J. J. 20, 100, 110, 123, 149
JACOBS David 844; J. J. 696; Jacob 129; John J. 390; Mary 129; Rev J. J. 26, 67; Samuel 27; Selonary W. 546; Thomas 546
JACQUES Elizabeth 814; Lancelot 129, 697, 814
JAMES --- 669; Abraham 234; Cordelia 654; David 669; Elizabeth 669; Henry 669; Isaac 669; Jacob B. 669; Mary Ellen 726
JAMESON Francis 9; Lionel M. 110
JENNINGS Mahlon 655; Rev 58, 608; Rev Dr. 401
JEWETT James 528; Rev 805; Rev A. M. 679
JOHNS John 267; L. H. 541; Leonard H. 637; Michael S. 407; Rev 467, 514; Rev L. H. 219, 230, 841
JOHNSON Anna 90; Benjamin 90; Bethsheba 741; Charlotte 717; Edward 464; Eleanor 556; Elizabeth 556, 823; Ephraim 174; Fanny 514; Henry 556; Jacob 556; James 796; John 22, 409, 556; Louisa 409; Maria 260; Naomy 778, 819; Susan 556
JOHNSTON Eleanora B. 712; Jacob 826; John 270, 431, 539, 693; Samuel 626; William 363
JOLLIFF Mary 288
JOLLISS Mary 438
JONAS Adolph 50; Ann 50; Catharine 50; Elizabeth 50; George 50; Hannah 50; Jeremiah 50; John 50; Lucia 50; Mary 50; Rachel 50; Samuel 50; Susanna 50; William 50
JONES Elizabeth 617; John 83; John R. 805; Rebecca 685; Rev 606, 695, 822; Rev W. 798; William 668
JORDAN Thornton G. 362, 495
JULIUS Elizabeth 776; John 234; Mary 715
JUSTICE Elizabeth 644; Mazy 698

INDEX

KADE Richard 70
KADLE Roena 310
KAFFMAN Samuel 654
KAGERISE Michel 256
KAGEY Henry 547
KAIGHN Lavinia 288, 438
KAPP Frederick 768; Jacob 676; Michael 379, 510, 768; Sophia Ann 768, 819
KAUFFMAN Amelia 701; Catharine 455; Christian 743; Jacob 701; John 739; Rachael 743
KAUSLER Christiana 494; Eliza 684; Jacob 684, 817; John 373, 494; Margaret 817
KAUTZ Catharine 768; Peter 276, 768
KEADY Rev 350
KEALHAFFER Catharine 686
KEALHOFER Christopher 576; Eliza M. 638; Elleanora 28; Henry 744; John 638, 825; Susan A. 825
KEAN Thomas 803
KEARN David 173; George 209; Sophia 173
KEARNES David 29
KEATY John A. 795
KECKRON John 371
KEEDY Daniel 704, 855; David H. 720; Elizabeth 751; George 235, 418, 453, 455; Henry I. 704; Jacob H. 751; John 604; John D. 313; John J. 623; Mary 848; Rev 405, 406, 407, 411, 459, 500, 515, 528, 537, 563, 619, 663; Rev G. 564
KEEFER George 656; Henry 278; Susanna 753
KEEN Gabriel Jefferson 789; William 809
KEENER Samuel 775
KEESECKER Jacob 592
KEHLER Jacob 234
KEISACKER Jacob 260
KELLAR Adam 829; George 750; Henry 738; Isaac 400, 568, 576, 593, 625, 626, 630, 642, 645, 655, 656, 665, 667, 730, 755; Jesse 494; Joseph 293, 440; Lewis 667; Philip 738; Rev 581, 614, 713, 715, 716, 719, 767; Rev I. 627; Thomas 675
KELLER Ann M. 835; Ann Margaret 620; Barbara 304, 676; Elizabeth 306, 625; Isaac 536, 572, 668, 675, 718, 763, 789; John 722; Joseph 306; Joseph C. 625; Mary 211, 573; Peter 253; Rev 565, 695, 788; Rev I. 171, 572, 573, 659; Sarah 563
KELLY Edward 139; Elizabeth 295; Henry A. 673; Joseph 57; Mary 201
KEMP Bishop 128; Edward 91; Elizabeth 639; Henry 91; James 639; John 91; Mary 91; Massey 91; Richard 91; Sarah 91
KENDAL Maria S. W. 316; Mrs. 776
KENDLE James 262; William 518
KENEDY Rev R. 685
KENEGE Elizabeth 604
KENNDEY Alexander 316, 476; Dorothea 614; John 704; John H. 98, 665; Rev 22; Rev R. 5, 562; Robert 29, 33, 98, 665, 746; Thomas 92, 614
KENNEY Jabez 540
KENNY David 549; Gertrude 837
KENT Eleanor Lee 79, 639; Joseph 79, 639
KEPHART Elizabeth 556; Henry 556
KEPLINGER Margaret 841
KERFOOT George W. 299, 446
KERNS Catharine 306
KERR Debra 809; Jacob 809; Walter 67
KERSHNER Andrew 516; Benjamin 614; Catharine 643; Christiana 607; Daniel 514; George 835; Isaac 607; Jacob 622; Jonathan 244; Joseph 501; Josiah 641, 794; Martin 297; Mary 835; Mary Ann 825; Michael 68; Nathaniel 839; Philip 607
KEYS Rev 566
KIEFFER John D. 359
KIESECKER Elizabeth 276; Simon 276
KILE Amelia 125
KILGOUR John A. T. 69
KILPATRICK Mary 743
KIMBERLY John 173; Michael 173
KIMMEL Gabriel 9; Michael 545; Nancy 9
KING Abraham 757; James 11; John 424; John O. 552; Martin 395; Rebecca 11
KINKADE Jacob 455
KINKLE Elizabeth 671; Jacob 431; Mrs. 790
KINSELL F. & E. B. 634; Jemima 463; Mr. E. B. 574
KINSLEY Elizabeth A. 767

141

INDEX

KIRBY Martha 598; William 516
KIRKPATRICK Alexander 521; James 546; Maria F. 753
KITCHEN George 817
KITSMILLER Eliza 580
KITZMILLER Nancy 757; Samuel 832; William H. 838
KLINE Benjamin 690, 752; Catharine 340, 397; Elizabeth 789; George 545, 547; Harriet 690, 752; Jacob 392; Mary 275; Samuel 514; Sarah 573
KLINK George 559
KNAFE Catharine 454
KNAFT Catharine 309
KNAVEL George 821; Mrs. 821
KNEEDY George 705
KNESELY Christiana 2; Joseph 2
KNODE Catharine M. 641; Elizabeth 340; Jacob 537, 565, 709; John 415, 417, 663; Jonas 346, 485; Margaret 537; William 415
KNODLE Catharine 572; Elizabeth 477; Mary 693; Susan 481; William 743
KNOWLTON Thomas 697
KOONS Harriet 826
KOONTZ John 563; Peter 641
KORN Henry 159; Maria 159
KOST Jacob 752
KRABER John F. 286
KRAUGHT Rev 459
KRAUS Peter 370
KRAUTH Rev 597
KREBS John M. 840
KREIGH Philip 827; William 814
KREPS Christian 156; Eveline 443; George 422, 443; George F. 636; Margaret 847; Michael 246, 847; Mrs. 422; Rebecca 156; William 306
KRETZER Daniel 629; David 629; Leonard 431
KRETZZINGER Susanna 640
KRICK Andrew 399; Philip 530
KRIEGER Abraham 847
KRIEGH Philip 521
KRINER John 705
KRING Mary Ann 814
KRISSMAN Michael 309
KROFT Jacob 681; Susan 681
KROH Henry 692, 722; Rev 644, 689, 712, 714, 721

KUHN Christiana 701; Elizabeth 701; Jacob 677, 701; John 701; Margaret 786; Moddelena 701
KUHNS Jacob 545; Nancy 531
KUNTZ Elizabeth 605; Peter 421
KURTZ Ann 568; Benjamin 208, 240, 361, 450, 478, 486, 490, 493, 495, 502, 567, 717, 735, 762, 765, 768, 809; Louisa Amelia 361, 495; Nancy 567; Rev 62, 231, 232, 234, 235, 237, 238, 241, 256, 258, 260, 262; 264, 299, 336, 339, 343, 404, 405, 407, 412, 425, 434, 446, 454, 464, 501, 518, 526, 545, 563, 574, 582, 598, 607, 615, 704, 705, 728, 792, 796, 832, 834; Rev B. 242, 243, 244, 248, 249, 251, 253, 254, 271, 275, 277, 279, 281, 283, 286, 288, 289, 291, 293, 295, 296, 304, 309, 310, 311, 314, 315, 317, 319, 320, 325, 329, 332, 334, 340, 344, 349, 351, 352, 353, 356, 358, 361, 369, 381, 383, 385, 392, 397, 399, 419, 421, 430, 435, 438, 439, 458, 461, 477, 495, 513, 514, 524, 530, 535, 543, 547, 549, 551, 553, 555, 557, 560, 564, 566, 568, 576, 579, 589, 590, 598, 600, 601, 602, 605, 612, 617, 713, 715, 718, 719, 720, 722, 723, 727, 737, 739, 741, 747, 748, 750, 751, 753, 755, 766, 769, 773, 774, 786, 791, 794, 797, 802, 803, 804, 805, 811, 812, 815, 817, 819, 821, 823, 825, 827, 828, 838, 847; Rev H. A. 242, 567

LAFEE Lewis 185
LAHM Catharine 607
LAMAR Colonel 393
LAMARR Archibald 825
LAMBERT Isaac 214; Jacob 348; Mary Ann 803; Sophia 348
LANCASTER Adeline G. 807; Margaret 689
LANDEGER Gideon 787
LANDEN Ann 279; Francis 279, 573
LANDIS Barbara 346; Christian 571; Elizabeth 712; Henry 346, 378, 845; Sarah 600
LANE Ann M. 618; Catharine 573; Charles G. 753; David 778, 819; Elizabeth 778, 819; Frances 111; James S. 378; John 778, 819;

INDEX

Julian 778, 819; Michael 111, 224; Sarah 778, 819; Seth 558, 573
LANTZ Catlett Clarissa 9; Clarissa 9; Daniel 9, 123; Eliza 9; Elizabeth 721; George 9, 106; Jacob 9; John 642; Julian 9; Margaret 9; Margarett M. 162; Samuel 449; Sophia 9, 123; Susan 9
LAUGH George 128; Sarah 128
LAUGHM Margaret 275
LAVIS Elizabeth 323
LAWMAN Henry 413
LAWRENCE John 369; Mary Ann Hoffman 252; Otho 369; Upton 8, 252, 525
LAYMAN George 187; Harriet 187
LAYTON Lowther 155
LEADY Barbara 563; Henry 563
LEAKIN Rev 40
LEAPARD Adam 330, 470
LEARY Mahala 701
LECHRONE Mary 637; Nancy 650
LECKMAN Benjamin 844
LECKRONE Jacob 664; Mary 840
LECOMPT Thomas D. 834
LECOMPTE Benjamin W. 296
LECRON Mary 275
LEE John 226, 631; Lewis L. 821; Mary Duncan 511; Rev 523; Richard H. 511
LEEDS Lodowick 774
LEFEBER Mary 309
LEFEVER Isaac 847; Maria 718
LEGG Basil 825; Mary Ann 825
LEGGETT George 528; James 452, 597, 703; Jeremiah 434; Martha V. 703; Thomas 597
LEIDY Joseph 286
LEIGHT Benjamin 286, 655; Catharine 655; Eliza 286; John 355; Mr. B. 531
LEIGHTER Mary 610
LEINBACH Catharine 545
LEISURE Elijah 291, 440; Henry 560
LEKRONE Margaret 667
LEMASTER Abraham 408
LEMMON George 362, 386, 396, 596, 620, 626, 676, 696, 704; Rev 346, 388, 481, 531, 548, 619, 647, 652, 704; Rev G. 701; Sarah 346
LEMON George 18, 36, 575; Rev 641; Rev G. 495, 515, 592
LENKHORN Clara P. E. 713

LEONARD Henry A. 777
LEPLEY Adam 172
LESCHER Augustus 761
LEVIS Charles 573
LEVY Maria C. 436
LEWELLEN Abegael 129; John 129
LEWIS Anthony Wayne 572; Henry 488; Malohn 113; William 108, 230, 286, 372, 677, 841
LEYDY Henry 332
LEYPOLD John 466
LICHSTINE Gotleib 704
LICKLITER John 628
LIDER Catharine 537
LIGGET Prudence 288
LIGHT Jacob 349, 486; John 829; Mary 536; Nancy 542; Peter 434
LIGHTER Joseph 722
LIKENS Ann 846
LILLICH Mary 574
LILLY William 618
LIND John 16, 243, 266, 316, 329, 365, 546, 642; Rev 462, 498, 533; William Young Campbell 642
LINEBAUCH Benjamin 694
LINGO Samuel 133
LINN Addis 367; Elizabeth 367; Mr. D. 247
LITTLE Christiana 606, 607; David 808; David T. 703; Elizabeth 557; Freeman 677; James 533; Joseph 416, 606; Liberty D. 703; Louisa Anna 795; N. B. 69; Nathan 287; Peter 207, 809; Rev 64, 135, 574; Rev N. B. 57, 59, 62, 83, 96, 98, 109, 113, 115, 136, 140, 142, 144, 159, 164, 171, 174, 175, 176, 191, 194, 225, 228, 561, 566, 569, 570, 572, 580, 586, 587, 601, 615, 624, 662, 795; Samuel H. 718; Thomas 369; William 591
LITTRELL William H. 46
LIZAR Henry 629
LIZER George 324; Henry 698
LLOYD James 229; Mr. 629
LOCHER and BRANDNER 381
LOCHER George 391; Henry 770; Mary 240
LOCKE Eliza 586; Sophia 804, 850
LOGAN Elizabeth 547; Mary 619
LOGSDON David 105, 196; John 105, 157; Joseph 105, 110; Joshua 105;

INDEX

Margaret 105; Ralph 105; Sarah 110; William 49, 105
LOMAN Mary Ann 700
LONAS Leonard 652
LONG David 240; John 499; Sarah Ann 164; Sophia 752
LONGMAN Susanna 411
LOP Jacob 640
LOR Elizabeth 690
LORSHBAUGH Barbara Ann 648; Catharine 590; George 325, 590, 609
LOSE Conrad 260; Mary Ann 260
LOUDERBAUGH Mrs. 20
LOUGH George 142; Sarah 128, 142
LOUIS Rev 376
LOUNS Mary 674
LOVETT Harriet 148
LOWE Ann Eliza 520; George 465, 520, 532, 640; John T. 381; Mary 532; Overton G. 688
LOWER Solomon 547
LOWMAN Daniel 589
LOWNDES William 482
LOWRY Mary Ann 844; Thomas 751
LUDY Ann 286; John 238
LUKENS Jacob 750
LUND Rev 270
LUPTON Rebecca McPherson 819
LUTZ Elizabeth 595; Henry 644; Isaac C. 632
LYNCH John B. 579, 750; Mary 638
LYNN Anna 69, 624; Capt D. 69, 624; David 41, 132, 153, 255, 267, 413; Francina C. 267, 413; Joseph 788; Mary G. 255
LYON Rebecca 768
LYTLE Thomas 500; Elias 430

M'AFEE John 571; Lucy 668
M'ALRATH James 277
M'ATEE William 694
M'CAFFERTY Dennis 503
M'CALL Mary 397
M'CALLMOT Harriet 665
M'CAMMON Alexander 809
M'CANDLASS Rev A. 619
M'CARDELL Lucretia 689; Rebecca Ann 238; Thomas 238
M'CARTY Edward 15; Joseph 171
M'CAULEY Charles 746, 804, 809; Hugh 384; James 531; Lydia S. 568; Rev J. 562; Samuel 727

M'CAWLEY Rev 453
M'CLAIN Elie 494; James 314; Josiah 541; Nancy 618
M'CLANAHAN Isabella 270; Matthew 573
M'CLANNAHAN Mary 305; Matthew 305
M'CLARY Jane 22; Mary 15
M'CLEERY Margaret 26; Peter 26
M'CLELLAND Arabella Eliza 598; John 678; Maria 678
M'CLENAHAN Samuel B. 547
M'CLINTIC Daniel 755; Mary 755
M'CLURE James 552
M'COY Edmund 714; Edward 253; James 619; John 605
M'CRAE Elizabeth 464; Rebecca 803
M'CRUSKER Rev 689
M'CULLOUGH John W. 776
M'CURDY Jane 452
M'DADE william 615
M'DANIEL Rebecca 495
M'DANNELL Eleanora 585
M'DILL Catharine 374
M'DOWEL Ann 495
M'DOWELL Nathan 808; William M. 595
M'DUFFIE George 186
M'FALL Ann 246, 653; Eliza 464; Maria 285, 519
M'FARQUHAR Colin 326
M'FEE Daniel 630
M'GAFFIN John 255
M'GONNIGAL Margaret 673
M'HENRY John 471
M'ILHENNY Joseph 631
M'ILVAINE Rev 509
M'KEE Mary 303
M'KENNA Ann 759; William 759
M'KINLEY Henry 14
M'KINNEY John 673, 702
M'KINSEY John 105; Margaret 105
M'KINSTRY Maria 805; William 805
M'KISSICK James 657
M'LAIN John 659; Maria 659
M'LAUGHLIN Catharine 277; Henry 642; James 721; Sarah 642
M'LENAHAN James 490
M'MULLEN Francis 711
M'NAMEE Job 765
M'NAUGHTON Rev 773
M'NEIL Archibald 30
M'NEILL Ann Maria 84; Francis A. 206
M'PHERSON Horatio 386; John 673, 800
M'QUINNY Thomas 699

INDEX

M'VITTY Rachel 399
M'WILLIAMS Robert P. 751; Sarah 751
M..TAG Susannah 809
MACGILL Charles 770; Dr. 542, 611; Mary 542
MACKEN Elizabeth 642
MACNAME Maria 143
MACNAMEE Mary 151; Moses 151
MADDEN Samuel 70
MADORE Francis 159
MAFFET Margaret 743
MAFFITT Mary 536
MAGAW Jesse 377, 775; Mrs. 654; William 775
MAGEE Daniel 602
MAGGILL William D. 397
MAGILL John 215; Samuel 61
MAGRUDER Burgess 131; Hannah Elizabeth 131; John B. 69; Jonathan W. 255
MAJORS Elizabeth 49
MALCOLM Caroline 185
MALONE John 279
MALOTT Daniel 699; Theodore 495
MANER Caleb 701
MANNING Wesley 770
MARCHAL Rev 196
MARESCHAL Most Rev Archibishop 604, 629
MARESHAL Ambrose 138
MARKEN Jacob 815
MARKER Elias 346; George 554; Mary 299, 446; Sarah 607
MARKWALD Margaret 796
MARMADUKE Sarah 741
MARSHALL Elizabeth 521
MARTENEY Amelia 533; George 533, 537
MARTIN Ann 847; Catharine 473, 803, 805, 816; David 389, 516, 620, 694, 738, 740; Eliza Jane 675; Elizabeth 88, 618; Esther 830; Joseph 173, 594; Lenox 88, 219; Margaret G. 839; Mary 540, 809; Nicholas 738, 740; Rev 28, 604; Samuel 540, 620, 633; Sarah 656; Stephen 805
MARTZ Squire 145
MASON Elizabeth A. T. 769; Jeremiah 476, 520, 688, 716, 846; John Thompson 769; John Thomson 558; Rev J. 422, 481, 773, Temperance 773
MASSEE Henry 856; Mary L.P. 856

MASTERS Henry 302, 448
MATHIES Jacob 483
MATTHEWS John 360, 668, 751; Rev 629, 698, 703; Rev Dr. 789, 790; Rev E. 464; Rev J. 422
MATTINGLY Baptist 34, 110; James 99; John 167; Nancy 110
MAUGGINS Nancy 557
MAUGINS Catharine 300, 447
MAXWELL James 806; Susan 806; Susan H. 774; William 774
MAY John 316, 678
MAYER Ludwig 688
McAFEE Archibald 712
McARTHUR Thomas I. 190
McATEER Hugh 577
McBEE Jemimee 721
McCALLMOT Harriet 98
McCAMMANT Elizabeth 58
McCARTY Edward 105, 119, 176; Elizabeth 176; Patrick 147; Sarah 105
McCAUL Margaret 704
McCAULEY Barbara 346; Hannah 582; Rev 726; Samuel 346
McCILTON Rev D. 825
McCL... Maria 775
McCLARY Hannah 778, 819; Margaret 814; Patrick 778, 819
McCLEARY Andrew 174; Jacob 827; Rachel 174; Robert 176
McCLEERY Peter 68
McCLELLAN Eleanor B. 700; John 700
McCLENNAH Malvina 813
McCLERY Andrew 180; James 180; John 180; Robert 180; Thomas 180
McCORMICK Helen C. 706; Otway 792; Thomas 787
McCOY Daniel 735; John 805
McCRACKEN John 222
McCRAIN Adeline C. Junkin 754; Richard 754
McCULLOCH Alexander 91; Daniel 91; Jeremiah 91
McCULLOH George 176; Joseph 201; Rebecca 176
McDONALD & RIDGELY 850
McDONALD John 158
McDOWELL Matilda 634
McFARLAND John 118, 329
McGILL James 218
McGINNIES Mary 677

145

INDEX

McGOVAN Sarah 321
McGUIRE William 158
McKAIG Thomas Jefferson 157
McKEE Rebecca 789
McKEY James 314
McKINLEY James 112; Margaret 112
McKINNEY John 133
McLANAHAN Catharine 828; Mary G. 631; William 631
McMAHON Owen 758; Sarah Ann 190; William 107, 190
McMECKEN Agnes 214; Sarah H. 214
McNARY Ebenezer 147
McNEEL Catharine 661; John 661
McNEILL John 84, 162; Rebecca 162
McPHERSON John 429, 514; Sarah 429
McSHANE John 124; Mary 124
McWILLIAMS Robert P. 542, 780, 827
MEALY Jacob W. 309, 454; Sarah Ann 317, 461
MEDCALF Benjamin 694
MEDTART Jacob 846; Rev 609, 618, 619, 620, 623, 627, 637, 640, 641, 642, 645, 650, 654, 660, 668, 677, 684, 689, 695, 812; Rev J. 685, 693
MEISNER Catharine 640
MEKIMMEY Jacob M. 846
MELONE Rebecca 713
MELVIN Mary 246
MENDENHALL Elizabeth 579; Mr. E. B. 579
MENGHINNE Joseph 629
MERCER John F. 287
MEREDITH Rachel W. 673
MERIDETH Maria Louisa 535
MERRICK Daniel 714; J. I. 542, 714; Joseph I. 345; Mary 345
MERYMAN James 529
MESSER Caleb 284
METART Rev 604
MEYER George 547; James 547
MICHAEL James 47
MIDDELKAFF Leonard 627; Samuel 627
MIDDELKAUFF Barbara 578; Christian 374; Daniel 272, 331, 419; Elizabeth 701; Henry 578; Jonas 500; Julian 272, 419; Juliann 331; Mary 276, 421; Samuel 358
MIDDLECAUFF Henry 717
MIDDLEKAUFF Christian 459, 623, 735; Daniel 352, 716; Daniel S. 575; Elizabeth 459; Henry 743; Jacob 845; John 759, 815; Lavinia 845; Mary Ann 623
MILES Joshua B. 643
MILLER Ann 444; Arawine 394; Baltzer 242; Catharine 244, 545, 547, 553, 806, 846; Christian 291, 440, 733; Christiana 232, 402; Conrad 385; Daniel 309, 631, 796; David 806; Eleanor B. 631; Elisha B. 655; Eliza 161; Elizabeth 607, 697, 837; Ellis M. 155; Erwine 394, 849; Eve 294; George 232, 373, 402, 556, 701, 837; Henry 169, 273, 607, 840; Hester 676; Hetta 221; Hezekiah 843; Isaac 627; Jacob 240, 400, 775; James W. 115; John 30, 244, 283, 298, 566, 598, 603, 637, 803, 840; John Henry 755; John I. 277, 421; John T. 625; John W. 283; Joseph 273, 687, 700; Juliana 484, 490; Lonas 701; Margaret 784, 803; Maria Ann 629; Martha 293; Martin 273; Mary 556, 641, 652; Matthias 501; Nancy 300, 447; Oliver 333; Otho H. W. S. 843; Peter 243, 255; Rev 165, 187, 569; Rev J. 171; Robert 490; Samuel 397, 718; Sarah 458; Sophia 704, 819; Squire 182; Susan 796; Susanna 286, 394, 849; William 320, 444, 697; William C. 88; William H. 383; William M. 513
MILLIGAN James 659
MILLS Levin 617; Samuel 697
MINNICK John George 185
MISER John 855; Romena 855
MISH George 632
MITCHELL Alexander 322, 669; Catharine 420; Hannahretta 678; J. 420; Nathaniel 483
MITTAG Gotleib 748; John F. G. 759; Mary 516
MITTOE Mr. 441
MIX Sarah 667
MOATES Jacob 406
MOATS Daniel 753; Jacob 340; Mary 554; Samuel 837
MOELLER Rev 778
MOGGINS Susanna 238
MOLER Elizabeth 464; Michael 464
MOLES Levi B. 830
MOLOR Mary 90; Matthew 90
MONAHAN Charles T. 784

INDEX

MONG Elizabeth 238; Margaret 700; Margaret A. 828
MONNTNGER John 799
MONROE Rev 806, 842
MONTGOMERY John 733; John C. 809
MOOR George 7
MOORE Alexander 366, 714; Daniel 559; Ellen 215; Enoch 118, 193; Francis 91, 673; George 422; James 180; James D. 240, 405; James M. 203; John 714; Larkin 413; Louisa 193; Mary 118, 604; Rachael 91; Rebecca 559; Richard 604
MOOTE Jacob 424
MOPPS Edward 44
MORGAN Isaac 782; Margaret 848; Samuel 309
MORRIS Mary 277
MORRISON Ann 735; Anna 753; David 480; James 24, 250; John 125; John H. 566; Manly 397; Mr. 835
MORROW Charles 489; Elizabeth 216; George 156; James 617; John 216; Sarah Ann 156
MORSE Jedediah Rev 631
MOTES Harriet 373
MOUDY Amelia 668; Frederick 572, 830; George 241; Matilda 665
MOUNTZ John W. 162
MOUSER Jacob 796
MOWDY Frances 644
MOWROR Lydia 730
MOWSER Margaret 593
MOYER Ann 723; John 367, 401, 609, 716; Lewis 547; Lydia 248
MOYERHAFFER Rev 598
MUIR Sarah Ann 746
MULLAN Edward 98
MULLANNIX Rebecca H. 495
MULLEN Charlotte 757; John 648
MULLENNIX Rebecca H. 362
MUMAU Katy 652; Sarah 174
MUMMA Elias 796; Jacob 855; John 428; Joseph 392; Rosanna 772
MUMMAW John 181
MURCAN Samuel 454
MURDOCH William 40
MURPHY John 415
MURRAY Basil 556; Elizabeth 597; James 604; Joshua 462, 680; Margaret 604; Mary Ann 690; Matthew 597, 680, 690, 732;

Stephen 537; Thomas 827; William 588
MURRELL John 163
MURROW Ruth 57
MURRY Elizabeth 516
MUSSELMAN Andrew 72; Christian 6, 72; Christiana 72; Daniel 72; Elizabeth 72; Jacob 72; John 72; Susanah 72
MYERS Adam 336, 560, 670; Catharine 21; Elizabeth 647; Isaac 701; Jacob 431, 469, 533; Jesse 459; John 568, 607, 701, 825; Margaret 659; Martin 307; Mary 234, 392, 568, 825; Mary Ann 533; Rev 406; Rosanna 726; Sarah 639; Susan 307, 454; Susana 524
MYRES John 787

NAIL Ann 685
NAGLE Charles 621
NASH Rev 66
NASHEE George 109
NAYLOR William 158
NECODEMUS Jacob 654
NEEDY Elizabeth 250, 566; George 250; Henry 250; Isaac 250; John 250; Margaret 250
NEFF David 545; Hannah 18; Henry 130, 216; Jacob 18, 45, 67, 126, 130, 134; Margaret 126; Mary 45
NEGLY Elizbeth 809; Jacob 809
NEIBERT John 707; Philip 604
NEIGHKIRK Henry 855; Nancy 855
NEIKIRCK Elizabeth 232; George 450
NEIKIRK Catharine 799; Daniel 799; David 799; Elizabeth 799; George 799; Henry 799; Jacob 799; Johanis 799; John 799; Joseph 799; Michael 799; Samuel 799
NEILL A. 531; Adam 646; Alexander 610; Isabella 610; Jonathan 538; Rebecca 531; Samuel 646; Thomas 531; William 51
NELSON Anne Maria 675; Madison 223
NEPPER Jacob 773
NESBIT --- 142; James Noble 619; Susan 142; Susannah 129
NESLY Barbara 669; Jacob 669; Joseph 669
NEVINS Rev 286
NEWBY Elizabeth 630

147

INDEX

NEWCOMER Amelia 721; Ann 765; Anna 546; Catharine 339; Christian 546, 563, 574, 765, 813; Christiana 574; Daniel B. 836; David 332, 604, 612, 649, 655, 721, 741; David C. 179, 771; Elizabeth 612, 722; Henry 275, 339, 717, 747; Jacob 684; John 309, 339, 454, 629; Maria 649; Martin 237; Mr. C. 658; Nancy 275; Peter 401, 609; Samuel 339, 361; Sarah 655; Solomon 658; Susan 361; Theresa 716
NEWMAN Christiana 795; John C. 121
NEYKIRK Elizabeth 759
NICHODEMUS Eliza 395; Henry 395; John 563; Margaret 563
NICHOLS Jemima 463
NIEBERT Catharine 336
NIGH George 844
NIGHSWANDER Daniel 752; David 752; Emanuel 752; Jacob 752
NIGHT --- 799; Elizabeth 799
NIKIRK Samuel 457
NITZEL John 661
NITZLE Mary 279
NOEL Catharine B. 637; William S. 221
NONEMACKER Samuel 283
NORTH Edward 452; George 173; John 164
NOURSE Ann 722; Charles 582; Gabriel 722
NOWELL Gilbert 581
NUNAMACHER Mr. 612; Mrs. 612
NUNEMACHER Susanna 518
NYMAN Henry 769
NYSWANDER Elizabeth 739; Susan 704
NYSWANGER Daniel 295

O'BYRNE Dennis 631
O'DONNEL Hugh 255
O'FERRALL Ignatius 390; John 333; Patrick 37
O'NEAL Elias 567
O'NEALE Lawrence 9; Mary A. 9
OGDEN Charles W. 445
OHLWEIN Catharine 792; Charles 792
OHLWINE Charles 845
OHR Henry 240
OLDS Lydia 26
OLDWEIN Sophia 845

OLDWINE Barney 357; Barney B. 452; Bernard 308; Charles 822; Elizabeth 822; Mary 288, 438; Sarah 276, 421
OLEWEIN Polly 759
OLIVER John 495
ONDERDONK Right Bishop 751
ONG Juliet Ann 841
ORNDOFF Christian 781; Elizabeth Ann 781
ORNDORFF Christian 379, 548, 855; Christopher 378; Elizabeth 598; Louisiana 627; Mary 379
OSBORN Margaret 40; Selleck 649; William 40
OSSIER Mary 541
OSTER David 800; Elizabeth 257; Jacob 843; Samuel 235
OSWALD Benjamin 104, 672; Eve 785; Henry 197; Margaret 575
OTT Adam 117, 686, 717, 779; Catharine 717; George 717; Jacob 717; John 64, 617, 717; Julian 717; Julianna 779; Margaret 717; Mary C. 64, 617; Mary S. 363; Michael 363, 717; Nancy Ann 722; Polly 717; Sally 717; Samuel 580
OTTENBERGER Philip 665
OWINGS Prudence 479
OYLER Henry 507; Michael 507

PADIN Margaret 827
PAGE Mary 549
PALMER Christian 340, 477; Daniel 696; Jacob 572; John 524, 601; Mary 832
PANELL Susanna 640
PARK Mary M. 383, 513
PARKER Ashford 474; John 61
PARRATT Susanna 329
PARRON Mary 397
PASCAL George B. 280
PATTERSON Joseph 193, 787; Solomon 640
PAYDEN John 323
PAYNE Benjamin C. 5; Rachel 362; Ralph 105; Wenny 105
PAYTON Sarah Ann 99
PEACOCK Neale 699
PEALE Edmund 153
PEARS Ann 415
PECKLEY Henry 685

INDEX

PEIFFER Margaret 395; Michael 678
PELTZ John 564
PENNELL --- 608; John 722
PENTZ George 682
PERRY Caroline Lydia 801; James 801; Roger 41, 132
PETERMAN Jacob 715; John 792
PETERSON Derick 767
PETMAN David H. 596
PETRY Catharine 834; Elizabeth 395, 569; John 375; Jonas 812; Mary Ann 755; Philip 395
PEYTON Rev 807
PFAUTZ Catharine 276, 421; Elizabeth 768; Henry 768; Jacob 768; John 768; Joseph 768; Michael 768; Nancy 768; Samuel 768
PHEASANT Sarah Ann 700
PHILIPS Rachel 166
PHILLIPS Jacob 166
PHILSON William 790
PHYSICK Dr. 287
PICKING Jacob 659
PIERCE John P. 783
PIERSON David 91; Hulda 91
PIKE Captain 845
PINCKNEY Thomas 851
PINOR Samuel 523
PIPER Aaron 839; Daniel 556, 580; Elizabeth 550; Henry 751; Jacob 556, 757; John 556
PITTIE Polly 729
PLEASANTS John H. 856
PLOCHER Anna 72; John 72
POFFENBERGER Christian 769; Elizabeth 782; Jacob 612; Rosanna 629; Sarah 502
POFFINBERGER Henry 413; Mary 413
POLAND Mary 197
POLLARD Louisa P. 146; Mary H. 32; Rabecca 1; Thomas 1, 29, 32
POLLICK James C. 560; Joseph 560
POOL William 773, 798
POORMAN Jacob 618
POPE Charles 177; Prissy 177
POPPLEIN Miss C. 606
PORTER Benjamin F. 110; David 105; Hannah 110; Henry 110, 105; Henry H. 557, John 105, 110; Michael 110; Nancy 105; Polly 110; Rewis R. 42; Samuel 110, Samuel Scott 49, 110; Thomas 105, 110; William 110

POST Capt. T. 793; Narcissa 793; Rev R. 706; Thomas 180, 772
POTTENGER Dr. 433; Mary 433; Robert 443; Sophia B. 296,443
POTTER Barbara 563; Benjamin 593; D. Steward 810; Daniel 563, 810; John 563; Sarah 319
POTTS Elizabeth 467; George M. 652
POUGH Nimrod 221
POWER William 279
POWLES Daniel 706; Jacob 706; Rev 426
POWLUS Jacob 428
PRAIME Solomon 623
PRATHER Basil 773; Benjamin 846; Elie 771; Mrs. 15; Perry 717, 829; Samuel 139; Samuel S. 721
PRATT Ellenor T. 36, 575; Mrs. 53; Thomas 36, 53, 575
PRECHFIELD Sally 749
PRETZMAN Samuel 719
PRICE Col. 387; Elizabeth 755; Henry 841; Jane 776; John 848; Josiah 356, 387, 519, 606; Levi 327; Mary 397; Samuel D. 422; Sarah 397; Washington 356; William 167, 821, 855
PRITCHET Ephraim 470
PRITTS Joseph 50, 598
PROTZMAN Ann Maria 425; Daniel 268; Elizabeth 812; Henry 307; John 281, 425; Mary 281, 344; Peter 704; Sarah 268, 547
PRYOR Hannah 412
PUI John De 361

QUANTRILL Judith Ann 844; Thomas 844

RADFORD Jane 426; Thomas 426
RAFTER Henry 130; Jacob 130
RAGAN Amelia 325; John 325, 716; Jonathan Hager 546, 747; Mary 770; Richard 770; Selenary W. 747
RAGER Amanda 25
RAHAUSER H. J. 721; Jonathan 570; Mary Elizabeth 570; Mrs. 600; Rev 50, 289, 438, 754, 772, 795, 809; Rev F. 324, 843
RAHOUSER Jacob 16
RAMSAY Col. J. 836; Eliza 752; Frances 752, James 752; John 635; John Van Lear 752; Mary Jane 752, 836; Matthew Van Lear 635; Nancy

INDEX

752; Sally 752; Sophia Allis 752; Susan Emma 752
RAMSEY James 777; Jane Van Lear 718; John 174, 718
RANDALL John 631; V. W. 397; Vachel W. 397
RANES Darcus 608
RANEY Hugh C. 778
RANKIN D'd 549; Mary 549
RAUHOUSER Rev 598
RAVENSCRAFT Abner 165; John 140
RAVENSCROFT John Stark 813
RAWHOUSK Rev 667
RAWLINGS Ann 668; Moses 176, 208; Nancy 208; Solomon 668
RAY James B. 740
REAM Michael 71
RECK Rev 835; Rev J. 848
REDMOND James 342, 479
REDMUND Rev 333
REED John 817; Josephus 598; Peter 194; Rev 581; Sarah 570
REEL Barbara 790
REESE Rev Dr. J. S. 805; William 730
REID Cornelia Rebecca 745; George 143; James 595, 603, 656, 661, 701, 735, 745, 749; Mary 22; Rev 638, 704, 706; Rev J. 594, 631; William 162
REIDENAUER Eleanort 446
REIDENAUSER Jonathan 446
REIDENOUR Jacob 441; Mrs. 441; Sarah 313
REILEY Rev J. R. 423
REILY Elizabeth 67; James 737; James R. 238, 738; Mary 238; Rev 341, 446, 531; Rev J. 399; Rev J. R. 23, 240, 241, 243, 244, 245, 246, 250, 253, 265, 273, 275, 276, 277, 279, 282, 286, 294, 300, 301, 302, 306, 307, 309, 310, 313, 315, 317, 329, 331, 335, 337, 338, 339, 342, 346, 348, 350, 351, 354, 359, 361, 370, 373, 374, 380, 394, 395, 397, 398, 415, 421, 447, 454, 460, 473, 480, 481, 485, 487, 494, 520, 522, 525, 530, 533, 536, 541, 545, 549, 550, 552, 557, 560, 567, 570, 572, 573, 849
REINHART Elizabeth 240
REITZELL Jacob 812
REMSBERG Sarah 772

RENALDS Angelina 46
RENCH Andrew 776; Daniel 96, 716; Elizabeth 716; Margaret 250; Otho 451; Peter 391; Samuel H. 171, 763; Theresa 626; Thomas H. 253
RENNER Francis 789; Maria 609, 816; Peter 356, 490; William 704
RENNEY Stephen 697
RENTCH John 329
RERNSPERGER Mary 726
RESIDE Edward 98, 665; James 71, 98
RESSLY Lydia 306
REUTTER Charlotte 331
REWLETT Harriet 619
REYNARD Susan 762
REYNOLDS Elizabeth 522, 558; George 274, 332; John 43, 244, 446, 558, 583, 615, 727; Maria 244; Mary 676; Mary Ann 615; Matilda 727; Rev C. 244; William 522; William M. 378
RHINEHART William R. 839
RHOADES Mary 279
RHOADS Massy 253; Rev 155, 157
RIBLET Augustus 373, 503; Daniel 373; Maria 581
RIBLETT Maria 568
RICE Anna 177; Catharine 166; Eliza 804, 850; Frederick 102; George 177; Henry 557; Jacob 177; John 43, 375; Mrs. 43
RICHARDS Henry R. 598
RICKENBAUGH David 348; Martin 803
RIDDLE Rev 208, 809
RIDENOUER Sarah 574
RIDENOUR Adam 264; Anna 590; Charlotte 603; Daniel 277, 806; David 753, 817, 845; Dorothy 734; Elizabeth 332, 769; Elizabeth C. 791; Jacob 693; John 734; John D. 547; Jonathan 570; Martin 264, 433; Mary 688; Nicholas 343; Susan 704
RIDGELY Charles 189; Nicholas G. 850
RIDOUT Addison 640; Harriet 644; John 479; Melrora 598; Samuel 644
RIELY George 98; James 84; Rev J. R. 554; Tobias 84
RIETZ Elizabeth 560
RIGERT Catharine 717; John 717
RIGHTSTINE Margaret 701

INDEX

RIGLER Barbara 589; Catharine 667; Stephen 667
RILEY Rev J. R 340; William 51
RINEHART Jacob 666
RINGER Catharine 336; John 337; Robert 265; Susanna 265
RINGGOLD Ann Cadwalader 18, 548; Charles Anthony 505; Cornelia 652; Edward Lloyd 324; Gen. S. 505; Maria 713; Mary A. 630; Samuel 18, 198, 324, 375, 488, 548, 652, 713, 794; Tench 630
RITCHEY Archibald 736
RITCHIE Mary Anna 828; Robert 17
RITENOUR Amelia S. 596
RITTER Elizabeth 319
RIVER Elizabeth 391; Peter 391
RIZER Benjamin 167; George 167; Joseph 109; Mary Magdalene 193; Rabecca 12
ROACH Jesse 670; Mary Ann 670
ROADS Catharine 642, 840
ROBERDEAU Isaac 167, 759
ROBERTS George 702; Mary Ann 587
ROBERTSON John 500; Thomas 279; William 322
ROBINETT Jairus 219; Joseph 217; Mazy 171; Ruth 217; William 172
ROBINSON Amelia 817; Archibald 777; Elizabeth 144, 589; Jane 777; Jonathan M. 828; Mary 514
ROBISON Francis 760; John 838; Mary 385; Robert A. 18
ROBY Owen 96; Statia 96; William 96
ROCKAFIELD Abraham 610
ROCKENBAUGH Maria Louisa 329
ROGERS Arthur 112, 142; Catharine 112; Lucinda Ann 770; Reuben 814
ROHRBACH Catherine 803
ROHRBACK Catharine 582; Henry 814; John 726; Mary 814; William 762
ROHRER Barbara 307; David 826; Frederick 377; Henry 811; Jacob 307, 312, 457, 572; Jacob M. 608; John 611; Joseph 751; Maria 826; Martin 841; Samuel 453, 620, 784; Susan 639
ROLAND Elizabeth 634; Isaac 634; Jacob 569
ROLIN Mr. 529
ROLLINGTON Sophia 621
ROOF Joseph A. 770
ROOT William 342
ROPER Dr. J. W. 749
RORRIOCK Ann O. 660
ROSENBERGER Anthony 802; Catharine Ann 802
ROSS Margaretta 830
ROTHRAFF Rev 364, 400
ROTHRAUFF Rev 280, 434, 661; Rev F. 666
ROTHROFF Rev 836
ROTRAFF Rev 240, 256
ROTROCK Mary Anne 306; Samuel 306
ROUNER Michael 669; Sarah 669
ROW Samuel 279, 423
ROWE Charles 785; Nancy 589; Thomas 764
ROWLAND Abraham 291, 440; Barbara 367; David 367; Elizabeth 315; Emanuel 526; Henry 367; Isaac 315; Jacob 367; John 367; Jonathan 367; Joseph 352; Mary 367; Rosanna 458; Sarah 658
ROZER Francis E. 629
RUCH Elizabeth 804
RUCKEL Samuel 718
RUCKLE Ann 818; Elizabeth 718; Paul 818; Samuel 842
RUDASIL Michael 716; Sophia 716
RULET Daniel 550
RUNIOR Mary 752; William 752
RUNNELS Col. H. 834
RUNYAN Mary 690; William 690
RUSH John 129; Rachel 129
RUSS George 686
RUSSELL Elnathan 191, 202; Mary 607; Mary Ann 191; Susan 291; Susanna 439
RUTH Joshua 215
RUTHRAUFF David 656; Frederick 809; John 677; Jonathan 616; Margaret 536; Rev 384, 508, 518, 537, 557, 569, 593, 619, 632, 637, 638, 640, 641, 644, 646, 648, 650, 653, 660, 671, 753, 789; Rev F. 104, 489, 516, 524, 535, 538, 560, 545, 608, 610, 618, 630, 643, 656, 659, 668, 672, 677, 700
RUTTAN Daniel 90; David 90; Peter 90; Phebius 90
RUTTER John H. 288; Mary Ann 811
RYAN Rev 49, 68, 142, 157, 167, 642, 673, 848; Rev T. 34, 98, 99
RYEN James 551

INDEX

SACKETT Milton H. 467
SAGER Mary 770
SAILOR Peter 664
SANDERS Mary Frances 240
SANDERSON Mary 683
SANDS George W. 434, 538; Thomas 257
SANFORD Catharine B. 13; Thornton 13
SAPPINGTON Sarah B. 615; Thomas 615
SAUNDERS Barbara A. 671; Cyrus 255, 465, 475; Henry 678; Joseph Crane 255; Mary Francis 405
SAYLAR Jacob 44
SAYLER Andrew 752; Catharine 814; Elizabeth 752
SCHAEFFER Jacob 99; Rev D. F. 568, 591, 802
SCHEIMER Susan 359
SCHELL Margaret 267
SCHLECT John M. 791
SCHLEIGH John 462, 815; Mary Ann 462; William 471
SCHLENKER Elizabeth 741; Mary 543
SCHLEY Francina Cheston 153; Frederick Augustus 267, 413; Frederick S. 153; William 18, 198, 548, 794
SCHLOSSER Mary 667; Sarah 351
SCHMUCKER Eleanora 497; Eliza 578; George 431, 615; Rev J. G. 578; Samuel 419; Samuel S. 497, 598
SCHMUTZ Elizabeth 359; Jacob 543; Sarah 769
SCHNEBLY Caspar 571; Catharine 236; Catharine R. 755; Col. 598; Daniel 236, 250, 793; David 238; Elizabeth 313, 706, 775; Ellen 793; Eve 799; George 799; Henry 706; Jacob 775; John 306; Mary 428; Mary C. 706
SCHNEE Rev 515
SCHNEIDER Sarah 273
SCHOEPFLIN Mr. W. F. 598
SCHOOK Jacob 225; Margaret 225
SCHOOL Elizabeth 598; Rev 845
SCHRIBER Rebecca 242
SCHROYER Juliann 677
SCHULTZ Elizabeth 620
SCHWARTZWELDER Margaret 794
SCHWEITZER Nancy 630
SCOTT Deborah 213, 819; James 70, 93, 154, 390, 659, 696; John C. 695; Julian 576; Mary 174, 390; Mary Ann 695; Rev 185; Sarah 696

SEARIGHT Anna B. 153; Catharine 86; James 86, 153
SEIBERT Amelia 342; Eliza 458; Mary Ann 747; Peter 342, 458, 709, 747
SEIFERT Maria 299
SEIFORT Maria 446
SELBY Arthur 72; Hannah 523; Mrs. 72
SELLARS Alexander 549; Mrs. 483
SELLERS George W. 773; Henry D. 328
SELSER Charles 808; Henry 330, 470
SENSEBAUGH Catharine 543
SENSEL John 755
SENSELL Peter 672
SENSEMAN Maria 514
SENSENBAUGH 397
SENSIL Maria 537
SEUTER Jacob 622
SEYMOUR Garret 59; Mrs. 59
SHACKLEFORD John 726
SHAFER Catharine 174; Delila 562; Elizabeth 392, 701; George 23, 557, 811; Henry I. 805; Jacob 42; John 265; Jonathan 265, 644; Leonard 367; Mary Ann 811; Mary C. 765; Rev 841; Samuel 569; Susanna 644
SHAFFER Catharine 744; Daniel 744; Jacob 662
SHAFFNER Charles 645; Eliza 246; Henry S. 673; Matthias 246, 593, 637; Sevilla S. 645
SHALL George 321, 703; Margaret 703
SHANAFELD Andrew 321, 381; Sarah 321
SHANE Sophia 560
SHANEBERGER Jacob 570
SHANEFELD Andrew 309
SHANEFELT Abraham 650; Andrew 664; Daniel 664, 814; David 664; Henry 664; Jacob 664; John 664; Peter 315; Sarah 567, 664; Susanna 664; William 664
SHANK Andrew 667; Catharine 619; Elizabeth 412, 616; George 619; John 794, 802; Nancy 802
SHANNON Joseph 679; Mary Ann 685
SHARER Mary Ann 571
SHATT Christiana 368; Samuel 368
SHAW John 614; Levi 191, 218; Mary 218; Rev 316; Samuel B. 322, 323
SHEAFFER Rev D. F. 770
SHEARER Eliza 713; John 713
SHECTOR Daniel 260
SHEETER Mary 737

INDEX

SHEETS Daniel 701; Elizabeth 701; Thomas O. 549
SHEETZ Adam 89; Henry 74
SHEETZE Harriet 89; Henry 89; Jacob 89; Joseph 89; Margaret 89; William M. 89
SHEFY Solomon 661
SHELDON Rev H. O. 798
SHELHORN Ann 9; Baltzer 9; Henry 9; Jacob 9; John 9
SHELLEBERGER David 574
SHELLER Elizabeth 358, 493
SHENAFELT Elizabeth 618; Henry 394
SHENEBERGER Amelia 722
SHENEFELT Andrew 454
SHENK Nancy 555
SHEPHERD Abraham 659; Ann 659; William 475
SHEPLER Mary 275
SHERERD Elizabeth 701; James 350
SHERRARD james 487
SHIESS George 773, 798
SHILLING Hannah 620; John 346, 485; Jonas 689; William 620
SHIMER Elizabeth 315
SHIP James 717
SHIPLEY Ephriam 65; Otho 676
SHIPPEN Edward Burd Yeates 446; John 446
SHIRCLIFF Honour 107; Leonard 107
SHIRLEY Frances 645; Richard 674
SHLEIGH William 332
SHOCKEY Ann 203; Samuel 156
SHOLL Rev F. 846
SHOOP Elizabeth 304; Jacob 514
SHOOPER Peter 692
SHORT David 799; Mary 799
SHOWAKER Martin 589, 815; Mrs. 815
SHOWECKER William 241
SHOWMAN John 452; Louisa 775
SHRINER Anna Maria 515
SHRIVER Catharine 693; Daniel 262; Elizabeth 26; James 26, 80, 640; Margaret 600
SHROEDER Henry 542
SHROUDS Mary 788
SHROYER Lewis 132; Louisia 132
SHRYER Elenora 115; Harriet L. 27; John 27, 115; Mary Ann 27; Rosanah 52; William 39
SHRYOCK Anna Maria Margaretta 448; Leonard 448
SHUCK George 159
SHUGERS Eliza 772

SHULL Rev 260, 585
SHULSE Frederick A. 522; Mary 522
SHULTZ Nicholas 391, 412; Rev 416
SHULZ Henry E. 522
SHUMAN Samuel 501
SHUMATE Deborah 79; Joseph 79
SHUPE Jacob 759; Mrs. 759
SHUTT Elias 848
SIDERSTICK Susan 821
SIDES Jacob 224, 303, 833
SIETENSTICK Elizabeth 545
SIGLER Adam 32; Eli 45; John T. 32; Lydia 620; Mary 407; Peter 620; Rev 19, 25, 39, 49, 61, 65, 74, 102, 121, 141, 143, 148, 151, 156, 161, 162, 166, 177, 215, 218; Rev A. 34, 42, 197
SILVER Lewis 665
SIMPKINS Christiana 195; Darius 310; Dicksey 95; Disey 195; John 113; William 170
SIMPSON Rezin 151
SINGHARS Christian 515
SINGLE Basil 41, 132; Kit 138
SINGLETON Mary Rebecca 186; Richard 186; Susan 171
SKINNER John 527; Rev 32
SLAGLE Ann Maria 642
SLANGE Mary 194
SLATER --- 401
SLAUGHTER Smith 542
SLEIDER Mary Ann 823
SLENKER Daniel 502; Rebecca 817; Regina 339; Susan 295
SLICE Barbara 826; Christiana 460; Nancy 241
SLICER George 175; Henry 173; John 138; Nathaniel 173; Priscilla 132; Samuel 373; Walter 82, 132
SLICK Christiana 315
SLIFER John 472
SLOAN John 544; Nancy 50, 598
SLY Matthias 620; Sophia 620
SMALTZ Rev 803
SMITH Abijah 309; Ann 718; Anna 350, 487; Catharine 701; Christian 543; Christoper 547; Dr 644; Edward 644; Elizabeth 675, 710; Elizabeth H. 435; Frederick 230, 662; George 373, 660, Henry 737; Isaac 732; Jacob 616, 753; Jacob S. 647; James 752; Jane 735; John 327, 377, 589, 693; Jonathan 717; Joseph 269, 535, 668, 761, 773;

153

INDEX

Joshua 701; Josiah 289, 693; Lydia 662; Margaret 296; Margaret S. 577; Maria 688; Mary 277, 421, 608, 764; Mary Ann 761; Nancy 281, 353, 490; Nicholas 435, 436; Peter 544; Rev 155, 777; Robert 855; Rosanna 585; S. 675; Samuel 334, 385, 514, 710; Sarah 240, 557, 715; Sohia 696; William 309
SMOOT George C. 634
SMOUSE Henry 228; Julian 228
SMYTHE Alexander 213
SNAVELY Adam 799; Catharine 752; Eliza 826; George 826; Mary 237; Ruhannah 799
SNIDER Amelia 436; Christian 426; George 560; Henry 557; Mary 616, 664; Peter 664; Samuel 656, 811; Sarah 242; Susanna 641
SNIVELY Eliza 839; J. 83; Jacob 642, 799, 839; Martha 845
SNOW Rev 610
SNYDER Adam 556; Anthony 712; Catharine 488; David 769; Elizabeth 556, 769; George 769; Gertrude 39; Henry 607; Jacob 39, 769; Jacob C. 809; John 353, 488, 490; Joseph 769; Mary 399, 572, 769; Nancy 769; Rosanna 698; Ruanna 769; Sarah 769; Solomon 769; Susanna 769
SOCKMAN Rev 417, 453
SOUTH Eliza 392; Gera 738, 823; Mrs. 738; Sarah 650; Sarah Ann 668
SOYSTER Jonathan 71, 145; Mary 71
SPANGLER Jacob 542
SPEALMAN John 407
SPEAR Matthew 630
SPEER Rev 721
SPENCER Amos L. 129; Benjamin 91; Daniel S. 129; Darcus 91; David 129; David G. 129; Drusilla 91; Edward 91; Eleanor 805; John W. 129; Joseph W. 129; Margaret 91; Moses T. 129; Rachel 91; Samuel C. 129; Sarah 129; William 457; William I. 129
SPICKLER Elizabeth 332; Samuel 839
SPIELMAN David 533, 814; John 487; Joseph 487; Rosanna 533
SPIGLAR Samuel 447
SPIGLER Catharine 761; Elizabeth 471; John 258; Samuel 300
SPITZEL John 638

SPITZNAGEL Barbara 545; Nancy 273
SPITZNOGLE Elizabeth 718
SPONG Elias 761
SPRECHER David 750; Jacob 784; John 570; Margaret 348; Mary 231; Philip 238
SPRIGG John McMahon 17; Joseph 177,301; Lucy 604; M. C. 177; Margaret 80, 639; Michael C. 9, 47, 80, 639; Osborn 9; William 690
SPRINGLE Sarah 828
SPURRIER Horace 162
STACHER Barbara 563
STAHL Ann 619; Elizabeth 281
STAKE Peter 318
STALEY Cornelius 799; Jane 737
STALLINGS Thomas 155
STANGE Mary 853
STANLY James S. 552
STANS... Elizabeth B. 401; John E. 401
STANSBURY Elizabeth B. 608; John E. 608
STARTZMAN Amelia 660; Ann 815; Daniel 619; David 815; Eve 581; Henry 581; Jacob 244; Peter 660; William 819
STATLER Nancy 65
STATTLEMYER Nelson 412
STAUBS Katharine 789; Susan 783
STAUFFER Magdalena 306
STAUNTON Catharine 602
STAUPS Jacob 459
STEED William 725
STEEL William 749
STEELE James W. 479; Samuel 797
STEENBERGEN Mary Catharine 598; William 598
STEFFEY Mary 535
STEFFY Catharine 572; Daniel 671; David 590; George 576; Peter 344
STEIN Henry 342
STEINER Thomas 306, 590
STEINMETZ John 307,454
STEMBEL Elizabeth 307; Henry 307
STEMPLE Christian 341, 665; John 275, 371, 735; Magdalena 665; Margaret 371
STENGER Chs. 591; Wilhelmina 591
STEPHENS Alexander 767; Lewis 275
STEPHENSON Ann 692; Margaret G. 765
STERETT Joseph 269; Nancy 527; Sarah Isabella 679
STERLING Frances 447; John 447
STERRETT Joseph 414; William D. 568

INDEX

STEUART Elizabeth 690
STEVENS Daniel 609
STEWART George 669; Jane 721; Mary 253; Nancy 669; William 847
STICKEL Samuel 458
STICKLEY Regina 814
STIER Frederick 805
STIFFLER Lydia 641; Mary Ann 667; Sarah 234
STILE John 717
STINE Catherine 794; Elizabeth 240; Jacob 400, 608; Jonathan 396; Matthias 396
STINEBAUGH John 701; Mary 701
STITZEL Henry 517; John 581
STOCKSLAGER Philip 769
STOCKTON Lucius W. 559
STODDARD James 219; Sarah Ann 219
STOKES Sarah 564
STONE Jpohn 556; Mary 556
STONEBRAKER Ann 727; Gerard 704; Maria 627; Michael 611; Sophia 704
STONER David 374, 839; Rachel 234; Sophia 619; Thomas 47
STOOPS Elizabeth 735; William 660
STOTLER Christopher 59
STOTTLEMEYER Mary 324
STOUDT Catharine 661; William 661, 683
STOUFER Amelia 612
STOUFFER Christian 744; Mrs. 744; Nancy 526, 700
STOVER Catharine 342, 385; Christian 779; Christiana Dorcas 112; Elizabeth 569; George 397; Harriet 112; Samuel 273; Sarah 310; Solomon 27, 112
STOY Dorothy 240
STOYE Dorothy 405
STOYER Absalom 66; Catharine 61
STRACH Joseph 434
STRAUSE George 434; Jacob 235
STREEPEY John 652
STREET Rebecca 83
STRICKER John 43
STRICKLER George 533
STRITE Elizabeth 809; John 273; Joseph 809; Nancy 240; Samuel 845
STRONG Rev 316
STUBBLEFIELD Mr. 206
STUCKSCHLAGER John 339
STULL Anne B. 92; Elie W. 92; J. I. 639; John I. 92, 744; John Louis 92; Matilda 92, 744; Prudence C. 639; Prudence H. 92
STUMP Elizabeth 110; Jacob 110; John 61
STURR Jacob 374; John 572; Samuel 535
SUCKLEY George 694
SULLIVAN Mr. J. 146
SUMERS Adam 667
SUMMER John 658
SUMMERS Catharine 381; Elisabeth 273; Mary 551
SURGHNOR John 551
SUTER Peter 816
SUTTON Theophilus 75
SUVER Catharine 788
SWAN George M. 520; Juliana 166; Robert 166
SWARTZ Andrew 495
SWEARINGEN Amelia 778, 819; Catharine 819; Charles 258; Charles V. 696; George 154, 173, 192, 196, 200, 390; J. V. 557; John 778, 819; John V. 23, 171, 763; Joseph 433; Martha B. 23, 557; Mary C. 154; Mary Catharine 154, 213; Susan 171, 763; Susanna 258
SWIGART Levi H. 637
SWINGLEY Elizabeth 544; Nathaniel 713
SWISLER James 674, 813
SWOPE David 816; Elizabeth 834; Jacob 286; John 755, 813
SYMMES John Cleves 185, 777

TABB Elizabeth 483; John L. 483
TALBOTT Hilleary 835; Hillery B. 650
TALIAFERRO John 100
TANLEY William 802
TANNEHILL James 826
TANNER Rudolph 593
TARLTON Mr. 645; Mrs. 500, 64; Susanna 369; Thomas 369
TAYLOR Andrew 690; Jacob 9; James 138, 162, 177; Joseph 776; Mary 9; Mary Ann W. 70; Orphit 623; William 42, 70, 121, 141, 836
TEISCHER John 795; Sally 663
TEISHER John 233, 329, 402; Mary 329; Nancy 374
TEMPLE Dr. 66
TEMPLEMAN John 227
THACHER Bartholomew 652

INDEX

THOMAS Daniel 415; Elizabeth 751; Gabriel 511; George 351, 842; Hannah 838; Jacob 802; John 585; Jonathan 772; Maria 802; Mary 575, 637; Michael 369, 501; Samuel 82; Susan 842
THOMPSON Eliza 92; Hilleary 92; Joseph 290; Josias 92
THOMSON Ann Cecilia 749; William C. 837
THORNBURG George 803, 845; George T. 276; Mary 475; Sarah 803; Solomon 309, 475; Thomas T. 421
THUMB George 598
TICE Eliza 717; John 243, 275, 317, 659; Jonathan 713; Mary 317, 716; Michael 521; Sarah 243
TIERNAN Ann Elizabeth 604; Luke 604, 751
TIGNER Richard 557
TILGHMAN Ann Eliza 393; Anne E. 833; Col. F. 833; George 69, 393, 624; Rebecca 207, 833; Thomas 207, 808
TIMMONDS Andrew 77, 110, 224; Ann 34, 77; Anne 110; George 77, 110; James 77, 110; Jerome 77, 110; Joanna 110; Johanna 77; John 77, 110; Margaret 77, 110; Nancy 77; Ophelia 77, 110; William 77, 110
TISSUL Elizabeth 91; Isaac 91
TOBY Eliza 759
TOD John 210
TODD Elizabeth 619; John 220; Mary Ann Elizabeth 283; William 283
TOMLINSON Jesse 303; Benjamin 3, 96, 662; Emily 197; Henry B. 58; Martha 96, 662; Rachael 3; Sarah 303
TOMPSON Daniel 515
TOOL Nancy 180; Peter 180
TOWLER Rev 744
TOWNSEND William 10
TOWSON Jacob T. 389, 700; John S. 700; Martha 389
TRACY John 666
TRAGO Abraham 826
TRAUBINGER Daniel 574
TRITCH Eliza 640; Jacob I. 704; John Jacob 706
TRITLE Lewis 805; Ludwick 803
TROUP Catharine 572; David 494; John 663; Nancy 256

TROVINGER Catharine 309; Christopher 263
TROXEL Abraham 391; Sarah 391
TROXELL Ab'm 829; Abraham 714; David 799; Elizabeth 799, 829; Margaret 799; Peter 799
TSCHUDY David 253
TUCKER St. George 700
TURNER Edmund H. 293; Thomas 36, 575
TUTWEILER Catharine 264; Jacob 264, 294, 446, 708
TWIGG Francis 50, 178
TYLOR Eliza 562
TYRROL Henry 846

UHL Archibald 143; Charles 94, 181; Eliza 181; Jesse 174; Levi 216; Rebecca 196
ULHURN Rev 620
UMBAUGH Mary Jane 338; Michael 338
UNGER Elizabeth 722; Frederick 712
UPDEGRAFF George 329; Samuel 756

VAN HORN Matilda 373
VAN LEAR Eliza 365; Eliza England 498; Horatio Nelson 369, 500; Joseph 365, 498; Mary 728, 752; Matthew 364, 369, 496, 500, 718, 728, 799; Mrs. 635; Sophia 799; Thomas Farmer 127, 696; William 127, 365, 498, 696
VAN METRE Abraham 667; Maria C. 667
VAN PETERS Harriet 235
VAN SWEARINGEN George 174; Mary Scott 174
VANSICKLE Annah 90; Ephram 90
VARNER Mrs. 571
VAUGHN Benjamin 120; Rebecca 120
VICKROY Mary 19; William 19
VINSONHELLER Robert 748
VINTON Rev R. S. 542; Robert S. 617
VOIGHT Rev 181
VOIGT Rev 143
VOIT Rev 174

WACHTEL Jonathan 610; Valentine 338
WADE Henry 581
WAGELY Catharine 250; John 250
WAGER Edward 646
WAGNER Benjamin 418; Joseph 503; Polly 250; Valentine 250
WAGONER Christian 279

INDEX

WALKER Aaron 608; Elizabeth Ann 798; George P. H. 116; John P. H. 115; Margaret 631; Philip 116; Thomas 529
WALKINGHOOD Hughes 634
WALLACE Alitha 855; William 855
WALLING James 350, 589; Mary 589
WALLMEYER Henry 668
WALLS Eleanor 142; Samuel 142
WALSH Rev 631
WALTMAN M. Michael 729
WALTZ Mary 369, 501
WARD Jacob 676; James 49, 137; Jesse 173; Sophia 173
WARNER John 697; Polly 405; Rosanna 453
WASHABAUGH Daniel 642
WATERBERRY Elizabeth 542
WATERS Phebe 809
WATKINS Benjamin 804
WATSON Conrad 275; James 666; Joseph 686; Simon 518
WATT Jane 791; Mr. A. 791
WATTON David W. 19
WATTS Elizabeth 847; Pamelia 579; Sarah 823
WAUGH Ann 674; Archibald M. 494; Rev 307, 676; Thomas M. 638
WAUGHTLE Margaret 598
WAYMAN Francis Deakins 442
WEAVER Ann 799; Catharine 761; David 799; Emeline 812; John 809; William 845
WEBB Letitia 535; Mary 604; Nathaniel 262; Pointon 677; William 604
WEEBER Lewis 706
WEIDMAN Susanna 545
WEINANDT Rev H. 563
WEINBRENNER John 331; Mary 346
WEINERT Ann 431
WEIS Christiana 485; John 360, 485, 620, 807; William 794
WEISE Daniel 535; Richard 573; William 656
WEISEL Daniel 578, 695; Elizabeth 768
WEITZELL Frederick 820; John 820
WELCK Elias 823
WELFLEY Isreal 55
WELHOUSER Elizabeth 752; George 752
WELLER Squire 174
WELLS Henry 725; Isaac 249; Jesse 725; John 144; Joshua 818

WELSH Harriet 283; James M. 435; Margaret 412; Mary 351; Richard 774
WELTY Elizabeth 397, 524, 557; Henry 521; Samuel 395, 701
WENGERT Elizabeth 69, 624
WENTLING Rhody 183
WENTLINGER Mary 512
WEST David P. 769; Eliza 730, 807; Elizabeth 234; Matthew 560
WESTEBERGER Catharine 755
WESTENBERGER David 292; Elizabeth 666; John 762; Nancy 514
WETHKNECHT Jacob 541
WETZEL Peter 723
WHARTON John O. 769
WHEELAN Martin 755
WHEELER Rev 407; Rev C. 559; Sarah 144
WHERRETT Margaret 262
WHERRIT Catharine 626
WHETSTONE Jacob 561; Henry 104; Isaac 70; Isaac S. 670; Joseph 118; Rosanna M. 266; Thomas 105; Wenny 105
WHITEHEAD John 56
WHITEMAN Mary Ann 61
WHITFIELD William 621
WIKES Isaac 640
WILCOX Aaron 696; Moses 696
WILES Sarah 529
WILKES Elizabeth 385
WILKINSON Thomas 534
WILKS Charlotte 646
WILLEY Alexander 89; Elizabeth 89
WILLHELM John 166
WILLIAMS Abner 737; Anne Barbara 92; Catharine 396; Col. O. H. 581; Edward G. 286, 695; Edward Greene 761, 762; Eleanor 659; Eli 341; Elie 373, 396; Elizabeth B. 581; Harriet Eliza 509; Henry 10; James F. 806; Jane 304, 394, 849; John Conrad 92, 373; John S. 92; Joseph 92; Martha 301; Mrs. 725; Naomi 92; O. H. 488; Otho 495; Otho H. 92, 365, 474, 752; Otho Holland 498, 761, 762; Susan 92; William 92; William E. 474
WILLIAMSON James 744; Rev 754; Thomas 755
WILLIS Elizabeth 673; William 673

INDEX

WILLISON Delana 155; John 155; Moses 164; Rosanna 164
WILMER Rev 829
WILMS Mr. 807
WILSON Ann Mary 369; Asias 172, 219; David T. 369, 488, 656; Ezra 142; Greenberry Barker 627; Jemima 219; John 175, 422; John K. 634; Lydia 705; Mary Ann 350; Mazy 172; Rev 194, 495, 573, 799, 846; Rev R. 773; Robert 717, 721, 804, 814, 850; Sophia 175; Thomas H. 235; William 634, 680
WILT Susannah 848
WINDERS Catharine 821; Daniel 641; Jacob 600; John 712, 817, 822; Nancy 572; Sarah 822; Susan 351
WINEBRENNER Christian 488; David 488; Peter 488; Sebastian 488
WINEOUR Henry 79, 812; Margaret 812
WINEOW Henry 209; Margaret 209
WINGERT Philip 96, 662
WINOUR George 170; Henry 41, 132, 170
WINTER Ann Mary 576; Christian 789; John 277, 675, 761, 762, 771, 780, 785, 814; Rev 715, 719, 749, 768, 821, 839, 847; Rev J. 718, 751, 767,. 784, 787, 788
WINTERS Anna 49; Elleanor 167; John 370; Mary 235; Rev 735, 826; Samuel 361; Susan 370
WIRE Elizbeth 475
WISE Catharine 373; Henry 373; Margaret 731; Richard 807; William 731, 765
WISONG John 765
WITHNEY Arthur 440; Elizabeth 292, 440; John 40; Mary 619
WITMER Daniel 787; David 802; Frances 362; Henry 261, 296, 362; John 235, 337, 616; Mary 261, 337; Sarah 787
WITNER George 10
WITT Teeny 166
WOLF Eve 373, 761; Jacob 761; John 199
WOLFE Matthew T. 214
WOLFERSBERGER Elizabeth 338; Frederick 297; John 338, 384; Margaret 395; Peter 395
WOLFERSPERGER Mr. J. P. 607; Mrs. 607

WOLFORD George 83; Henry 481; John 278
WOLGAMOT Andrew 317; Elizabeth 335; John 335, 389, 516, 685, 738; Mary 795; Susan 389; Susanna 516, 795
WOLSLAGER Samuel 351
WOLTZ Mary 396; Peter 396
WOOD James 596; Joseph 306; Mary 306; William 652, 659, 677, 717
WOODMAN Eliza 845
WORKMAN Andrew 184
WORLEY Eve 738
WORSTER Frederick 517
WORTHINGTON Reubin 81; William 81
WOTRING Mr. A. 570
WRIGHT Barbara 245; John B. 180; Peter 783; Polly 180; Samuel 34
WYATT Harrison L. 175; Rev 751; Rev Dr. 147
WYETH Francis 774

YAKLE John 593; Susanna 369, 501
YANTZ Henry 173; Sophia 29
YEAKLE John 694, 728, 852; Mary Ann 677; Mrs. 694; William 752
YENTER Casper 12
YERTY Sally 757; Benjamin 354, 647; Benjamin F. 793; Elizabeth 354; Sarah Ann 647
YONTZ John 748; Martin 785; Sarah 748
YOST David G. 272, 418
YOUNG Catharine 600; Daniel 297; Henry 762; Jacob 416; Jane C. 777; John 316, 765; John C. 797; Ludwick 257, 600; Margaret 655, 677; Margaretta St. Clair C. 316; Matilda 258; Rev 203, 777, 804, 850; Rev C. B. 214, 221, 227; Sarah 291
YOWLER Eleanor 802

ZACHARIAS Daniel 780; Catharine 275
ZEIGLER Andrew 607; Ann 722; David 341; George 341, 439; Mary Wilhelmine Fustin Caroine Louise Fredericke 823
ZEILER Daniel 568
ZELLAR Jacob 514, 542
ZELLER Daniel 568, 795; David 626, 721; Elizabeth 376; Jacob 376, 385
ZELLERS Samuel 655
ZENTMYER George 820; Sarah 847

INDEX

ZIEGLER Elizabeth 767; Frederick 767
ZIGLER Elizabeth 30; George 291
ZIMMER Elizabeth 780; Mr. 224
ZIMMERMAN Henry H. 825
ZIPPERER Christopher Seigman 412
ZOLL Elizabeth 668
ZUCK David 809; Henry 577; John H.
 577; Mary 648; Nancy 500
ZWISLER Charles 563; Christiana 541;
 James 541

Other Heritage Books by F. Edward Wright:

Abstracts of Bucks County, Pennsylvania Wills, 1685–1785
Abstracts of Cumberland County, Pennsylvania Wills, 1750–1785
Abstracts of Cumberland County, Pennsylvania Wills, 1785–1825
Abstracts of Philadelphia County Wills, 1726–1747
Abstracts of Philadelphia County Wills, 1748–1763
Abstracts of Philadelphia County Wills, 1763–1784
Abstracts of Philadelphia County Wills, 1777–1790
Abstracts of Philadelphia County Wills, 1790–1802
Abstracts of Philadelphia County Wills, 1802–1809
Abstracts of Philadelphia County Wills, 1810–1815
Abstracts of Philadelphia County Wills, 1815–1819
Abstracts of Philadelphia County Wills, 1820–1825
Abstracts of Philadelphia County, Pennsylvania Wills, 1682–1726
Abstracts of South Central Pennsylvania Newspapers, Volume 1, 1785 1790
Abstracts of South Central Pennsylvania Newspapers, Volume 3, 1796–1800
Abstracts of the Newspapers of Georgetown and the Federal City, 1789–99
Abstracts of York County, Pennsylvania Wills, 1749–1819
Bucks County, Pennsylvania Church Records of the 17th and 18th Centuries Volume 2: Quaker Records: Falls and Middletown Monthly Meetings
Anna Miller Watring and F. Edward Wright
Caroline County, Maryland Marriages, Births and Deaths, 1850–1880
Citizens of the Eastern Shore of Maryland, 1659–1750
Cumberland County, Pennsylvania Church Records of the 18th Century
Delaware Newspaper Abstracts, Volume 1: 1786–1795
Early Charles County, Maryland Settlers, 1658–1745
Marlene Strawser Bates and F. Edward Wright
Early Church Records of Alexandria City and Fairfax County, Virginia
F. Edward Wright and Wesley E. Pippenger
Early Church Records of New Castle County, Delaware, Volume 1, 1701–1800
Frederick County Militia in the War of 1812
Sallie A. Mallick and F. Edward Wright
Inhabitants of Baltimore County, 1692–1763
Land Records of Sussex County, Delaware, 1769–1782
Land Records of Sussex County, Delaware, 1782 1789
Elaine Hastings Mason and F. Edward Wright
Marriage Licenses of Washington, District of Columbia, 1811–1830
Marriages and Deaths from the Newspapers of Allegany and Washington Counties, Maryland, 1820–1830
Marriages and Deaths from The York Recorder, 1821 1830
Marriages and Deaths in the Newspapers of Frederick and Montgomery Counties, Maryland, 1820–1830

Marriages and Deaths in the Newspapers of Lancaster County, Pennsylvania, 1821–1830
Marriages and Deaths in the Newspapers of Lancaster County, Pennsylvania, 1831–1840
Marriages and Deaths of Cumberland County, [Pennsylvania], 1821–1830
Maryland Calendar of Wills Volume 9: 1744–1749
Maryland Calendar of Wills Volume 10: 1748–1753
Maryland Calendar of Wills Volume 11: 1753–1760
Maryland Calendar of Wills Volume 12: 1759–1764
Maryland Calendar of Wills Volume 13: 1764–1767
Maryland Calendar of Wills Volume 14: 1767–1772
Maryland Calendar of Wills Volume 15: 1772–1774
Maryland Calendar of Wills Volume 16: 1774–1777
Maryland Eastern Shore Newspaper Abstracts, Volume 1: 1790–1805
Maryland Eastern Shore Newspaper Abstracts, Volume 2: 1806–1812
Maryland Eastern Shore Newspaper Abstracts, Volume 3: 1813–1818
Maryland Eastern Shore Newspaper Abstracts, Volume 4: 1819–1824
Maryland Eastern Shore Newspaper Abstracts, Volume 5: Northern Counties, 1825–1829
F. Edward Wright and Irma Harper
Maryland Eastern Shore Newspaper Abstracts, Volume 6: Southern Counties, 1825–1829
Maryland Eastern Shore Newspaper Abstracts, Volume 7: Northern Counties, 1830–1834
Irma Harper and F. Edward Wright
Maryland Eastern Shore Newspaper Abstracts, Volume 8: Southern Counties, 1830–1834
Maryland Militia in the Revolutionary War
S. Eugene Clements and F. Edward Wright
Newspaper Abstracts of Allegany and Washington Counties, Maryland, 1811–1815
Newspaper Abstracts of Cecil and Harford Counties, Maryland, 1822–1830
Newspaper Abstracts of Frederick County, Maryland, 1816–1819
Newspaper Abstracts of Frederick County, Maryland, 1811–1815
Sketches of Maryland Eastern Shoremen
Tax List of Chester County, Pennsylvania 1768
Tax List of York County, Pennsylvania 1779
Washington County Church Records of the 18th Century, 1768–1800
Western Maryland Newspaper Abstracts, Volume 1: 1786–1798
Western Maryland Newspaper Abstracts, Volume 2: 1799–1805
Western Maryland Newspaper Abstracts, Volume 3: 1806–1810
Wills of Chester County, Pennsylvania, 1766–1778

www.ingramcontent.com/pod-product-compliance
Lightning Source LLC
Chambersburg PA
CBHW060537100426
42743CB00009B/1560